Murder

Murder

A Tale of Modern American Life

Sara L. Knox

Duke University Press Durham & London

1998

© 1998 Duke University Press

All rights reserved

Printed in the United States of America

on acid-free paper ∞

Typeset in Janson with Lettres Eclatees

display by Keystone Typesetting, Inc.

Library of Congress Cataloging-in-Publication

Data appear on the last printed

page of this book.

To my parents, Heather and Ray,

for their love and support,

and to Emma

Blood is not a thing at all but is a tale . . .

Cormac McCarthy

Contents

Acknowledgments

I acknowledge gratefully the aid of Barry Grennan, chief
of the Major Offenses Bureau, Office of the District Attorney,
Mineola, New York, and, naturally, his staff, for making available
the transcript and case materials of *People* v. *Fernandez*. My thanks
also to Mr. Grennan for his courtesy in allowing me to share his
office for the duration of my stay there. Thanks are due as well to
Mr. Henry Devine — retired assistant district attorney for Nassau
County — for his willingness to share his recollections of the
Fernandez case with me, and to John Guastello, clerk of the New
York Supreme Court, Queens, for his aid in helping me run to
ground the transcript. To my supervisors at the dissertation level,
Professor John Salmond and Dr. Lucy Frost, whose faith in my
sometimes wayward enthusiasm was invaluable, I am grateful.
Special thanks are due to my sister, Elizabeth, for her editorial
suggestions on the manuscript, especially her attention to matters
of tone and style. Lastly, I am indebted to Cathy Davidson,
Duke University, for her encouragement.

Introduction

It was night when I arrived, disorientated, at the international terminal of Salt Lake City airport. Until then America had been to me the long stretches of blue carpet and rubber tiling that I had wheeled the luggage trolley over as I trailed from Immigration to the Delta terminal at LAX. Outside, through the burnished glass of the windows, the Los Angeles sunshine was dirty with smoke from the still-burning fires out at Malibu. The air cleared and paled as I flew across the Mojave desert and on over the snowcapped ranges rimming Provo and Salt Lake City. I had spoken then only a little to flight attendants, immigration officials, and airline employees. Everyone seemed to want to call me "Ma'am." Personally, I felt that I fitted the title poorly.

The cab driver who ferried me from the airport to Salt Lake City itself did not call me "Ma'am." He mildly wondered at my accent and seemed vague about its origins, even after my explanation. As I eyed the billboards and freeway exit signs, he asked me what I'd come to America for. I had my summary ready, the blurb I'd be repeating in clubs, bars, and dinner parties for the next two months.

"I'm writing a Ph.D. on murder in modern American culture. Not how it happens, but what people want out of the retelling of stories of murder."

At that I faltered, trailing off into silence. The taxi driver was quiet too.

"It's sort of a cultural studies thing," I added lamely.

The driver half-turned, laying his arm over the back of the seat.

"Well you sure have come to the right place. People are getting killed all the time."

The driver told me how he'd come to Salt Lake City for its peace and quiet. He had lived too long, he said, in big cities. I told him that I was headed for New York. He nodded, and kept nodding, almost as if he were sorry for me somehow.

"That's the place to go for murder."

"Yeah." I agreed, trying to shift the vowel sound so my assent would come out properly, prosaically, American.

When he dropped me off outside my motel he told me to be careful. I said I would be.

But I wasn't, necessarily. On my first night in Manhattan I locked myself out of my apartment. While I squatted in the sixth-floor corridor, staring ruefully at the closed door, I heard — for the first time in my life — the distinctive sound of automatic gunfire, coming from somewhere over in Harlem. I wasn't careful when I decided, after a late night out in Greenwich Village, to take the 1 or the 9 home. I wasn't careful the days I walked alone through Riverside Park, where four women had been raped during the past month.

I had been given a pragmatic definition of "careful" by the woman I was staying with. She told me not to walk the extra distance from the 116th Street station to home. I was more likely to be stabbed, shot, raped, or have my bag snatched as I sauntered through Sakura Park, dodging the bundled-up dog owners exercising their pets, than I was crossing Tiemann onto Riverside Drive. She told me not to buy into the "segregationist bullshit," and to do my shopping in the stores nearest us, in Harlem, rather than in the overpriced delis scattered throughout the Columbia district. And so I did.

I did pride myself on the care I exercised in my research out in Mineola at the county courthouse. I caught my train out on the Long Island Railroad every morning and chatted to the district attorney's secretarial support staff to show I was keen, and friendly to boot. The District Attorney's Office had never had its own scholar before, and they extended me every courtesy: coffee and photocopying, and a chair and desk in the office of the chief of the Major Offenses Bureau. I was clearly visible there daily, sitting forward in my chair, doggedly reading through the nine volumes of *People* v. *Fernandez*. My presence elicited much curiosity. I had my spiel ready. The tall, wide homicide detectives who seemed to be forever conferencing in low tones out in the hallways were particularly intrigued by me. They extricated themselves from the latest speculation on the *Buttafuco* case (then being heard in one of the courtrooms below) and drifted in to chat with the chief of Major Offenses. Being big men, they proceeded to crowd out the office and were forced, then and there, to make my acquaintance.

They made me nervous. I was conscious of how odd I looked to them. When they asked me what I was doing there, I could barely manage to squeeze out a single line in reply.

"Oh, I'm studying murder."

Their eyes lit up; they warmed to me immediately. They called me "Ma'am," offered me gum, coffee, cigarettes, donuts. They started to tell me about murder: their terrain, their expertise. I listened and nodded — their very interest part of the evidence arrayed before me.

When I had finished with the trial transcript, the chief of the Major Offenses Bureau, Barry Grennan, set me up with a date at the Mineola Police Department to examine the police files on the case, a source that promised to fill in some of the more worrying gaps in my research. The night before I was due out there, a man named Colin Ferguson boarded one of the outward-bound trains to Mineola and, after crossing the county line, walked through the carriage firing his automatic weapon into the seated bodies of the homeward-bound commuters. That night, when the mass killer was taken into custody, he appeared on the TV screen flanked by the two big detectives who had earlier been swapping stories with me. The Mineola Police Department was in an uproar, functionally cordoned off by the press and their cameras. I decided that it would be better if I didn't go out there. A practical definition of safety weighed out over the scholarly ideal of care.

Researching murder is an ethically ticklish occupation, although historical and sociological research per se carries with it ethical as well as methodological problems. Part of that ticklish quality is the reaction of others to one's project. If I say I'm interested in murder, I lay myself open to the charge — as Wendy Lesser has put it — of "sleaziness."[1] Yet even the horrified reactions of those who mildly enquire after the research topic point to an interest in murder that is general, if not universal. That interest has spurred a small number of scholarly enquiries and a much larger number of mystery, detective, and "true crime" works (not to mention the many literary works that deal to some extent with an epistemology or metaphysics of murder). All these works attest to the "interested-ness" of American culture in murder narratives.

Murder stories elicit more interest, in their power to plumb the mysteries of mortality, than might seem justified by the frequency and variety of murders that daily occur in the United States. According to the vital statistics, a white man aged between twenty-five and forty-four is more likely to die in a car accident, succumb to an AIDS-defining illness, or die by his own hand than he is to be a murder victim.[2] African American men and women (and, to a lesser degree, Latino men and Latina women) are *less* likely to die by their own hand, but are conversely much *more* at risk of violent death than their white counterparts. That discrepancy is significant, and it is one that will be returned to throughout this book. If we remain, however, with the law of large numbers, we can see that the interest in murder within contemporary America (whose majority is made up by those least likely to die by violence) does not derive from experience — from some common cause of death that inexorably claims family, lovers, friends, and acquaintances. The "facts" of death attested to by the survivors are out of step with much of contemporary American culture's *narrative reckoning* of threat. Nor can the excessive interest be solely the product of news media that consider murder to be infinitely more interesting than the AIDS pandemic, suicide, or the willy-nilly slaughter enacted on American roads. (After all, the phenomenon of "newsworthiness" cannot be reduced to the proposition that news creates an interest not already there.) This book is an exploration of the various means by which the tale of murder claims the interest it does in contemporary America; it is an exploration of the constancy and change of that interest dependent upon the particular conditions of period, disciplinary framework, medium, and genre.

I intend to deal, generally, with the cultural impulses that drive the narrator of the tale of murder — whatever its medium, form, or ostensible genre — to tell a story that will encompass and address questions ancillary to the actual subject. Mine is an analysis preoccupied, therefore, with mediation and with the structure of authority in the murder narrative. For the *A*uthor and the *a*uthor of a murder are not, of course, necessarily identical. It is the author/mediator, rather than the author/murderer, who is the focus of this book — along with the sensibilities of the storyteller, whose tale of murder must somehow necessarily be about the storyteller's own distance from the murderous subject. This is the case even when the author/mediator and author/murderer *are* identical. Nathan Leopold's autobiography, *Life plus 99 Years*, is fundamentally concerned with demonstrating the difference between his "mature" self and that "unstable" nineteen-year-old who was sentenced, with Richard Loeb, to life imprisonment for bludgeoning to death Bobby Franks.

The first chapter sets out my definition of the "interestedness" of American culture in the tale of murder, and in the legal homicide enacted in the public's name. By brief reference to the tropic relationship of death and femininity and the difficult relationship of the "real" to its representations, my opening chapter also establishes the general parameters of enquiry for the critique in the chapters following. Chapter One investigates an early study — one of very few that provide a cultural and historical frame for American fictional studies of murder — namely, David Brion Davis's *Homicide in American Fiction*. Davis's analysis of the nineteenth-century tale of seduction and the moral underpinnings of the sentimental novel allows us a first glimpse at the discursive characteristics of murder narrative: the psychiatrization of the murderer; sexuality and gender as pathology; confession, secrecy, and truth; metaphysical speculation and the mystification of mortality.[3] The contemporary work of Bill Ellis and Joel Black, on the other hand, is concerned with the relationship of representations of murder to the actuality of violence. Ellis, discussing the scare around satanic cults, has concluded that the rumor, the report, and the urban myth combine to concretize the possibility of events previously only conjectured. Ellis's work on "ostension" and Black's analysis of the "hyperrealization" of violence together offer an analytic springboard for my own critique of the ability of murder narrative to survive, so to speak, "out of the womb" of fact to which it supposedly refers.[4] Attention to the works of Davis and Black is obligatory in a project of this sort because they (along with Wendy Lesser, whose work is dealt with in the final chapter) have provided practically the only scholarly studies of *murder in narrative* or *murder as narrative*.

The second and third chapters demonstrate the ways in which texts of the earlier period (1946–1956) sought to harness the meaning of murder, whether metaphorically (as a moral tale) or actually (in law or forensic psychiatry, where classification of the murderer is aimed at revealing greater psychological or social "truths" about the genus from which he arises). I have chosen Willard Motley's *Knock on Any Door* and William March's *The Bad Seed* because their works seem to fall squarely between "high" and "popular" fiction — between, say, the metaphysical and the commonsense explanations of murderous violence in America after the Second World War. By writing this I do not mean to suggest a continuum of complexity and simplicity, with high literature at one end and pulp at the other. The complexity of a narrative encoding of murder is neither governed nor necessarily limited by discipline, medium, genre, or style. In the quite different texts of these two chapters, fiction and nonfiction alike, authority is inscribed in the narrative by reference to the commonsensical, the banal, and the everyday as well as the metaphorical and the mythic. Whatever the authority referred to, the narrative coheres around something quite other than actual *events*. Beneath the descriptive narrative structures of myth that Dr. Fredric Wertham employs to unravel his patients' psyches there lies the scientific expert's desire to classify and to contain.[5] And within the grimly deterministic naturalism of Motley's picture of slum life,[6] or the cynical fatalism of March's portrait of humankind's essentially violent nature, lies a naive adulation of innocence and redemption, a fear of precocity and corruption.[7] Like Wertham, Judge Curtis Bok writes his fictional account as a sociological tract, using the lyricism of metaphor to elucidate the meaning not just of a particular murderous act and its agent, but of a proper moral response to violence in general.[8]

These earlier texts use murder to define "civilization" and to determine the shape of an evolving and therefore malleable humanity. The sensibilities of the authors range from the classically liberal — with an attentiveness both to right and rights — to the progressive, critical of institutional inequality. Of the four authors selected, William March focuses more narrowly upon the "intransigence" of evil, an intransigence that Curtis Bok and Fredric Wertham qualify.

Wertham's *The Show of Violence* has been selected because of its popularization of forensic psychology and because of the author's status as a forensic psychologist. Curtis Bok, on the other hand, has been chosen not because *Star Wormwood* itself was influential, but because Bok enjoyed distinctive status as an "expert": he was a seasoned jurist, had served on the court of last resort in Pennsylvania, and came from an esteemed family of lawyers. I aim, then, at a critique of the "expert" in order to show the importance of expert authority in the reauthoring of nonfictional tales of murder. Wertham and Bok backtrack along the trail of their patients' disturbed minds, seeking to explain and ultimately control their difference. To inscribe pathology with the metaphorical structure of myth was to strip the murderer of all idiosyncrasy, to make of him or her a historical exemplar in a particular topology of violence. Such a classificatory enterprise was also an attempt to advance a science of mind for social ends, by means that — given the narrative structure of myth and metaphor — constituted an ineluctably *literary* form of analysis.

There is a real confidence both in Wertham's and in Bok's work, a sense of some expected imminent order (if not utopia). That confidence is what allows these two authors their generosity of spirit. Crime, for Curtis Bok, is a "disease of civilization" and, like civilization itself, can be "studied" and, while civilization can be "improved," crime can be remedied by the handmaiden of law: psychiatry. Both Bok and Wertham believe in the concept of "incorrigibility" and give tacit (or, in Bok's case, overt) support to capital punishment.[9] It might perhaps require a bit (or a lot) of fine-tuning by the expert, but nonetheless "the future of penology is treatment."[10] Unlike March and Motley, whose fictions positioned the author tacitly (and falsely, as we shall see) outside the text, the professional expertise of Dr. Fredric Wertham and Judge Curtis Bok tends to explode the critical distance between author and subject, bringing the latter to heel as part of a *classificatory* enterprise. The interest of these latter two authors in murder, then, is explicit. It is not *disinterested*, the ethical vocation of the expert notwithstanding.

The central sections of this book, Chapters Four, Five, and Six, detail the progress of a particular "case" from the courtroom (in which the press were restricted in the content of their reporting, if not in their access to the trial) out into the canon of true crime and the cult crime film. The anecdote with which I begin Chapter Four describes my meeting with one of the principals in a murder case forty years old, and its tone gestures toward some of the contrary impulses of identification and mystification that exist at the heart of "true crime" literature that I deal with in the final chapters of this book: the hope of the storyteller that nothing important will be left out; the intoxication of researchers with the subjects they re-create; the feeling that the "truth" is near at hand. Such a space of wonder and affect is not one of revelation, but of mediation.

The tale of murder gains authority in the context of cultural readings not always obliging or expected. The sensational case of the "Honeymoon Killers" with which these central chapters deal was a cautionary tale set not exclusively in the generic mold of the crime story, but as a *romance*. Such culturally contingent readings also reveal more fundamental narrative structures of the tale of murder. The odd combination of narrative stylings for the testimony of Martha Beck and Ray Fernandez was not merely a matter of the news media's hand in distributing the story. The press was gagged, but the women attending every day of the trial were not, pointing to one of the significant characteristics of murder narrative — its informality. The professional media are not the only vehicle for news and information. Gossip and speculation (and the ossified form that embraces it, folklore) are the very lifeblood of the tale of murder. As in the later film satirization of the case, the gallery audience was filled with those women (middle-class and middle-aged housewives) most likely to consume that quintessential literature of domesticity, the romance. "True" crime and "true" romance blended into a renegade genre in the accounts of the "Hearts Killers," even though Martha Beck herself was bound not to measure up as a romantic subject. The press called her "fat, dowdy Martha,"[11] and at one moment she pointedly (and rhetorically) asked whether she was being "tried for murder, or because I'm fat."[12] Her body, her gender, and her sexuality were all subjected to an intense scrutiny. And, make no mistake, Martha Beck became the central figure in the case and in all incarnations of the story to follow because of the intensity, and the nature, of that scrutiny.

The many versions of the story of the Hearts Killers revolve around an indeterminate center, the assumed "truth" of the events. An authoritative version of what happened (and its meaning) is arrived at not through a narrative arranged to accommodate the "facts," but from out of the ungainly but remarkably resilient structure of the "backwards narrative": murder foretold through the unraveling of the murderer's developing psychosis. Narrative conventions in the tale of murder work on a system of portent, of *presque vu*. The murder happens because of the murderer, and yet there is no murderer until the murder. This paradox is the very engine of narration in the tale of murder.

I have already indicated that the prediction of dangerousness relies upon the classification of the murderer through analysis — an analysis that reauthors the act *and* its original author. The true crime genre as a whole is similarly implicated in the reauthoring of its subject, even as its subject exceeds the focal point of the narrative: the figure of the murderer. The popularity of the pulp genre of true crime (in which the tale of murder reigns supreme) can be taken as partial evidence of the importance of the murder narrative in the American cultural consciousness. The conditions of possibility for the true crime detective magazine and the forensic psychiatrist's report are obviously different, but the direction of meaning in the tale of murder is governed by similar cultural impulses. The question asked of murder by legal process is unusually narrow. The "How?" investigated in the trial becomes, even in the expert psychiatric testimony it contains, the much more insistent "Why?" ruling the murder narrative. *The business of the murder narrative lies with the murderer, and with the enigma of origins.*[13] In true crime, as in other tales of murder, there is the expectation that a definitive version waits, somewhere at the end of the author/detective's trail. Yet that authoritative version must remain, mirage-like, on the horizon of the murder's telling. The questions are insistent, the answers elusive.

The true crime genre has its own topology of murder. Crimes can be grouped by the criminological tag for the killer (lust or serial killers), by the profession of the killer (doctors, police), by the age or gender of the killers (kids who kill, women who kill), and by the relationship between the killers or between killer and victim (couples who kill, children who kill their parents, abused women who kill their husbands). These aggregates repackage a finite number of sensational crimes and allow for their recontextualization in the subgenre that describes them. The inflection is significant, for established tales of murder — like that of the Honeymoon Killers — change from category to category. The telling of the story of the Hearts Killers as a true romance (analyzed in Chapter 4) will give rise to a slightly different narrative from that of the *folie à deux* (discussed in Chapters 5 and 6), although both share elements of the romance. Regardless of the framework, however, the tale is told to render "truth" from the great mystery that is murder.

Chapter 6, the final piece in the section dealing with the Hearts Killers, attends to the incarnation of their story in a film made in 1970 that was to assume cult status. The dark satire of *The Honeymoon Killers*[14] is but one example of a more general shift in the 1960s toward a "critical" narrative form quite unlike the confident, authoritative narratives of such liberal humanists as Fredric Wertham and Curtis Bok, or the social critiques of Willard Motley and William March. The political critique of authority in the West, culminating (in Europe) in the upheavals of 1968, had an impact also on philosophy, social criticism, the new journalism, and literature. While "postmodernism" may be merely a marker in the overall development of modernism during this century, the move toward self-reflexive narrative has been a significant one in the past thirty years. Thus the predominantly ethical, though prescriptive, concerns of writers like Wertham and Bok give way to what might be seen as more complex, and less certain, forms of narrative. The modern tales of murder dealt with in the final three chapters of this book demonstrate, generally, not just that "facts" are difficult and often spare, but that authority within and without the text is inherently suspect. Narrative cohesion still demanded the construction of authority within intelligible historical and cultural horizons — but the horizon, and all it took in, had changed.

Chapters Seven, Eight, and Nine deal with narratives of murder that belong to an era where authority, within and without texts, is suspect. These texts demonstrate a quite different set of allegiances and concerns from those of the earlier works, and all of them try in some way to put the killed back into the tale of murder. The work of James Baldwin on the child murders in Atlanta and that of Kate Millett on the torture murder of a teenage girl in suburban Middle America both refuse in different ways the narrative impulses of an increasingly aestheticized discourse of murder.[15] James Baldwin has written in *The Evidence of Things Not Seen* a devastating critique of American racism. His analysis of the creation of a single controversial "case" out of the so-called Atlanta Child Killings demonstrates how the trial of Wayne Williams and his condemnation elided the more pressing — and central — issues of racial ghettoization, endemic poverty, and racism. Kate Millett, in her eloquent revisitation of a murder scene, critiques the violent workings of patriarchal institutions in capitalist America. Baldwin and Millett hold in common a broad social critique and a refusal, therefore, to make of the murderer a scapegoat. And yet, the signal difference between the two works is their object: race, on the one hand, and gender on the other. Although both accounts attempt to deconstruct hierarchies of difference that are structurally encoded, their terms are pretty much mutually exclusive.[16] For this reason, I scrutinize the inscription of gender in Baldwin as well as Millett's silence about race.

The last chapter is, if you like, the return of the prodigal. It draws together the earlier analyses by returning to the problem of the ability of the tale of murder to fascinate. How and why does the figure of the murderer become the focal point of mediation in narratives from the earlier as well as the later period? What, finally, is it that compels people to tell murder stories? (Which question must also become: What do they listen for in such stories?)

For Willard Motley and William March, Dr. Fredric Wertham and Judge Curtis Bok, the matter in writing about murder would seem to be "I am doing this for. . . ." There is, after all, an *end* to all of this: a better understanding of what poverty and lack of caring can inure the soul to, an understanding of the nature of evil, of madness, of justice. For later writers, like James Baldwin and Kate Millett, the *question* at the heart of their tale is different: "Why did this happen — this way — to this man, this child, this girl, this woman? How easily could this have happened to me?" And that, perhaps, is what I must finally call a more "fitting" way of writing about murder: a witnessing that identifies not with the fundamental fragility of *all* bodies confronted with violence, but with the greater vulnerability of some who must confront the invulnerability, or blind hurt, of others. The fragility of one's own body is thus written into the text, a figural space for the murdered to appear as something other than a corpse, more substantial than a sign.

Part 1
The Killers

Other 'en killing,

I have been nice to everybody all my life.

Henry Lee Lucas

1. Here There Be Killers

Things least to be believed are most preferred
All counterfeit as from truths sacred mint
Are readily believed if once put down in print.
John Clare, "St. Martin's Eve"

In 1866, early in that period of violent social change known as Recon-struction, a paper carried in its column of curiosities a snippet of news from Mobile, Alabama. In a vacant apartment a headless body had been found. Accompanying the corpse was a note that read: "To prevent iden-tification I have hidden my own head where you will never find it."[1] This anecdote is a perfect example of the conundrum of murder: the story of the lively corpse or the blithe murderer. The report provides no resolu-tion to the mystery, its wry brevity attesting to the publishers' confidence in a reader's love of the paradoxical quality of the tale of murder — not necessarily the more *orderly* satisfactions gained from the narrative of crime, detection, apprehension, punishment, and redemption. By the "lyrical fiction" of this particular "murderer's song,"[2] the body in the vacant room becomes at once murderer and victim: a sign of its own disappearance. Any layperson knows that the best evidence of murder (upon which to hang a prosecution, at any rate) is a corpse, yet the mod-ern tale of murder turns attention away from the victim to the mur-derer — the corpse becoming little more than a relic of another's trans-gression and transcendence. The metaphysics of modern murder makes the victim a sign of the murderer.[3]

The cultural resonance of the narrative of murder arises from its uneasy position at the borderline of ethics and aesthetics. In a culture wherein the communication and entertainment media are more varied and accessible than ever before, the "fact" of murder and its representations grow close indeed: "That murder is the most unrepresentable and yet one of the most represented of acts in our culture points to the fact that rather than take one out of discourse, murder ironically leads one back into it, with a vengeance, to which the vast and ever-expanding plethora of murder literature bears witness: horror stories, detective stories, criminological literature, video nasties, and so on."[4] Murder as a fundamental expression of immanence and abjection has a presence that consumes the corpse of victim and murderer alike. And yet the visceral, brute fact of murder is itself a false, or insufficient, foundation for narrative. All that is given in the tale of murder is the corpse; everything else remains to be found.

Murder belongs only partly to the juridical and penological realm, where it becomes, in the discourses of the modern social sciences, a "problem" effected by period and place, evidence of the changing relationships of power between classed, raced, and gendered actors. The disciplines of sociology, criminology, penology, law and, not least of all, forensic psychiatry have traditionally laid claim to scientific status (with the exception of the law, for which quite other truth claims are made).[5] The positivistic assumptions at the root of the development of these disciplines are quintessentially ethical and implicitly political.[6] The quest for topology and classification that underpins the disciplines of criminology, penology, and psychiatry can exist only on a discursive landscape against which the "discovered" object can have its form defined and its shadow cast. Every psychological classification for the "insane" murderer; every analysis of the degree or gravity of the crime; every determination on gradation, technique, or site of punishment for murder; and every study of the environmental milieu of the violent individual makes a decision about the meaning of murder: its origins, its impact, its "nature."

The crime story is a critically significant narrative frame in modern Western culture — whether the scripted broadsheet "confessions" of the murderer on the scaffold in the eighteenth and early nineteenth century, or the compendium of sensational trials in the Ordinary of Newgate Account, or the detective fiction of Poe, Dickens and (later) Hammett, Chandler, and Spillane.[7] The true crime genre that has enjoyed an unsurprising renaissance since the 1940s (and not only in the United States) is the direct descendant of a genre of crime reporting that treats the "facts" at issue as a good deal less important than the narrative rules of the genre.

Throughout the eighteenth and nineteenth centuries there could not be said to be a clear demarcation between a high and low literature of crime, nor between the stories of actual and fictional murder. Thackeray satirized the style of the *Newgate Chronicle*, and Henry Fielding, in *Jonathan Wild*, drew on the *Chronicle* for a panoply of characters and crimes. The vogue of the crime story by the mid-nineteenth century should not be underestimated. What contemporaries perceived as the degenerative horrors of urban culture were enthusiastically chronicled from the 1860s in both Britain and the United States.[8] By the later nineteenth century, eugenic thought—haunted by the spectre of the "born" criminal and atavistic degeneration—existed side by side with more progressive social analyses of violence. As the century waned, the tale of murder as fact or fiction moved progressively further from its description of the murderous act to an analysis of the murderer.

Between the early part of the nineteenth century and its apogee, the murderer grew in stature; the meaning of murder, its metaphysics, was no longer evident in the event but in its main actor. That discursive shift belongs to a more general historical process within which the individual subject grew more complex, and more affecting: the subject a synecdoche for the greater social "whole." As part of that epistemological shift inward from the world to the soul and psyche of the subject, the "murderer" was invented—along with (and, often, part and parcel of) the "hysteric," the "homosexual," the "adolescent," the "criminal," and the "psychotic."

In the following chapters I will be examining both the representation of actual murder and murder in fiction. By dismantling various narratives of murder it will become possible to expose the cultural meaning given to murder, that irreplaceable taken-for-granted quality of a murder that, when narrated, says so much about *what a culture knows* and *what it will not let itself know*. While this work is in part a general analysis of the compelling quality of murder narratives in the West, it is also an investigation of the interestedness of modern and contemporary American culture in the tale of murder. Americans consume murder as a daily fare, sometimes—during the trial of O. J. Simpson, for instance—to the point of biliousness. Most states have legislation allowing trials to be televised whole or in part, and an adept channel surfer can always find a murder covered in detail: on the news; in "true crime" miniseries; in the urban folklore of programs like *Unexplained Mysteries;* in the tabloid format of disaster and police work series; and, of course, on twenty-four hours a day of *Court T.V.* Television talk-show hosts regularly address the topic, programming fatal violence along with more banal, folksy wisdom on the control of weight, excess or insufficient body hair, and relations with one's in-laws. How can one not be riveted by Oprah Winfrey's tongue-in-cheek questioning of a woman deeply smitten by the younger of the Menendez brothers, a man she knows only from a miniseries, from news and *Court T.V.?* Oprah on "Woman in Love with Serial Killers," or Donahue railing at the National Rifle Association, or Sally Jesse Raphael on adolescent drug use, all have in common their reference to a popular understanding of how violence is lived in contemporary America. To say that Americans have an interest in murder is to use "interest" both as a noun and a transitive verb, to show "curiosity" and "concern, affect, and relation to," to signify the "personal" and "public." It is to show the *implication* of the curious in the object of their curiosity. And yet that "interest" is not a unitary one, shared by one and all in a unified, undifferentiated culture. "Cultural interestedness" is a general term that embraces a varied set of local effects, as evidenced, say, by the difference between pro- and anti-death-penalty lobby groups (not to mention the difference of both of these again from the people most likely to find themselves on death row).

Michel Foucault has observed that the relationship of power to death in modern democratic societies is, in appearance, benevolent or, at least, passive. It may "*foster* life or *disallow* it to the point of death."[9] The main business of technologized power is to maintain and extend life, and that preoccupation has been accompanied by a kind of "occulting" of death. Death is sequestered in modern Western culture, becoming private in its actuality yet increasingly public as representation. Death, like power, has become dispersed. It is everywhere and nowhere. In a culture that has located so much meaning in self-identity, in individuality and in the body as "person,"[10] it should not be surprising that it is the psyche of the criminal, rather than the crime itself, that fascinates. Death takes up residence in the figure of the murderer. Execution — killing the killer — is contrived to exorcise the *presence* of death, but such a presence cannot be exorcised (for where can death *go?*). Death is a symptom, and, like the symptom in psychoanalytic practice, it is all there effectively is — the limit and extent of meaning, yet a limit that points beyond itself (What is death?). Execution, as the last great secular ritual surrounding death in American culture, is still important, if not critical, to that culture's sense of its own *life*.

The last chapter of this book will deal more closely with the question of execution and with the stature of the murderer as death's "agent" in contemporary American culture. That discussion demands an analysis of one of the most recent, and exemplary, works on the place of murder in American culture: Wendy Lesser's *Pictures at an Execution*. Two earlier critical works also deserve attention, for despite their quite different pre-occupations with murder in (or as) literature, both David Brion Davis and Joel Black provide ample evidence of the cultural importance of the murder narrative.[11] The differences between the two texts suggest the historical contingency and particularity of the tale of murder. Davis's is a liberal text produced during the Cold War, one concerned with the social values exposed by American literary accounts of murder from the Revolution to the Civil War, and Black's a "postmodern" account that ranges through the fiction of four languages and two countries to arrive at an analysis of "hyperrealized violence" in contemporary American culture. Both works are motivated by presentist and manifestly "social" concerns, notwithstanding their historical, comparative, and more or less "literary" subjects. Both works treat, in different ways, a familiar question: How does an individual act of violence relate to the culture that gives rise to it, and how is that act of one (the murdering individual) *owned* by the community of others? Davis's work addresses this conundrum as a question of "social values." Black, on the other hand, considers the interchange between representation and "reality" and, in choosing to study simultaneously fictional texts and sensational cases, opts for an interrogation of the aesthetic approach to murder.[12] The problem of murder that looms large for Davis is the problem of a society that gave birth to the collective domestic homicide called the Civil War. His is not a simplistic conception of the "mind" of society (in the form of its "imagination"), for he does recognize the unpredictable and contradictory nature of the symbolic level of his texts. But the movement of meaning remains one-way: killings stay in the world and are mimicked in texts; the texts themselves are never murderous.

In the prosperous but still ideologically troubled United States of the mid-1950s it is not surprising to find Davis arguing that a study of the literary treatment of murder should "elucidate more general problems in American civilization." His aim is to establish a kind of intellectual history of both American aggression and the sanctions against it; to explain the contradictory nature of a "sparkling, smiling, domestic land . . . where it is estimated that a new murder occurs every forty-five minutes."[13] Yet Davis's attention to a discretely American culture of violence makes his concern no less universal than an examination of the extent and range of reasons put forward for mankind's "extraordinary capacity to kill." By examining the reasoning, reflective, and mimetic art of literature, Davis strives to produce an empiricist account of murder's reason.[14] Significantly, this account of reason becomes, by its own critical strategies, an inescapably gendered one.

As part of his discussion of the triumph of the tale of seduction, Davis analyzes a notorious homicide in New York in 1836. James Gordon Bennett provided extensive and detailed reporting for the *New York Herald* concerning the murder of Helen Jewett, a cultured and successful prostitute, by a disgruntled client, Richard Robinson. Jewett was axed and then, in a failed attempt by the murderer to dispose of the evidence, her body was slightly burned. Despite the brutality of the murder, Bennett dwelt at length upon the beauty of the corpse:

The body looked as white, as full, as polished as the purest Parian marble. The perfect figure, the exquisite limbs, the fine face, the full arms, the beautiful bust, all surpassed, in every respect, the Venus de Medici. . . . For a few moments I was lost in admiration of the extraordinary sight, a beautiful female corpse, that surpassed the finest statue in antiquity. I was recalled to her horrid destiny by seeing the dreadful bloody gashes on the right temple.[15]

Although "recalled to her horrid destiny," Bennett goes on to enumerate the other accomplishments of the victim, now a corpse. Davis describes Bennett's minute attention to Jewett's rooms — from the furnishings and the titles of the books on her shelves to the beautiful penmanship and delicate turn of phrase of her private letters. The scene of death in this way becomes an extension of the "beautiful female corpse." In his discussion of the Jewett case and its successive mediators — from Bennett and H. R. Howard[16] through to the fictional study of the Jewett case by

Joseph Holt Ingraham[17] — Davis shows the shift of emphasis, enacted through the aestheticization of the corpse, from the victim to the murderer: a naive boy beguiled by the harlot's accomplishment and beauty.[18] An excess of stimulation deranges the murderer's previously controlled passions. The reversed tale of seduction, in which female corruption dislodges male reason and is thereby punished, vindicates the murderer while banishing the victim to the borders of the moral frame. In Bennett's early "true crime" narrative, an ugly act — the outcome of two degraded lives in collision — begets a scene of "beauty."[19]

Recent scholarship on the tropic relationship of femininity and death in Western culture suggests that the feminine partakes of much of death's "allusive" qualities: its "unrepresentability" as well as its immanence. Death, like femininity, is both "limit and excess."[20] While Death is *nowhere*, Woman is simply *not*. As Sarah Goodwin and Elisabeth Bronfen put it, "[O]ur culture posits death and the feminine as what is radically other to the norm, the living or surviving masculine subject; they represent the disruption and difference that ground a narcissistic sense of self."[21] While an analysis of the allegorical relationship of Woman and Death is a fascinating project in and of itself, what most concerns me here is the insight that relationship provides to a reading of certain historically contingent tales of murder. If, as Goodwin and Bronfen point out, "femininity and death are Western culture's two major tropes for the enigma," then women would seem to be killed (both in and out of texts) not because they are dispensable objects, but because they are *indispensable*. To put it another way, the instability of the category of the Feminine is essential to the maintenance of an illusory stability of the Masculine. In concrete terms this perhaps means that Woman (as sign and substance?) is *indispensably dispensable*.[22] The ineluctable symbolic quality that attends the flesh made feminine is part and parcel of the murder narrative, because — in a sense — where Death appears so too must the Feminine. The gendered tropic strategy of the tale of murder appears in and around the interrogation of the murder's origin in the murderer's psyche. It appears in the discussion of the victim's sexuality, class, and race, all categories which are themselves coded by the pathologizing of the murderer into the idiosyncratic rather than the social: "character," "predisposition," or "environment." The following work is, if you like, a way to return the idiosyncrasy of violence to the context of its culture. The act of narrating murder, for all its drive to make that act an aberration, and its actor pathological, makes murder culturally intelligible by reference to *things known:* that which is taken for granted, everyday, familiar, and common to all. Murder is part of an everyday grammar, its mark acute, but final only for the one killed.

The conjunction of femininity and death is clearly visible in David Brion Davis's erudite study *Homicide in American Fiction.* Although much of Davis's work deals in depth with changing perceptions of homicidal "madness" throughout the nineteenth century,[23] his concentration on the popularity of the tale of seduction in the second half of that century leads him toward a critique of the representation of women in such texts. In the sentimental tale that Davis analyzes, Woman primarily represented what she could bestow upon or take from a man — whether that be land, family, love, fidelity or, ultimately, his reason. Woman, in turn, could have her own moral soul (writers less readily spoke of lost reason for women) destroyed by seduction. The final blame for that fall, however, did not lie with the seducer but with the seduced who allows her own "murder."[24] Like Guy River's mother, that "weakly fond, misjudging woman who gave me birth" whom River blamed for his own murderousness, a woman could also be held responsible for the dead moral sense of her murdering son. Largely, then, women could be seen to be both the source and the arena of corruption. As such, Woman became the representation of nightmare, not of reason. In the discourse of murder, sex is Woman and sex is Death: therefore, Woman too is Death.

As a historian, Davis is careful to contextualize the symbolic use of Woman as transcendent figure, yet his contextualization (male fears derived from a change in the status of women) tends itself to reinstate Woman as the object of a male historical subject — whether he be an author or the gendered generic of "American society." Discussing the preoccupation of nineteenth-century authors with the destabilizing power of sex, Davis notes that "nothing was so common in popular fiction as the hero who struggled simultaneously for his father's estate and for his heroine's hand. Sexual conflict could symbolize all conflict between human egos, every contest between men for possession and power."[25] In this way Davis not only describes the predilection of popular writers for the use of Woman as symbolic prize, but he is himself excluding her from the discursive realm of competition.

Commenting on the growing obsession in the popular fiction of the 1840s with the evil in Woman, Davis provides what could be read either as his historicization of that hostility and fear or his *own* theory as to its cause:

De Tocqueville shared the view of many foreign travellers that Americans were unique in their respect and admiration for women. It was also true, however, that many American men were unhappy over the extreme idealization of the fair sex, which inevitably brought restrictions for men. Sentimental writers might glorify motherhood, but mothers also exercised more power in America than in most other countries.[26]

Davis here works within — rather than opposing — the discursive frame of a secular idealization of Woman. When he goes on to discuss the dualistic character of Woman in nineteenth-century fiction, he is therefore able only to deal with the increased ability of men to discriminate between "various feminine stereotypes."[27] At issue is the use to which Woman is put as symbol, but not her wholesale status *as* symbol. In Davis's exposition, as in the texts he analyzes, symbolic Woman becomes a lesson in the social values of a society-gendered male. By reinscribing the symbolic strategy of sentimental literature as part of an ethical discourse on murder, Davis produces a gendered discourse of murder in which Woman becomes both the ethical agent of her own destruction and the aesthetic object of that destruction. The beauty of the female corpse that so hypnotized James Gordon Bennett comes both from the aura of exemplarity in the female victim (she who is *by her very sex* corrupt but whose perfect corpse resists, momentarily, corporeal corruption) and from vestigial traces of the murderer's presence left on the body, a presence impressed, by quite another aura, upon the scene of the murder itself. Because Robinson has killed her, his presence cannot be excised from the scene; Bennett, the observer, stands in for the murderer who has fled. It is Bennett who, in contemplating the corpse, is "recalled to her horrid destiny" — like the murderer who suddenly realizes what he has done.

The dark renown of the murderer, and, indeed, the "beauty" of his act, is eloquently explored in the framing of the narrative of a nineteenth-century French parricide by a research group at the Collège de France. Michel Foucault, with his colleagues, explained their reasons for not interpreting the lengthy confession of Pierre Riviere: "[O]wing to a sort of reverence and perhaps, too, terror for a text which was to carry off four corpses along with it, we were unwilling to superimpose our own text on Riviere's memoir. We fell under the spell of the parricide with the reddish-brown eyes." Elsewhere Foucault declares that "its beauty alone is sufficient justification" for reprinting the murderer's text.[28] The song of the peasant murderer is—for the Collège de France group—such an unlikely sound, such a rarity, that they cannot bear to provide a new arrangement for its startling score. The text of the confession is beautiful because surprising that it ever was articulated at all, and the act—of which the confession is but a part—can therefore be viewed as one of rebellion.[29] By virtue of the "murderer's song" to which they so intently listen, the Collège de France scholars become witnesses to a crime that initially had no witnesses but the murderer. In taking up his text, they are converted to an audience as the crime plays out again before them.

"Murder," wrote W. H. Auden, "is unique in that it abolishes the party it injures, so that society has to take the place of the victim and on his behalf demand atonement or grant forgiveness; it is the one crime in which society has a direct interest."[30] His definition of that "uniqueness" was founded upon a qualification of the antisocial nature of the crime, yet that moral response can also be read as having implications for an aesthetics of murder. What, for instance, might be a phenomenology of murder when the only subject is the witness to the crime and the murderer?[31] If "murder abolishes the party it injures," this must indeed be the result, and society's "direct interest" should be seen not only as ethical and punitive, but as aesthetic.

Explaining the notion of the aesthetic response, Joel Black writes:

[A]ny object or idea may be experienced or interpreted by a beholder (or witness, in the case of someone who is present at an event or an act) as a work of art— again, according to whatever the beholder's definition of "art" may be. . . . [Such a response] refers exclusively to the beholder's subjective experience, regardless of whether or not the object of this experience was intended as a work of art or designed for the beholder's aesthetic enjoyment.

The theory of aesthetics developed by the Romantics took account of "painful as well as pleasurable perceptions"—not least of which was fear. Terror, or the spectre of terror, was thought to have a more powerful effect than pleasure. Black's explication of this theory of the dark sublime hinges upon his revisionist analysis of Thomas De Quincey's essays on murder. Black argues that De Quincey's "aesthetics of murder" was an attack upon the "rational, bourgeois ideology of detective fiction" that parades as an ethical literature of murder. De Quincey, therefore, foreshadowed modern works within which

the classical idea of mimesis — the view that art is in some sense an imitation of nature or a representation of reality — is subverted to the point where being and appearance, ethics and aesthetics, are no longer distinguishable, but have become virtual simulacra of each other.[32]

Jean Baudrillard's epigraph to *Simulations* defines the simulacrum as "never that which conceals the truth — it is the truth which conceals that there is none. The simulacrum is true."[33] If the mimetic collapses into the "real," we all become, somehow, witnesses to murder in a culture of pure spectacle. The dark sublime of terror becomes a tool both for the murderer's performance and for the performance of murder. In the former case, Black provides the example of the "serial killer"[34] who is given a media fanfare that greatly enhances his murderous prestige, his ability to horrify and, ultimately, his desire to kill.[35] The latter case describes the ability of writers and filmmakers to "play on the fantasies and fears of their mass audiences . . . profoundly aware of the effect their actions will have on their enthralled spectators."[36]

Death fascinates. Although the circulation of images of murder is controlled and the television media follow certain guidelines of public "taste" — shielding the public from some of the most abject scenes captured by the news teams — those images of feigned violence proliferate, providing the means by which violence, as Black puts it, is hyperrealized:

Officially, the act of taking another person's life, either as crime or punishment, can be represented only as an artistic fiction or simulation. In this guise, murder is no longer a social reality; it has been neutralized and tamed as a supposedly harmless form of popular entertainment.[37]

Feminist critics of pornography, among others, have argued that images of sexual violence directly affect the incidence of actual violence on women.[38] However, no *causal* link has been firmly established, and the meaning of the correlation between representations of violence and actual acts of violence is still hotly debated.[39] That relation can be seen either as a quantitative or a qualitative one — or, indeed, it may be both. Commonly, those who theorize about the negative effects of media violence see its representation as increasing the incidence of actual acts of violence by making it easier for offenders to objectify their potential victims — to make them "unreal" and, therefore, disposable. Another argument suggests that murders represented sensationally are an invitation to copycat crime. More often than not, such killings are the reenactment of an already reenacted crime.[40] Both scenarios are, in a sense, largely quantitative: they increase the chances that a murder will be committed. A qualitative correlation, though, implies a more subtle relation of the image to the act. Discussing the example of the pornography and censorship debates in the context of the United States, Ian Hacking presents one possible way to tease out the complicated nature of the "qualitative" relationship of representation to actual violence:

Pornography of the vilest and most sadistic sort, it is argued, invites imitation. The evidence for this claim is poor, but it may be the wrong claim to examine closely. The real evil may lurk one stage higher up. Distributing pornography is distributing knowledge of new kinds of action . . . [increasing] . . . the range of possible demeaning actions.[41]

While this is perhaps an instrumental view, not so different in fact from a feminist critique that treats pornography as a blueprint for the misogynist objectification of women, Hacking concludes his discussion in a more problematizing, and Foucauldian, way. The "new modes of action, new descriptions, verbal or visual," do not merely give rise to implementation by the ill-meaning, but to a whole "looping effect of human kinds." The category of the "wicked" expands to contain both new *actions* and new categories of wicked persons — to embrace *types* of "wickedness," and new processes and classifications to contain that wickedness. In short, a complete and complex ascription of meaning to the violent, to crime, to the "criminal."

Joel Black is rather more long-winded in his explication of the "hyper-realization" of violence evidenced by the media-motivated assassination of John Lennon by David Chapman and the attempted assassination of Ronald Reagan by John Hinckley. Black refuses the simplistic notion that the killers merely wanted to "realize" the novel or film obsessing them.[42] Rather than argue that Hinckley and Chapman were psycho- or sociopaths who mistook "fantasy for reality, fiction for fact, art for action," Black proposes that they should be seen as "supreme literalists" who tried to see the world ("where violence is routinely sublimated into art") as it "really" is, "in all its unsublimated, sublime violence":

Artistic representations of slayings provide fictional displacements or simulacra of the act of murder for everyone except the artistically illiterate. Such persons are unable to recognize art as art, not simply because they live in a world of make-believe fantasy . . . but because they are absolute Realists who find no truth or meaning whatsoever either in their own private fantasies (the Imaginary) or in the collective fantasies of art and the media (the Symbolic).[43]

The artistic illiterate, essentially blind to the aesthetics of murder (in the sense of its "routine sublimation into art"), resorts to a dangerous ethics of murder as "a code or principle of action."[44] Black describes not a confusion of art for the real, but a supreme realism that banishes the "unreal" altogether.

There are other, more interesting, ways of looking at the qualitative relationship between representations of violence and actual violence. Bill Ellis, investigating the connection between urban horror folklore[45] and certain incidences of animal mutilation and murder, theorizes the existence of several modes of "ostension" — the conversion of narrative, or the legendary, into fact. Ellis reminds us that the definition of the legendary should be kept as broad as possible, that legends are "normative definitions of reality, maps by which one can determine what has happened, what is happening, and what will happen."[46] Legends are both descriptive and prescriptive narratives.

Ellis develops his analysis of ostension in a discussion of a satanist scare sparked by the discovery of certain "inexplicable" animal mutilations in the rural heartland of America, suggesting that the people thereabouts tended to interpret evidence in the light of existent narrative forms. Cattle mutilations, dismissed by the FBI as the work of foxes, presented to other eyes the work of "cults" long believed to exist — if quiescent — in the area. This act of interpretation Ellis designates as "quasi-ostension." "Pseudo-ostension" also seems likely to have played a role in the Texas satanist panic when practical jokers arranged unholy shrines or dismembered the already dead carcasses of animals to imitate a sacrificial scene. Pseudo-ostension was therefore defined as "imitating the outlines of a known narrative to perpetuate a hoax."[47] A third variety of ostension identified by Ellis has remarkable resonance with Black's analysis of an aberrant ethics of murder. "True ostension" involves not only taking the legend at face value, but writing oneself into it: in this case, actually sacrificing animals or even humans in order to "raise a spirit."[48] Such a version of murder as performance is quite different from the common understanding of copycat killings, for it involves the annexation of legend as positive action. The narrative frame to an act of literal ostension only makes easier the inversion of "reality." If someone kills two teenagers as a sacrifice to demons, then that person is acting upon a version of the world in which demons exist. If, when the crime becomes known, the community attributes it to satanists (in the face of a more rational alternative), then the wider frame for that murderous act is, epistemologically speaking, in agreement with it. "Legends about satanic murder and mutilation are not just expressions of fictive horror, they are paradigms for making the world more horrifying."[49]

Ellis's analysis of ostension is in some ways a more subtle sketch of the interrelationship of representation and reality than is Black's, for all the sophistication of the concept of those "supreme literalists" of violence. Yet Ellis and Black both describe cultural mechanisms (legend and media, respectively) that create the terms by which "reality" can be actively interpreted — can, in effect, be made.[50]

2. *Parens Patriae*

The depravity of mankind is so easily discoverable that nothing
but the desert or the cell can exclude it from notice.
Samuel Johnson

The problem and origin of evil looms large in Willard Motley's naturalistic fiction and William March's novelistic study of psychopathology in
the making. Motley and March present apparently polarized conceptions
of murder's genesis: culture on one hand, and bestial nature on the other.
To get to the bottom of the matter and to argue a case, both writers stray
out of the fictive into the realm of fact, of evidence — of sociological and
criminological models. Taken in tandem, Motley's *Knock on Any Door* and
March's *The Bad Seed* demonstrate the developing relationship of the
critical crime novel with true-crime, as well as a more broadly 'sociological' scholarship. Willard Motley explores the corruption and inequity of
juvenile detention systems, and William March the unforeseen results of
adoption in a world of inherited traits (or, in this case, "taints"). Motley's
critique seems, initially, to be directed at the social realm, while the latter
focuses on the micro, individual, or domestic level. Both texts work in
reference to theories of degeneration, although March wavers toward a
belief in "innate depravity."[1] Motley's *Knock on Any Door* follows the
materialist and naturalistic turn of Theodore Dreiser and Frank Norris,[2]
and March's *The Bad Seed* deals explicitly with the issue of genetics, enun-
ciating a quasi-Lombrosian theory of degeneration.[3] The idea of degeneration can turn in more or less deterministic ways, its effects apocalyptic
or merely of the moment. I would like to detour from an analysis of
degeneration at the level of the race or nation (or, in Foucauldian terms,
the "species body") to examine these texts at the level of their approach to

the individual body.[4] To elide the "species body" is not, however, to lose sight of it altogether, for both of these works provide a unique opportunity to look at that which unites the species body with the individual body: the discourse of sex, the "deployment of sexuality."[5] It is not just the construction of "deviancy" that joins the discourse of sex with that of the criminal, but also the practice of confession, the power of truth in the revelatory secret, the soul exposed through the body's penance.

Foucault writes in volume one of his *History of Sexuality* that

we . . . are in a society of "sex," or rather a society "with a sexuality": the mechanisms of power are addressed to the body, to life, to what causes it to proliferate, to what reinforces the species, its stamina, its ability to dominate, or its capacity for being used. Through the themes of health, progeny, race, the future of the species, the vitality of the social body, power spoke of sexuality and *to* sexuality; the latter was not a mark or a symbol, it was an object and a target.[6]

Both of these novels are, if you like, "saturated" with sex, if sex is understood in this way. The "four great strategic unities" that Foucault identifies as the "specific mechanisms of knowledge and power centering on sex" provide a useful discursive horizon for both texts.[7] Nick, the angelic altar boy turned criminal, who is the protagonist of Motley's novel, registers his dissolution at the sexual level and at the level of his masculinity. Christine, who mothers a monster (and, in turn, discovers she was mothered by one), is the subject focus for a constellation of doubts about what Foucault calls the "biological-moral responsibility" of the Mother. The figure of Rhoda, the "bad seed," marks another set of related anxieties about a "precociousness" that, while not overtly sexual, must partake of the sexual by virtue of a general quandary about her "adult-like" qualities, as well as her position as the object of desire of the adult, LeRoy. Rhoda can fruitfully be read as a " 'preliminary' sexual being, on this side of sex, yet within it, astride a dangerous dividing line."[8]

The ubiquity of violence and its endemic nature are core concerns in both works. Although Motley's novel is by far the bleaker — describing a society massively abusing and disfiguring its citizens — March, on balance, paints the most irredeemable picture: evil exists as an essential but random force in human nature. Evil essentialized means not that *murder will out*, but that it may *not*. Worse still, genocide and the full panoply of human-

kind's supposed "inhumanities" would then seem as natural (though spas-
modic) in their incidence as earth tremors in the California basin.

Suffer the Children

Although Willard Motley's work was published in the late 1940s and
found an audience sufficient and sympathetic enough to warrant its conversion into a film in 1949, the novel was written in the early years of the
war.[9] Its fidelity to the then declining naturalistic genre should not be too
surprising in an era still haunted by the Great Depression and the social
consciousness of the Popular Front era. The novel warrants inclusion
here because its themes found a receptive audience in a changed America
of the late 1940s and early 1950s.[10] Motley, an African American writer
who was accused by some of his contemporaries of ignoring the central
issue of race in his work, consistently claimed that his concern was the
"human race." The broad focus of his work reflects that sensibility and his
commitment to write of lives that he — brought up in a middle-class black
family in a comfortable white neighborhood — had only lately come to
know. Motley chose the life which others, during the depression, had no
hope of avoiding and he was jailed for vagrancy. Struck by the very or-
dinariness of the people he met in jail, he took the cause of their criminal-
ization by society as his own.[11]

The most interesting aspects of *Knock on Any Door* are thematic and
symbolic. Certainly the violence done to Nick, the young protagonist, is
more of a moral focus to the novel than the violence he *actually enacts*, and
in that sense Motley's novel is closer to Wright's *Native Son* than to
Dreiser's *An American Tragedy*.[12] Yet the distinctiveness of Motley's novel
comes from its sexual and gender coding of the poverty and brutality that
makes a killer of Nick. Nick is not taunted by the apparent accessibility of
the American Dream, as Clyde Griffiths was, nor is he completely excluded from it as was Bigger Thomas. Nick, the angel-faced altar boy, is
momentarily an *emblem* of the American Dream. But the boy who was so
good that he'd "go straight to heaven" if he died unfortunately *lives*, and
he endures a world so remote from heaven that it belies the goodness
supposedly severing the saved from the damned. That goodness is wholly

reliant upon the condition of its expression, a reservation that signals Motley's refusal to entertain the idea of humankind's *essential* goodness. Aunt Rosa's hopeful assessment that "there's something good in everybody" only underlines this, for even she admits the crucial proviso that people "don't do no wrong . . . *when they're left alone* [italics mine]."[13] But they are not left alone.

There is a bewildering amount of description of male beauty in Motley's novel. Initially, in his "innocence," Nick is unconscious of his good looks. His awakening to his own beauty precedes his discovery of its uses (a discovery that coincides with the revelation of sexual desire). Nick first perceives the *virility* of beauty through the lens of his attraction to Rocky, a fellow Borstal boy. Rocky is Nick's first mirror, reflecting a panoply of desires. Nick desires Rocky's assurance and swagger, and his freedom. The sign of that freedom is itself physically manifest in the names pinched into the skins of the gang members. Nick progressively steps into the space of these most wonderful and strong bodies around him: he beats Bricktop, the reformatory's champion fighter, and befriends Allen (an African American youth shunned by the other inmates), becoming — spiritually and physically — "Champ of the Hill." He steps into Rocky's place when the other has gone, adopting his swagger and his gang.

These figures, Nick's surrogates, represent an illusory masculinity that Nick adopts as his own, with disastrous results. Degraded "manhood" is certainly not an unfamiliar theme in the naturalistic novel, occurring in different ways in both *An American Tragedy* and *Native Son*. It was a theme of great concern to Motley, one that he coded quite differently from his peers Richard Wright and James Baldwin.[14] In *Knock on Any Door* the issue of "manhood" becomes a meditation upon sexual corruption and the liminal space of adolescence. Nick's is an "arrested" manhood, tied to the trauma of his brutalization as a boy in the reformatory, and tied, by the very concept of trauma itself,[15] to the permanently fragile, threatened yet threatening, state of childhood.[16] Theodore Dreiser's Clyde Griffiths grows to physical maturity, but retains a peculiarly adolescent naivete. He is unable to find a model with integrity among the overwhelming array of dream figures confronting him. By attempting to move out of his class without fully understanding the meaning of class, Clyde demonstrates that he is beguiled by the *image* of American society. He mirrors the surface of those images confronting him, never piercing the reality beneath.

There lies the source of his fundamental immaturity, and his tragedy represents the possible misanthropy of many young men in a morally duplicitous society. Clyde's failure is written as individual yet exemplary. Bigger Thomas's manhood is denied him completely — is, and yet is not, an individual tragedy. Wright suggests the impossibility of *any* black man asserting his humanity (for which one can hardly avoid reading "manhood") without a contradictory act of violence that destroys the newly created self. Of course, it is of critical importance that Bigger's transcendent act of violence involves his scramble to "stand tall" as a man on the bodies of the two *women* he has slain.

Knock on Any Door represents the bravado and fragility of the Masculine in a duplicitous society. Nick parades his virility and his good looks but, like Clyde, has adopted an essentially hollow quality of masculinity, one that will inevitably implode. Unlike Dreiser's and Wright's masculinist sagas of the tragically forestalled quest for manhood, Motley's novel is complicated by its deployment of the Feminine — not as opposition to the ideal Masculine, but as its vulnerable underbelly. Nick's body is muscled and lean and tan: archetypically masculine.[17] Yet his face — the window of the soul — has a peculiarly feminine beauty and is topped by a shock of dark, curly, unruly hair. What is more, Nick is always staring into mirrors:[18]

Sometimes now he'd stand in front of the mirror combing his curly brown-black hair and looking deep into his own eyes, admiring them and thinking how innocent they were. . . . And he knew girls and women on the street glanced at him curious-like. And men too, in a sort of admiration.[19]

Nick is conscious of what his looks mean *to other people*, and in this sense his vanity is coded as feminine:

He'd practice his innocent stare on people. On women, men at the poolroom when he was trying to mooch a dime, girls older than he was, Ma when she got after him about something. It always worked like magic. People would just melt in front of him. It became a regular trick. He could always work people by just staring at them kind of sad-like and innocent like.[20]

Nick uses his beauty, is not appreciative of it in itself. His beauty closely corresponds to that of the archetypal figure of the beguiling, cunning, and self-serving woman. It is unsurprising, therefore, that Nick goes on to make money from sexual favors to women and men alike. Motley, deferent to the mores of the time, is cautious in his portrayal of Nick's first homosexual encounter:

Barney, going across the room with the glasses that gently tinkled together, laid his hand on Nick's shoulder. And, in his mind, behind his tightly clenched eyelids Nick could see Barney's arm. The black-haired arm. The heavy, blood-filled veins. A man's arm.

"What's the matter, kid?" Barney asked.

"Nothing."

Nick felt like he was going to cry. To keep from bawling, to stop his bottom lip from trembling, he put his teeth over it and fastened it down.[21]

Barney is a man's man: hairy-armed, big-veined. Nick's own body is smooth and hairless. His fear before the threatening masculinity of Barney has a particularly virginal, maiden-like, quality about it. Nick begins to regularly woo for money those men so attracted to him, then spends his earnings on girls, as if he were trying to "cleanse" the money.[22]

Nick's homosexual contacts are not all a matter of business, however. He is befriended by one man who makes, initially, no sexual demands. Owen does Nick small acts of kindness, offering him friendship and sanctuary from his family. While their friendship is still new, Nick suspects that Owen, like all the others, just wants to use him sexually. But when his suspicions are confirmed Nick demurs to Owen's desire with little complaint and some affection, although consummation can't occur till they're both drunk.[23] Thereafter, Nick often stays with Owen, always warning him that he's "no good" and "money-crazy." When Nick takes money from Owen it is not as a "scam" but part and parcel of Owen's accommodation of the terms of their relationship.

Nick's "confused" sexuality is ostensibly Motley's way of describing the systematic destruction of Nick's humanity, and, of course, his manhood, by a hostile society. Nick is made delinquent, and thus, in essential ways, he is not responsible for his own degeneration. And yet there is something contaminating about Nick's delinquent sexuality, a sexuality arrested by trauma before its attachment on a settled and appropriate object. The story of Nick's marriage to Emma makes this clear. Emma adores and is adored by Nick, and her love theoretically offers him escape and redemption. But the offer comes too late. Nick has never learned how to do wage work and cannot hold down a job. His return to old haunts comes not just through financial exigency but from the pressure of social and sexual habit. Worse still, Nick is unable to make love to Emma. Their first coupling (so long desired by Emma) is cursory, rough, and aimed only at Nick's satisfaction. Not long into their marriage Nick loses desire for his wife altogether. His sexuality is structured on the borderline of the child/adult, masculine/feminine: it is liminal, abject, and dangerous. The traumatic arrest of Nick's sexuality has an exponential power; that is to say, his delinquency, while crippling, is actually fatal to his wife. Emma dies: a slaughtered innocent and quintessential "child."

While serving a short prison sentence for theft, Nick has a telling nightmare:

In his hand he held a huge key. The end was broken off. Lost. He held the butt of the key in his hand. The jagged, broken end was dull metal and blunted. On a higher level of yellow cube was Emma. She stood on a precipitous, smooth-sided vertical with a flat and narrow top. There were no steps up to her. At the foot of the yellow cube, far below her, was a yellow sea of crashing waves. . . . There was no boat to make the crossing in. . . . The broken key in his hand. He could feel the coldness of its metal. It crept up into his arm, crept through him, making his arm metal. . . . [H]e couldn't move. The boyishness was frozen in his eyes, on his cheeks and lips. . . . Then he was moving . . . away from Emma. He was faced into yellow space. At his foot he could see a dismembered arm. Swollen. The tissues ragged at one end. The nerves throbbing in it. An arm with thick, curling black hairs on it. A man's arm . . .[24]

The broken key signifies Nick's impotency, yet the castration symbolism is complicated by the image of the severed arm. While that image initially suggests Nick's first homosexual experience with Barney, it also recalls Fuller, the sadistic reformatory superintendent whose one remaining arm does such brutal works. Strength masks lack. The dream sequence not only points to Nick's degraded manhood, but creates doubt about the whole category of masculinity itself.

Nick is feminized, and his experience betrays the fragility of a masculinity grounded in mere appearance. Interestingly, few characters in the novel do represent a well-balanced and easy sexuality. Rocky is one of those few, and his sexual identity—like that of his "place" (he is a vagrant)—remains liminal, untested. The sensuality of Rocky that Nick mimics cannot be maintained. Rocky survives by traveling; his true virtue is his lack of engagement.

Emma's initially healthy sexual persona becomes a casualty of the contagion of self-doubt and loathing carried by Nick. Nick finally tells Emma why he cannot "be a real husband to her":

"I was no good from the time I was sixteen. There were men and women. A lot of them." He could hear his own voice rush on loudly, scaring him. "They gave me money. I always needed money. There was every whore and slut on West Madison." . . . Inside the room it was so quiet he could hear his conscience condemning him; he could feel the rope his conscience had put about his neck.[25]

A few days after this revelation, Nick returns home to find that Emma has gassed herself.

Throughout the novel, Nick has as his motto: "[L]ive fast, die young, have a good-looking corpse."[26] As "Pretty Boy Romano" awaits his execution in the death cell, he searches anxiously for his only remaining possession — his good looks:

He wanted — awfully — to see himself. Look at himself. He wanted that more than he had ever wanted anything in his life. He sat on the edge of the cot, looking around the dark cell wild-eyed, for something with which to see himself. Some reflecting surface. Numbly he arose and walked around the five-by-eight cell. . . . He stooped down, looking at the porcelain of the water fountain. Nothing reflected back. He rolled back the mattress and stared at the iron bar of the bunk. No reflection! He looked at the toe of his shoe. No reflection![27]

This last mirror scene is crucial. The lack of reflection symbolically prefigures Nick's execution. So long reliant upon image for sustenance, Nick's imminent real death lacks substance for him until it is translated into *how it will look*. ("Would it burn? How would he look?") Even Nick's body betrays him when he cannot *see* it. Motley's materialist theory of degeneration envisions a society that robs Nick of his humanity not just by reducing and imprisoning him in the corporeal realm, but by a further decrement of the body to its mere *image*.

Murder is not an incidental event in *Knock on Any Door*, and it was certainly not incidental to the novel's screen version.[28] Although the central murder narrative — murder as event — involves Nick's shooting of Riley in the alley at the back of the poolroom, murder as event is less important than the way in which murder is deployed as *metaphor*. Nick's lawyer's admonition of society for "murdering" Nick is the most obvious suggestion of the violence endemic to an unequal American society, and the whole novel resonates with images of symbolic and literal violence. The materialist determinism of Motley's naturalistic novel suggests that no violence should be naturalized, whether that naturalization occurs in the conceptual framework of society or in "nature."[29] Motley's analysis of the social extends beyond the structural and superstructural elements common to materialist analysis to include family and the other primary relationships which are veiled as private by classical liberal discourse. In such a critique of endemic violence, "murder" becomes an *exemplary* act of violence, both literal and symbolic. It is an inbuilt effect of the logical structure of violence culturally. Murder for Motley is discrete evidence of greater forces at work impeding both individual and social progress.

Knock on Any Door is replete with metaphorical incidences of murder. Fuller's flogging of Tommy, Nick's friend, can be read as a "little" murder (one that kills not Tommy, but Nick). The misnomer of the reformatory as Boys Home is suggestive. The doctrine of *parens patriae* is nothing but the false benevolence of a brutally authoritarian paternalism — the disciplinary function of family made overt.[30] The violence of Fuller, the bad father, is unappealable and irrevocable. This linking of Family and Institution as different agencies of the same disciplinary regime is further suggested by the sullen rage of Nick's father. Disappointed by his son's apparent delinquency, Pa Romano drags his seventeen-year-old son from his bed and beats him severely — echoing the earlier scene where Nick is beaten in bed for oversleeping the first morning of his stay at the reformatory. The sleeper punished for sleeping (a crime the commission of which he cannot be conscious of) is like the child punished *for being a child*. Pa Romano punishes Nick for not conforming to rules that Nick has never really been made aware of; for not being *part of the family* the way he should be.

Arguably, Nick's killing of Riley could not have occurred without the buildup of violence preceding it; yet that cumulation is essential to the narrative structure of the novel. The punishment dealt out to Nick by society comes home to roost in his murder of the police officer (himself a killer). The story of Nick's life — predisposing him to murder — is interpreted by his lawyer and advanced as a defense. Morton's summary of Nick's life, for all the insight of its polemics, is partial, and in fact completely omits the main element of this etiology of crime. Nick confesses to Riley's murder when he is accused, in an inspired foray of prosecutorial rhetoric, of the moral murder of his own wife. Clearly, Emma's death has greater moral weight than Riley's, and Nick chooses to hold himself to account for it. Later, when he is awaiting execution, it is the emotional "death" of his mother that ratifies his conviction for murder. Nick's acceptance of his failure as son and husband, and his construction of that failure as murder, indicates the central place of gender in Motley's degeneration theory. Of all the things that have gone wrong in his life, it is Nick's ambiguous masculinity that marks the site of the irreparable harm, of murder. Clearly, for Motley, none of this uncertainty is Nick's *fault*, but Nick's guilt indicates his embodiment of the blame, regardless. And I do not use the word "embodiment" idly: it is Nick's body (his impotence) that announces the train of circumstance that will end in Riley's death.[31] Of course, the irony is that Nick's failed masculinity is not a physical but a psychological phenomenon. Nick reads that failure as immanent because he mistakes his body for his self, and image for reality. It is that unintentional irony which signals the real strength of the novel. *Knock on Any Door*, by virtue of its deployment of shifting masculine and feminine values, adds new depth to an already rich literature of realism. The materialist premise is enriched by the sensuality of Motley's narcissistic bodies. And given the problematic relationship of the body to identity formation demonstrated in the character of Nick Romano, murder becomes more than a moral problem or event. Murder as metaphor — in the context of the beautiful, deluded bodies that people the novel — is one's own death witnessed in a mirror.

Strange Fruit

When William March was twenty-four he enlisted in the U.S. Marines and caught the tail end of the war in France, where he was gassed, wounded, and decorated. The croix de guerre was not his sole memento of the Great War, for he remained burdened by the cross of war long after he'd divested himself of the bauble on his dress jacket. His early novel, *Company K*, grappled with his experience of World War I, attempting to test that experience "empirically" through a microcosmic focus on the individuals caught up in it. War was a marshaling ground for a mass of complex human feelings and actions; not evil in and of itself, but a stage for individual acts of cruelty and heroism.

Somewhere between the bounds of free choice (how one acts in war) and the blind, unreasoning hand of fate (the peculiar contingencies of war) might lie the etiology of human evil. Arguably, the lesson of war for March was that free will came out a poor second, if at all. Humankind seemed an excellent vessel for all manner of evil, albeit a vessel shaped by circumstance.

One critic wrote of William March that "he tends to see all people as either mentally or psychologically deformed, and all relationships be-tween them, particularly close family relationships, as endless variants of sadism and masochism, hatred and answering love, murder and expia-tion."[32] Writing just as America was in the thick of a second world war, Stanley Hyman reads March with a jaundiced eye. How could the rela-tionships binding the human family *not* be pictured as an "endless" acting out of the fearful mutuality of sadomasochistic connection?

The Bad Seed was March's last novel, published just a couple of months before his death in May 1954. Within the space of a few years, the novel had been converted into a stage play by Maxwell Anderson and a film based upon Anderson's adaption. March did not live to appreciate the impact of his final work.

For March, the novel represented the refinement of a lifetime's strug-gle with the problem of human evil. His ideas had not become more generous. *The Bad Seed* clearly shows his belief (confided to a friend) that some people — without any cause at all — "are truly evil."[33] March's prin-cipal source for his imaging of the "true evil" of Rhoda Penmark (the precocious multiple killer of the novel) was his substantial collection of true crime stories that dealt with "seemingly 'no cause' types of mur-der."[34] The empirical foundations of the novel then become clear but, unlike Motley's critical attention to the social laboratory that constructed Nick Romano, the data on "criminality" informing *The Bad Seed* are of an entirely different order.[35] March's collection of evil precedents for Rhoda

Penmark turn up, either explicitly or in composite form, throughout the novel. March's inclusion of these notorious murderers indicates his own trust in the true crime tale as an explanatory tool.

The Bad Seed is a novel dominated by its women characters, but it is a world created by absent fathers.[36] Kenneth Penmark, Rhoda's father, is present only at the novel's conclusion and in snatches of remembered conversation. Richard Bravo, Christine's father, is long dead. Her biological father, August Denker, was an ephemeral figure in her early life, conjured by the adult Christine from faded photographs or the memory of his cornet-playing. All the men of the novel, particularly these three, are sheltered by a naivete that is astonishing. They are oblivious to the evil they have married, fostered, or begat, and their innocence sustains that evil. Reginald Tasker, the true crime writer who is a friend of Christine's describes for her the man who is her real father: "[He] was the preordained one who turns up over and over in the career of the mass murderer — the one who, through his natural trust, and the innocence of his outlook, makes possible the murderer's triumphs. . . . [H]e was blond, with delicate, almost feminine, features; and his eyes had looked out at the world with innocence and candour."[37] Similarly, Kenneth Penmark and Richard Bravo are to be held to account for their naivete.[38] Rhoda's father returns too late to the home and therefore remains ignorant of his daughter's true nature. Kenneth is also to blame for generously discounting the early evidence of his daughter's monstrosity.[39]

Kenneth's absence is useful to Christine. She is able to position him as a standard of rationality and faith against which to measure her own irrationality and doubt. She must protect his innocence but also utilize it, and does so in the unsent letters to him in which she wishes that he would "rub [his] cheek against [hers] and tell [her] not to worry so." Christine's determination to keep Kenneth out of the brewing trouble with Rhoda shows her concern for his career, but it is also aimed at keeping unsullied the figure of husband (and father). She reasons that "Kenneth must go on with his work untroubled and unhindered, and she must go on with hers as best she could. The problem of Rhoda was basically her problem, and she must solve it."[40] While later in the novel Christine momentarily considers Rhoda a "joint problem" to be solved upon Kenneth's return, the revelation of the genetic "taint" forces her once again to take full responsibility for Rhoda.[41] Then, rather than use the figure of her husband as the measure of normality and rationality that signals redemption and security, Christine warns him that he must "abandon" his wife and daughter on his return lest the "hateful taint" afflict him further. Both strategies attempt to protect her husband's innocence and to maintain him as a standard. This technique for the displacement of her own rationality, faith, and goodness describes one of the central discursive maneuvers of the novel. The private realm of the Family and Woman has innocently propagated an evil that the public realm of the Father is powerless, in its ignorance, to correct. But it is the very dichotomization of the two realms that makes for their vulnerability: why should the "problem of Rhoda" be Christine's alone?

The lesson of Richard Bravo, Christine's biological father, demonstrates the problematic nature of dualistic constructions: public/private, culture/nature, and environment/genetics. Bravo is an exemplary Lockean rationalist vainly trying to shape the Hobbesian world. His belief in the social and environmental origin of crime spurs him on to conduct his empirical research in the laboratory of his own family. But Christine is not saved by environment, as the unpredictable but inevitable genetic "taint" reemerges in her daughter, signaling the true inheritance not of rationality but brute evil:

They shared a bond of horror that bound them together, that tied them to a common past: a community of guilt that could never be changed through thought or word: they were fixed together by the life of Bessie Denker. There was no going behind that fact. There was no escape for either of them.[42]

Bravo, as an apostle of the social, has been a false prophet. Ironically, his commitment to culture has provided nature with the conditions necessary for the propagation of the "bad seed." Bravo's cheerful belief in the malleability of the individual is passed on to his daughter, not to be shifted until the revelation of her own "biological destiny." Thus, even at the first signs of Rhoda's atavism (the suspicious circumstances surrounding Mrs. Post's death in Baltimore and Rhoda's dismissal from school there for "thieving"), her parent's naive solution is to opt for a change of environment. Rhoda is placed in the traditionalist and conservative Fern School in the hope that its emphasis on "discipline and the old-fashioned virtues . . . would eliminate, or at least modify, some of the upsetting factors of her temperament."[43] The residue of this optimism is Christine's protectiveness toward the child, even after the truth of Rhoda's murderousness has fully dawned upon her. Her determination to own the "problem of Rhoda" and keep the truth even from her husband results in the eventual liberation of Rhoda to her criminal future. Thus the sanctity of the private realm — the kernel of familial sentiment represented by the maternal bond — is as dangerous a construct as the optimistic rationality of Bravo's social realm.

March's novel maintains a kind of cynical ambiguity in its figuring of the relationship between nature and culture. While it seeks to naturalize evil as the constant and ineradicable companion of progress, it criticizes the distinction between natural and social realms. Undeniably, March adopts an essentialist position of human evil as the Monstrous becomes merely the extreme end of a continuum of natural human brutishness.[44] The Monstrous is humankind's nightmare in the sleep of reason. And yet, the novel is not entirely biologically deterministic. The "bad seed" is quite able to skip whole generations, and may come out in one child and not another: it is a blind force and curiously random. Thus Leroy Jessup, the handyman, who is undeniably bad (though not so bad as Rhoda), is pointedly described as coming from a good family, with no suggestion of either bad blood or poor environment.[45] Although March uses Leroy's bad character to take a swipe at environmental liberalism, the origin of that character remains unknown. Society may be responsible for its inability to recognize and take seriously men like Leroy,[46] but it is undecided whether society is in fact responsible for his creation.[47] Despite the random and unknowable nature of human evil, it is its ever-present threat that typifies modern society. Thus, early in the novel, well before Christine begins to suspect her child's monstrosity and her own "taint," she gets an intimation of the blight soon to be cast on their lives. She overhears two men discussing the "age of anxiety and violence" they live in:

It seemed to her suddenly that violence was an inescapable factor of the heart, perhaps the most important factor of all; an ineradicable thing that lay, like a bad seed, behind kindness, behind compassion, behind the embrace of love itself. Sometimes it lay deeply hidden, sometimes it lay close to the surface; but always it was there, ready to appear, under the right conditions, in all its irrational dreadfulness.[48]

This crucial passage demonstrates the ambiguity of an evil that is a "natural" human quality, but one that is propagated and acted out in the social realm. Although evil shelters in the "heart," it may manifest itself only "under the right conditions"—conditions which are ineluctably *social*. Humankind's perpetual vanity is the drive to obliterate "nature" with history, and its attempts are ill-fated. That vanity is perhaps signaled most eloquently by Christine's revelatory research into her mother's life. She does most of her work in the Trellis Library, which is a noble structure built upon the site of an old graveyard. Knowledge and history vie with death, but cannot banish it.[49] Death also has its history.

Murder Memorialized

March's novel evinces a peculiar relationship to the genre of true crime, assuming an ironic distance from it while utilizing not just its descriptive but its supposedly explanatory force. True crime is the passion of at least three characters in the novel: Monica; her brother, Emory; and Reginald Tasker. Crime writing also represents Richard Bravo's most famous work. True crime in March's text is an important facet of both popular culture and sociological theory, and its devotees describe a whole spectrum of talent and scholarly rigor.[50] Monica Breedlove domesticates murder in her description of her brother's interests, reducing the murder narrative to just another form of recreation:

What are Emory's deepest interests in life; what are the things that occupy his psyche? . . . They are fishing, murder mysteries that involve the dismemberment of faithful housewives, canasta, baseball games, and singing in male quartettes.[51]

Although Monica is here indicating that her brother enjoys detective fiction, rather than the true crime tale, crime fiction gets considerably less of a look in throughout the novel than does crime "fact." Detective fiction appears throughout the novel as a means to cover or code the tale of true crime. Christine masks her research into murder and her own family's murderous history by telling Reginald Tasker that she needs help with the plot of the mystery story she intends to write. Tasker responds not with advice on techniques of writing detective fiction or opinions on the genre repertoire, but with case histories of actual murderers. Tasker outlines for Christine the "type" that is his "specialty":

They never killed for those reasons that so often sway warm but foolish humans: they never killed for passion, since they seemed incapable of feeling it, or jealousy, or thwarted love, or even revenge. There seemed to be no element of sexual cruelty in them. They killed for two reasons only: for profit, since they all had an unconquerable desire for possessions, and for the elimination of danger when their safety was threatened.[52]

Tasker tells Christine that he has been "clipping and saving reports of such cases" for years. Thus March's own file of "no cause" murders finds its way into the novel. *The Bad Seed* makes clear that this is just the criminal "type" March himself is interested in. All of the many murderers mentioned in the novel killed for insurance, property, or possessions.[53] A "no cause" murder, then, is one committed in cold blood for gain.[54]

At this stage in the novel, Tasker has already shown his predilection for a good murder. At a social gathering, he tells the guests about a murder he is covering "for one of his murder magazines." Tasker's tale, told with great gusto, entertains all present but Christine, who confesses to an aversion to "anything concerning crime." Such stories "depressed her and made her anxious."[55] It should therefore be quite surprising to her friends when Christine later announces her decision to write her own murder tale. That lack of surprise attests to the degree to which Tasker and the Breedlove siblings are beguiled by the tale of murder. Effectively, whether the tale is fiction or fact makes little difference. To the true crime devotee the integrity of the *story* is all-important. Monica confides to Christine her assessment of Tasker as a crime writer, comparing his considerable but lesser talents to those of Frederic Wertham, William Bolitho, and William Roughead.[56] Tasker's gift, in Monica's assessment, is a "compassionate irony."[57] While irony is much in evidence, "compassion" is not; and it could be argued that the ironic mode is antagonistic to critical reflection and, therefore, to compassion.[58]

Tasker is but one indicator in March's novel of the tendency of true crime to aestheticize its subject. Monica Breedlove adopts exactly the same amused and ironic tone in her synopsis of the life of a neighborhood man recently indicted for murder. Not long after she has embarked on the research "for her novel," Christine imagines the kind of notoriety lying in wait for her daughter should her story get picked up by the media: "*Tot Kills Two.*" In the writings of "Madison Cravatte" on Bessie Denker, Christine first encounters the banality of sensationalism and the delight that murder seems to engender. Cravatte, with "the tittering wit so typical of his speciality" (more kindly termed "irony" by Tasker), proclaims: "I make no secret of my admiration for this endearing lady. Bessie Denker was tops in my book. We're going steady now. Bessie Denker is my sweetheart, and I don't care who knows it."[59]

Tasker has himself labeled the file in which Cravatte's biography, *The Unparalleled Bessie Denker,* is found — demonstrating that he too has made a murderous icon of Christine's mother.[60] Sentiments such as these from Cravatte and Tasker describe the extent to which true crime can be described as a generic form, intertextually dependent upon both the fictional crime genre and upon other forms not recognized as fiction. The supposedly critical facility of true crime (played out in the debate on heredity versus environment in the etiology of crime) is overshadowed by its generic function as entertainment. Reginald Tasker, an apostle of degeneration theory,[61] ignores the implicit threat of his own philosophy in favor of the joys of plotting the outcome in the cases he collects. Ironically, therefore, his whole classificatory enterprise — to document the "natural" origin of crime — is diverted into the creation of a literature and *culture* of crime.

The discourse of true crime becomes, in effect, indistinguishable from the fictional genres of crime in the detective and mystery story. This elision of the "fiction" and "fact" of murder is eloquently illustrated by the scene toward the novel's conclusion wherein Christine is advised by a crime fiction buff on a fitting end to her "novel." Of course the plot of Christine's "novel" is in fact the unfolding progress of her own cursed life. Miss Glass, to whom Christine had formerly confided the problem of what the mother should do about her child, tells Christine that she took the "problem" to a group that "pondered trends in writing." In the ensuing hour the group had "discussed every possible solution":

It had been like a jury discussing an actual case, really. They'd debated the possibilities of psychiatric treatment, reform school, or blind faith in the future; and in the end they'd taken a vote: it had been unanimously decided that the only possible way to end the book was for the mother to keep her secret, kill the child, and then commit suicide.[62]

Christine concurs, opining that that ending "is the one" she'll "have to use." There is a curious form of doubling here. The fictional fate of the mother and her murderous daughter is determined by Miss Glass and her friends, constituting themselves as a "jury" — an assembly that, in the realm of actual justice, determines fate. And yet the novel is a ploy, a ruse to cover the facts of Christine's life. In accepting the determination of the "jury," Christine accepts an actual judgment which condemns both her and her daughter to death. The actual becomes fictional, then returns to the actual again.

Although true crime provides the means by which Christine discovers the truth about herself, and the solution to the situation presented by that revelation, she manages to prevent her case (or, more properly, Rhoda's) from coming under its lights. Her determination to save Rhoda comes from her abhorrence for the devotion accorded the infamous. Not for Rhoda that "specialized literature of legend" that made one "better known for the . . . evil they'd created" than were "the most compassionate people" known for doing good. Nor did Christine want her daughter to "end up in a blare of publicity and sentiment: in the gas chamber, at the end of a rope, or lunging forward as the current struck her, and hurtled through her blood."[63] Christine covertly makes her own life and Rhoda's into a story to stop them from overtly *becoming* one.

The previous discussion outlines the case for the novel being, in part at least, a critique of the true crime genre. March's reiteration of a catalogue of murderers, however, and his acceptance of a classification of "no cause" crimes, is evidence of his own belief in the explanatory power of "true crime." His parodic criticism of the sensationalizing and aestheticizing excesses of true crime cannot disguise the fact that he too is the product of a culture of mediated violence (though not as yet a "hyperaestheticized" culture, as Joel Black would term it). This is demonstrated by his figuring of Bessie Denker as a composite of two *actual* murderers, Belle Gunness and Ruth Brown Snyder. As a "type," Bessie Denker might just as well have been a complete fictional creation: representative instead of "real." March just cannot resist Belle Gunness — considered an exemplary villain in the history of American crime.[64] Snyder, executed in 1928 with her lover and accomplice, Judd Gray, contributes only one element to the life of Bessie Denker, but it is a crucial one — her execution:

Her mother's death in the chair had been a sensation that had been featured everywhere. There was a photograph of her mother at the time of her death. A reporter had smuggled in a camera . . . and at the instant the current hit Bessie Denker . . . the picture was snapped.

. . . Everything was there for the eye to see: the black mask that covered her mother's face; the bound hands raised from the wrist, trembling, and out of focus from movement; the fingers spread apart like the talons of a predatory bird; the thick, dead white, hairless legs, strapped down and bulging outward under the power of the current.[65]

Only the detail of the raised fingers is an addition to the photograph of Ruth Snyder that appeared on the front page of the *New York Daily News* beneath the banner headline "DEAD!" Like Ethel Rosenberg (in the year of the novel's writing), Ruth Snyder became the "natural prey of pornographers," yet she did not rate an explicit mention by March.[66] Only her death is useful: she was executed for murdering for "love," rather than for gain.[67] Just as Christine Penmark justified to Tasker her enquiries into murder for a "book to be reinforced and supported by the details of actual cases," March claims authority for his fiction through the use of true crime.[68] Given his intention that the novel should be more than mere entertainment, that authority was essential — representing, in fact, his last word on the problem of human evil.[69] On the face of it, March's use of the true crime genre marks his resistance to the use of murder as metaphor. Yet this instrumentalism veils with cynicism his investment of the murderous impulses of humankind with a distinctly mysterious nature.

Although the contest of heredity and environment is immediately apparent, the philosophical core of the novel is not so much expressed by the theme of degeneration as by its brand of crisis theology. This is revealed through a number of references to eschatology and also by the ironic position the novel assumes vis-à-vis psychoanalysis. Fundamentally, the mind of God is unknowable, and the mind of mankind — that creature created in his image — is equally opaque. This philosophy finds its voice in Octavia Fern, the headmistress at Rhoda's school. When Christine Penmark visits the school, Miss Fern — shocked by the inexplicable death of the Daigle boy — waxes philosophical. Christine, appearing to listen, is actually in one of her peculiar reveries, and it is therefore the reader who is Miss Fern's sole audience. Having just dismissed the idea that Rhoda could have had anything at all to do with the boy's death, Miss Fern falls to musing about the ubiquity of guilt in humanity, an irrational guilt that attaches itself to any and all acts and ideas:

[I]t was only natural to expect that we all have our particular guilts, since our development, our very place in the world we live in, is based on that premise. We are taught from the beginning that . . . man himself is entirely vile: that his very birth is the end result of a furtive sin to be wailed over and atoned somehow.[70]

This passage introduces a critical position on doctrinal Christianity, while also suggesting that the relation of conscience to act is inscrutable and possibly arbitrary. Musing upon the relativity of morality, Miss Fern asks:

How can we know that our own concepts of good and evil concern God in the slightest? How can we be so sure He even understands our tests and definitions? Certainly, there's nothing in nature, in the cruel habits of animals, that should lead us to think He does.[71]

God, it seems, is as ignorant of his creation as we are of him — although we retain the conceit of knowledge. Miss Fern's final comment, as she wryly dismisses Monica Breedlove's characterization of her as "that romantic Whistler's mother amongst school ma'ams," completes the existentialist direction of this monologue. Monica Breedlove, it should be recalled, is a noisy advocate for the critical and therapeutic force of psychoanalysis: "Actually, it's the other way around. Monica thinks man's mind can be changed through lying on a couch and talking endlessly to another man who is often as lost as the patient. Really, Monica is far more trusting and romantic than I."[72] Although Miss Fern suggests that man's mind cannot be "changed" by psychoanalysis, the implication is that neither can it be *known*.

Understanding March's crisis theology is necessary to unpack the conception of evil in the novel. God's and man's moral languages do not coincide: even the doctrine of the received word of God represented by the Old Testament cannot be taken as evidence of the dialectic between God and man, let alone as moral direction. It is pointedly observed that

Rhoda herself shows a great affinity for, and understanding of, Old Testament chapter and verse: "there is something as terrible and primitive about her, as there is about them."[73] *The Bad Seed* portrays a world in which neither humanist rationalism nor religious devotion can guard against, or trace, evil. Evil is an "inescapable factor of the heart"—that which "lies behind" all the veneers of human affection and civilization itself.[74] It is both essential and worldly. As God is unknowable, the problem of evil—presumably part of a divine plan and therefore *natural*—must be insoluble. Humankind, severed from God, must own an evil that it can never rationalize away. Yet to own that evil, ironically, means to make it of the *social.* March's existentialism serves ultimately to mitigate the biological determinism that is the supposed rationale of the novel.

The film version of the novel came out hard on the heels of the stage play, still running while the novel was in its first imprint. The film brought the play to the screen, retaining many of the mainstays of theme and plot from the novel. But, for all that, somewhere in this process of adaption the complexity of the novel was lost. The director, Mervyn Le Roy, had had a checkered career but could be credited with one of the early masterworks of the crime genre: *Little Caesar.* Potentially, *The Bad Seed* could have figured as an interesting twist in the development of the crime film; but, still bound by the standards of the Breen Committee, Le Roy was committed to showing that crime doesn't pay. Rhoda does not survive to carry on her criminal career in the film—but neither could the screenwriters (following Anderson's lead) have any truck with suicide and the murder of children. Rhoda and Christine survive Christine's radical plan to "protect" her daughter, and Rhoda is dispatched by the handy but highly unlikely intervention of a bolt of lightning.

The film proclaims a confidence in both God and man that the novel pointedly lacks. God *must* "understand our tests and definitions" of good and evil if he sees fit to intercede to avert the death of the innocent (Christine) and to annihilate the guilty (Rhoda). Equally, faith in man is evinced by the film's gesture toward the remedial influence of environment (even after the lengths to which it has gone to prove the theory of genetic taint). After the final credits have rolled, Rhoda comes onstage and is given a sound spanking by her grandfather, Richard Bravo, who tells the screaming child that this is just what she's always needed.

One of the major weaknesses of the film is its reinsertion of the "absent fathers." Kenneth is present at the beginning of the film and we cut to him occasionally in his Pentagon office. Richard Bravo also appears, and he confirms the identity of Christine's true parents when she asks him, "Daddy . . . father . . . who's child am I?" The return of "daddy" and "father" (in the guise of both Kenneth and Richard Bravo) removes the central tension from the plot: Christine's virtual isolation with the "problem of Rhoda." The dilution of this isolation — signaled in the book by Christine's solitary and covert pursuit of the truth about her past — is at least partly the result of the exigencies of the medium. The scene of action was necessarily contracted for the theatre, meaning that the solution to Christine's questions comes to her, rather than she going to it.[75] Accordingly, though Christine remains the central figure, the drama no longer issues from her. She is its object, not its subject.[76]

The film lacks March's commitment to describing what he considered "true evil"; the characters of Leroy and Rhoda are softened. Leroy is cleansed of his lascivious obsession with the child (and, importantly, Rhoda's character is aged to keep at bay the troublesome border of childhood and all the suggestions of precocity, sexual and otherwise, that it implies). Rhoda is even made to express a kind of mawkish love for her mother toward the end of the film. March's Rhoda, on the other hand, *enjoys* her mother's increasing remoteness. At no time does she express any genuine desire for her mother's company. The trend shown by these changes to the lead characters — the creation of composites, the reinsertion of Christine's husband and father into the plot — brings the ambiguous gender order of the book into line with a more homogenized, palatable, and unifying ideology of the family.[77] The result of that redrawing of the formerly shaky line between gendered spheres was an increasing tendency to locate murderous evil (as well as other manifestations of deviance) outside the norm. That commitment to a qualitative differentiation of the pathological from the normal was instrumental in the discursive shift in forensic psychiatry toward the identification of the relatively new categories of "delinquent" and "psychopath" (among other inventions).[78] Given this tendency in positivistic criminology and psychiatry (and a true crime genre that had always favored the monstrous), the intellectual cowardice of the film versions of *Knock on Any Door* and *The Bad Seed* is singularly unsurprising.[79]

Here I have described two different responses to the problem of violence in contemporary American life. While Willard Motley deploys the metaphor of murder to describe the degenerative effect of an unequal society, William March uses murder as the extreme edge of a continuum of human evil not recognized by liberal society. Both novels are deterministic in their conception of evil — Motley describing the structural and material determinants of crime and March bidding, at least nominally, for a biologically essentialist causation. Motley's structural interpretation compels him toward the utilization of murder as metaphor, figuring the life story of Nick Romano as a series of "little" murders that culminate in the actual killing of Officer Riley. March, on the other hand, tends to use murder as an empirically given category, as the seed (pun intended) of "fact" about which the remainder of his tale shapes itself. Thus, although *The Bad Seed* is explicitly concerned with the problem of human evil evidenced by murder, the meanings of murder advanced by the novel are strictly limited. March even restricts his empirical category to what he erroneously terms "no cause" murders — those committed for gain. March's delight in the genre of true crime (tempered by his criticism of its tendency to aestheticize murder and to heroize the murderer) undermines his ability to examine critically its meaning-laden category. *Knock on Any Door* ironically advances a much more complex set of meanings for murder: scrutinizing the act of murder and employing murder as metaphor to describe the actual and symbolic violence done to the individual by society. Murder — as cultural artifact and as individual act — is wrapped in meaning. Murder, as a central part of the action and the metaphorical structure of both novels, cannot fail to partake of the wider developmental (or degenerative) themes. William March is concerned with Rhoda's precocity as well as with the process of her mother's policing of those already breached moral borders. The threats and taints of genetics must also become a discussion about generations, about adult responsibility, abuse, and the "premoral" precocities of childhood (and adolescence). The following chapters will go on to unpack some of those meanings with a critical analysis of the discourse of true crime, both in its scholarly guise as forensic psychology and as popular literature.

3. Min(d)ing the Murderer

Nothing beyond the speech of common mortals can be
spoken save by the agitated soul.
Aristotle

Mythology and classical literature have furnished many murderous archetypes, from Thyestes, Agamemnon, Orestes, and Oedipus to Clytem-
nestra and Medea. Tragedies of revenge and ritual sacrifice unpurified are
still used to rechart narratives of murder. These mythical archetypes and
their metaphorical foundations can clearly be seen in two explicit reauthorings of the tale of murder.[1] The process of navigation by such stars
has significant implications for the construction of murder narratives;
although of course neither transhistorically nor transculturally constant,
these archetypes or metaphors indicate the structural effect of both gender and genre within such mythic master narratives.[2]

In 546 B.C. Herostratus set ablaze the temple of Diana at Ephesus,
knowing that even though the heat of the flames would abate, the heat of
the controversy would not, and in that longevity would lie his fame. Like
later generations in that long pedigree of murder in the West, he sought
to die by killing, and to gain glory by that sacrifice. The term "Herostratus complex" is still sometimes applied to those who kill for glory. Dr.
Fredric Wertham's reading of this and other mythological archetypes is a
significant part of his analytic project. Both he and Judge Curtis Bok
wrote as *experts*, apostles of increased psychiatric intervention and the
reform of existing judicial and corrective procedures. Their expertise was
founded upon the subtlety of their understandings of the "deviant" mind,
an interpretive power that owed much to their work with literary modes
of analysis.

The Show of Violence and *Star Wormwood*, Bok's philosophical-juridical treatise, construct "reasonable" stories out of the apparent madness of the murderous acts they treat. Their projects locate the meaning and significance of murder in particular ways, in that the object of wonder they construct (from their own desire) is neither crime nor victim, but murderer. Their narratives are critical and culturally located, both in their investigation of the role of arbiter, expert, and author (Wertham the psychiatrist, Bok the judge) and in their emphasis on the life story and psychic history of their subjects.

Both writers untangle anecdote and symbol through psychoanalysis of their subjects to create these "reasonable" stories. This desire to create order is partly a narrative or topological impulse, but it is also the logical outcome of the humanistic assumptions of the authors. The search for the possibilities of existence for a rational society can be achieved only through a systematic assault upon the silence and open-endedness of the psychoanalytic project, until the doctor and the judge are able to fix both psychoanalysis as a therapeutic science *and* the particular pathology of their subject. The interpretive process of classification makes the analyst, not the analysand, the apparent master of signification in the analytic discourse. For both authors, murder/murderer — properly decoded — furnishes a single, stable meaning, psychically and socially.

Wertham, a German-born, Edinburgh-educated disciple of Freud, was one of America's leading forensic psychiatrists for three decades at mid-century. Like most of Freud's followers in America, Wertham had gone the way of an emphasis on object relations, rather than in the direction of a more purely Freudian (or Lacanian) analysis of the vicissitudes of subject formation. Such an ego-centered philosophy of mind had radical results for Wertham's preoccupation with diagnostic classification. His emphasis on object relations lent itself explicitly to the interpretation of murderous "psychoses" in the context of social control theory. Wertham's liberalism overlays a confident belief in the ability of sympathetic experts to tinker with the interface of individual and society in order to make entity and collective progress equally.

Wertham was not just one more of the many experts then engaged in the struggle for hegemony in the new science of therapeutic psychiatry. He had effectively gained the ear of the public and was to become an important interpreter and champion of the intervention of medical expertise in judicial process. Along the way, he would also become an influential mediator on the meaning of murder in American society as it entered the boom age of the 1950s.

For Wertham the urge to classify was paramount. His main interest in analyzing murder was to perfect psychiatry's supposed ability to predict and prevent acts of violence by the insane.[3] Classification, and the principle of ordering, are logical (i.e., integral) instruments in an interpretive system of knowledge that aspires to the status of a science.[4] Wertham described the positivist core of psychiatry: "Psychiatry is not a young science, but it is still in a stage of development where description is on a firmer scientific ground than interpretation, where experienced clinical judgment still has to count more than objective laws about dynamic processes. In all the sciences in that stage, classification remains a big issue."[5] The emphasis here on classification is best read in the context of his primary distinction between "description" and "interpretation." That distinction is a symbolically violent one that obscures the dependence of description upon an interpretive, or tropological, act. Classification — the listing and ordering of data to fix the various "real" objects of scrutiny in either hierarchical or apposite relation — is a *narrative* act.[6] It is an interpretive process aimed at creating a *history:* whether of the evolution of a genus, the demise of a city-state, or the life span of a virus. Such an understanding of the classificatory impulse has interesting ramifications for a study of the analytic or "high" literature of true crime dealt with here.

The making of meaning, both in the talking cure of the ego-dominated psychoanalytic process and in the interpretation and construction of a murder narrative for which the *murderer* is the focal subject, is essentially a bid for the creation of a "reasonable" story. Poised at the brink of unraveling the troubled psyche of Robert Irwin, Dr. Wertham describes that moment as a transition from inarticulacy (chaos) to meaning (reason).[7] Through a process of "trust, if not reason" the doctor eventually passed through the barrier of Irwin's disorganized communication, his "heated words and violent gestures," until "eventually the pieces of his life story began to fit together."[8]

Wertham and his patient are both telling a story, but they do so differently. Irwin is prompted to tell his story in a certain way, and that telling is structured by the process of analysis provided by the psychiatrist eliciting it.[9] For the doctor, Irwin's recollections must "fit together" to become a "reasonable" story in that the order of its elements will inevitably reveal the condition of the patient/storyteller, and that condition in turn will reveal the *meaning* of the murder. The doctor is therefore creating order and meaning both out of disorganized narrative and out of the disorganized personality of his pathologized subject. The desire of the analyst to classify his patient's pathology, and then — *for the protection of society* — to coax the patient toward self-recognition of that pathology, is a movement that inevitably disables the free compact of analyst and analysand that Freudian analysis is founded upon.[10] Critical to consider here is the particular structure of analysis undertaken as a study of the criminally insane. The whole project of *forensic psychiatry as analysis* is problematic.[11] The act of transference must go awry when the analyst is positioned within the juridical realm.[12]

Contested Narratives:
The Story of Robert Irwin

In April 1937, Robert Irwin, an unemployed artist who had been in and out of various institutions for years,[13] murdered his ex-landlady, her adult daughter, and their lodger. Irwin told the police that he had gone to the boardinghouse under the impression that the older daughter, Ethel (his ex-lover), was still living there. It was, he said, Ethel whom he had intended to kill. After the murder Irwin left town, remaining at large for two months until he gave himself up to the *Herald and Examiner* in Chicago. On the occasion of his initial interview by the police, Irwin (who had already engaged a renowned lawyer, Samuel Leibowitz) called Dr. Wertham to ask him to come down to the police station. Irwin had refused to talk to the police until the doctor was present.[14]

Wertham had a long-standing therapeutic relationship with Irwin, having first seen him at Bellevue in October 1932 and continuing to interview him thereafter throughout the time of Irwin's stay at various institutions. Irwin, in fact, had allowed Wertham to interview him before an audience of sixty of the doctor's esteemed colleagues, although Irwin was present only because he had escaped from the state hospital (to which Wertham dutifully returned him after the meeting). The deliberations of that meeting formed the basis of a paper entitled "Catathymic Crisis: A Clinical Entity" which Wertham delivered at Johns Hopkins in 1936.[15]

The paper was published in a scholarly journal just as Irwin was giving himself up to the Hearst papers in Chicago.

Irwin and his story therefore had a particular context, a *history*, before the moment of Irwin's presentation of his scoop to the Hearst papers. That context was not lost on the press, as a telling bit of doggerel verse suggests:

IT'S ALL DONE BY MIRRORS!

He did not murder anyone
And such a charge not nice is:
He's just the charming victim of
A "Catathymic crisis."[16]

Naturally, the Hearst papers were as concerned to find an origin and cause for the murders as was Dr. Wertham. They were more inclined, however, to settle on the already conveniently constituted and present body of Robert Irwin, without the messy encumbrance of a psychic history into which both responsibility and guilt could be dispersed and lost.

For the news media, and for the public that formed the circuit of meaning for which the media are both source and conduit, the real boon of the murder story lies in the identification of the murderer, the process of his detection and arrest. (Needless to say, quite apart from the tale, the exposure and confinement of the murderer was an attractive *practical* prospect.) The narrative lure lay, therefore, in fixing the figure of the murderer — from the early origins of a sketch or profile issued by investigating police, through the tracing of his path as he eludes capture, to the revelation of his arrest and, with it, the "capture" of his story. Reconstructing the period of the manhunt for Irwin, the crime reporter Quentin Reynolds wrote: "The hunt and the literature continued (even the lad who had been out with Ronnie [the murdered daughter] on the fatal Saturday night sold his story to a tabloid at twenty-five dollars an instalment), and *now the figure of Robert Irwin began to emerge more clearly.*"[17] Like every history — whether a life story or that of the psyche — the story is projected backwards, existing as an entity only retroactively.[18] Reynolds describes the construction of Irwin, *or the story that is Irwin*, as a process of reconstruction: the police had "backtracked his life."[19] What is described as revelation is also constitutive: Irwin is both *made* and *found*. In this way Irwin, the embodied story, becomes a point of contest.

Disposable as it is, the doggerel verse above suggests a number of interesting readings. First, there is the struggle between psychiatry and the law for the murderer. The media — fearing the dispersal of blame and the loss of focus on the figure of the murderer — is naturally predisposed to side with the law in wishing to claim Irwin as sane (or he can be *mad* but not *irresponsible*). Their caricature of Wertham's "Catathymic crisis" shows an anxiety that the dispersal of responsibility will result in the loss of the tale of murder: "He did not murder anyone." For the media, then, the primary and originating force of the murder must be the *act* itself. Although this interpretation appears to contradict my previous assertion that the delight of murder lies in fixing the murderer, these are not incompatible theses. The corpse too quickly disappears — murder, like any event, is a transitory thing. The essence of the act can only ever be captured in its *author*. If the murderer is found to be irresponsibly insane, that vital element of authoring intent is lost and the status of the event is thrown into doubt. The insane murderous act becomes merely a kind of automatic writing, its origins obscure and unintelligible. Then, it is madness *itself* that becomes the subject of scrutiny, not murder.

The Herostratus Complex:
Murder as Transcendence

There is a story to be told about Herostratus that *cannot* be told: all that points to the real meaning of the act is its outcome. Thus, for Wertham, Herostratus is doubly a cipher, for the origin of his impulse to fame remains veiled: "We know nothing about Herostratus's personal life, but it is safe to speculate that he must have suffered from some tremendous frustration, some overwhelming inferiority, that made him seek acclaim and punishment at the same time."[20] Wertham's use of the Herostratus complex had a particular constructive effect on his telling of the tale that is Irwin, and that telling remade the joint subject of the tale, the doctor himself. Wertham tellingly described psychiatry as "the science of sympathy."[21] Wertham and Irwin, analyst and analysand, are intimately tied to one another by the act of authoring the story of the subject that is Irwin. As Irwin's lawyer, Samuel Leibowitz aptly put it, "The Irwin case is the Wertham case."[22] This echoes Freud's famous equation, "where it was, there I shall become." Thus, Wertham's description of Irwin's Herostratus complex, his desire for undying fame, is not merely a classificatory tactic, it is a parable of transcendence. In attempting to characterize Irwin's murderous act as a *failed* strategy of transcendence (the "catathymic crisis"), the doctor constructs the murder/er as *his own fantasy of transcendence*. Wertham desires the transcendent (because fixed) meaning of an authoritative interpretation of Irwin's psychic history. That history will in turn explain the crime. Despite his compassion and the generosity of those judiciously dispensed silences through which the story of Irwin appears, Wertham, as analyst, is unable to facilitate the "original pact" of analysis.[23] The triple murder forms the impetus for Wertham's reconstruction of the information derived in previous sessions with Irwin. Yet, after the killings, Irwin is less the patient and more the prisoner — awaiting the disposition of the state. Under such conditions, analysis is geared toward ascertaining the danger posed by the patient to society, rather than to himself. That change in the material condition of the narrative of murder has significant ramifications.

Early in the period of his analysis (before the triple murder), Irwin related to the doctor a dream he had once told his mother: "I dreamt I was walking on a road and an angel came to me and patted me on the head. (I was supposed to be a cute kid.) And the angel said, 'What do you want?' And I said, 'I want you.'"[24] The story of the angel becomes a particularly mobile metaphor in Wertham's deployment of the Herostratus complex. On one level, of course, the story points to Irwin's desire to improve himself, to plug in to the divine: he "wants" the angel; that is to say, he wants to *become* the angel in a clear exchange of identities. But the angel is neuter: Irwin provides no pronoun by which to sex his companion. In Oedipal terms, the angel could be the figure of Laius, struck down by the son who does not know him. A less simple exchange of identities: "Thou seek'st this man of blood: Thyself art he." The analysand, like Oedipus, becomes both murderer and detective. Alternatively, in Orestean terms, the angel becomes the figure of the mother. There is an undeniably threatening tone to the child's reply to the angel. To say "I want you" is to state an impossible violation, an unimaginable violence. How can the child "have" the angel? He can consume or rape the object of his desire, or he can "become" it, and that is all (that is enough).

In his summation of Irwin's catathymic disorder, Wertham wrote that "it was to his mother that he wanted to return in the glory of his attainment."[25] However, "The alternative between this infantilistic conquest of his mother and elimination of her image by flight or by violence was the secret unconscious blueprint that guided his life. His whole life was a flight from his mother."[26] Wertham's proposition that Mrs. Irwin was her son's object of ultimate desire tends to flatten the complicated lineaments of Irwin's psychosis.[27] From the story that Irwin himself offered the media, the police, his various doctors and, in short, anyone who would listen, it becomes apparent that Irwin's problem was his inability to separate self from other: a confusion of boundaries that gives rise in turn to that paradoxical formulation of "killing and dying."

The two integral tenets of the Herostratus complex that Wertham applies to Irwin are a desire for "glory" and the related urge to "die by killing." Murder as self-sacrifice has been extensively analyzed in reference to the crime of Pierre Riviere (briefly discussed above in Chapter One).[28] Riviere wrote in his memoir not of his intent to kill, but to die: "by my death I should cover myself with glory"; "I should immortalize myself by dying for my father."[29] This is a paradoxical rendering of the crime: the killings, though logically prior to his own glorious death, and the foundation of all future action and reaction, are effectively banished. Pierre Riviere exemplifies the authorial status of the murderer. Murder is the medium in which he works to make plain his skill and right to fame. And yet, there is also apparent in Riviere's memoir a determination of *what should be* — who, in the history of the family, should be subject; *who should live*. There *is* a sacrificial element to Riviere's murderousness. The renovation of his father and his maternal grandmother requires the sacrifice of particular victims, including the not immediately obvious choices: his father's beloved younger son, and — by implication the last victim — himself. His erasure of the greater part of the bloodline allows its *essence* to be invested in the remnants: the paternal line. The sum of his murderous act is therefore not subtraction but addition. Riviere's decision murderously to reconstruct the family demonstrates his belief that the thing itself existed above and beyond its constituent parts. A confusion of subjective boundaries.

Wertham characterized Irwin's Herostratus complex as a desire to "seek acclaim *and* punishment." Discussing Irwin's suicidal urge, Wertham noted the young man's comment that he had "often thought of suicide" but that he had never thought of "killing himself." Irwin told the doctor that, once, when he had been embarrassed and rebuffed by a girl he had tried to pick up, he was "thinking of killing her and going to the police station and saying 'Here I am.' "[30] When Wertham blandly noted the consistency of Irwin's "pattern of suicide without killing himself" through various episodes, he colluded in Irwin's own translation of the urge to kill into the will to die:

I was living with a nice old lady in Brooklyn and she was just like a mother to me. I was only there two weeks and I was so miserable and so sick that I thought I would commit suicide. But I wasn't going to kill myself. I thought I would kill her and go to the electric chair.[31]

Irwin recollected several instances of his desire to "kill somebody so I would be hung."[32] And who appears as the victim of choice in what here must be read as a murderous, not a suicidal, strategy? Women. This is remarkable to Wertham only insofar as the victim conforms to the role of the mother substitute, either by her relationship to Irwin or by her age. Veronica Gedeon's murder is thus explained:

Mrs. Gedeon was one of those psychological mother-substitutes which recurred throughout the course of his life. Her first name, by which he called her, was the same as his mother's. Her murder, precipitated by her refusal to let him see Ethel, was in its deeper motivations a symbolic matricide.[33]

The death of the daughter fits this theory less comfortably, but Wertham is able to advance a tentative explanation for both her death and that of the boarder. On the fateful night of the murder, "the original family constellation was repeated."[34] Ronnie and Frank Byrnes were slaughtered because of their situation as rival "sibling" figures. But did not Ronnie (short for Veronica) also have Irwin's mother's name? This girl, toward whom Irwin had always felt "comradely" (in the doctor's words) becomes, for Wertham, the victim of Irwin's "frustration" at not killing the one he wished to kill. But this is no simple surrogate. Irwin's full statement to the

police on the night of his surrender to the media shows him as rather less than uninterested in the *actual* victims:

Ronnie asked me to sleep with her in July because she was very lonely. I never touched her any time. She stripped for me on another occasion. I gave her a bath once. I stayed with Ronnie for three nights when Ethel and her mother were away and she went around the house half naked. . . . She fooled around with me a lot. . . . She was a nice little brainless, blue-eyed blond, a beautiful fluffy thing.[35]

Irwin's description of Ronnie as "a nice little brainless . . . fluffy thing" stands in contradistinction to Wertham's appraisal of their relationship as one of equals: "colleagues in art, she a beautiful model, and he an up-and-coming sculptor." This sanitizing trend in the doctor's interpretation leads him to demur to Irwin's assertion that there was no sexual element to the killings. Describing Irwin's strangling of Ronnie, Wertham assures the reader that "there were no sexual thoughts in Irwin's mind at that time."[36] When setting out the circumstances of Irwin's original statement, the doctor further notes that Irwin

almost hit the district attorney when he asked whether Irwin had done anything to Ronnie while she was lying on the bed. He was in a rage at what he evidently thought a horrid accusation: "I didn't attack either of these two women."[37]

The sexual element to the crime is absent because of the way in which the sexual is defined. The police and the doctor seemed oblivious to the profusion of sexual imagery in Irwin's own description of the murders.[38] Possibly his rage at being accused of rape shows the prisoner was more sensitive to the excess of meaning in his murder narrative than were his captors.

Wertham tends to ignore anything in Irwin's story that does not sit comfortably with his theory of the victim as surrogate. Irwin describes his murder of Mrs. Gedeon:

She put up a hell of a fight. . . . I had Mrs. Gedeon by the throat and I never let loose of that throat for twenty minutes.

She fell back on the floor with her legs back over her head and her dress over her head. She was all bare. She scratched my face like nobody's business. When she was on the floor I knew what the damned dog's place was in that family.

My face was scratched. My hands were full of blood. I smeared it on her, on her breast. I threw her in the bedroom under the bed.[39]

Just after the description of Ronnie as that "beautiful fluffy thing," Irwin goes on to tell how, after having held the girl for hours "just so that she could breathe," he is finally prompted to strangle her:

I only used my hands, nothing but the pressure of my hands. . . . I held her for a long time, at least an hour. I was holding her on the bed and strangling her. Afterwards I went out because she immediately became the most repulsive thing I had ever seen in my life when she was dead. It was like just blue death oozing out, a spiritual emanation oozing out.[40]

And, when discussing the original object of his murderous desire, Ethel Gedeon, Irwin told the police:

I wanted to kill Ethel because I loved her and hated her. Even when I knew her before when I made a bust of her I was going to model her on a straight block, beheaded with her hair hanging down and her eyes closed.

If Ethel had come in first I would have killed her and nobody else, if she had come in while I was drawing her mother's picture.

I don't know whether it was love or hate that made me want to kill Ethel. My choice was to either die or to put myself under pressure.[41]

Woman, easily objectified and in a kind of a subjective double bind,[42] can easily become merely a representational figure, a "stand-in." In Irwin's case, the selected victim stands in for his own death. Wertham, like his patient, tends to put Woman and Death, as interchangeable and related tropes, in the same place.[43] Wertham figures Irwin's victims as mother surrogate, thus making of the real woman a double cipher.[44]

Here is the slippage between killing and dying, between sacrifice and glory. Irwin's aim, his choice, is "to die" or to put himself "under pressure." The latter is of course achieved by killing, but the ultimate aim of the act is not its external but its internal effect. Just as Irwin tells the angel on the road that his only possible desire is *it*, his explanation for the murders, framed by Wertham, is predatory and synecdochic. Irwin is creating a new set of subjective borders: he "wants" the angel; he tries to cut off his penis to distill his energies;[45] he kills the Gedeons, then claims he can re-create them (the power he calls "visualization") whole and entire. Irwin is attempting to gerrymander his physical and psychic limits to contain the uncontainable and, ironically, to exclude the integral.

Irwin's bizarre strategy of aggregation is obscured by the appellation "Herostratus complex."

Wertham's analysis of his patient's desire for self-emasculation falls short of Irwin's complex delimitation of the sexual. The doctor prefers Irwin's earlier explanation (that he "cut off his penis in order to 'bottle up his sexual energy' ") to the extended rationale — provided, importantly, to *another* analyst after the murders: "You can say sex is the cornerstone. I wanted to make myself so that I would have an ever present awareness of the fact that I didn't belong in this scheme of things — so that would always be a goad after me to drive me to what I was doing."[46]

It is this question of the penis[47] as *source* and *site* of sexuality that, therefore, remains surprisingly unexamined. For all that Wertham argues that Irwin was confused in his attack upon his own body ("What was he trying to accomplish? Just to remove his penis as one removes a hat?"),[48] the doctor will not entertain, as his patient does, a more complex concept of the sexual. Irwin counters his analyst's reductionism with a *symbolic* and negative use of the sexual. Irwin's self-emasculation was a doomed attempt to *cast out* the other, and with it the mechanism of desire itself. That eviction could result in the refiguring of desire, its redefinition in reference to *lack:* present absence, remembered loss.[49] Irwin's complicated strategy of aggregation and disavowal cannot be reconciled with the dyadic model of object relations to which Wertham adheres.[50]

Nor, in the final analysis, can he allow his patient the luxury of explaining (thus constructing) himself. Irwin's insistence that the night of the murder passed him in a "daze," taking only moments, provided the doctor with the means to occlude Irwin's agency as murderer:[51]

Irwin said that during that night he felt as if in a blind alley, in a blue daze, as if it all passed in half an hour. His situation was that of a man walking in a fog who barely sees some of the road. His was a waking dream, a nightmare, instead of a waking reality.[52]

In a sense, Irwin is not present at the time of the murder. His act becomes the consequence of the catathymic crisis: it is authored by delusion. But who is the author of the *narrative* of delusion? The crux of this issue of authority is demonstrated by Wertham's willingness to position himself as the arbiter of meaning:

Speaking of the night before Easter Sunday, 1937, Irwin said "every bit of it was accidental." That was a sincere statement. He intended to annihilate Ethel — and instead killed three other people. But when he uses the term "accidental" that means only that the causes, the design, were hidden from him. If one understands the conscious and unconscious workings of the mind there are layers of patterns woven into one another.[53]

Wertham clearly suggests that *he* understands. As Irwin's interpreter, the doctor gathers together disparate and hidden clues to create continuity for a definitive story of the analysand's psyche, becoming in the process coauthor of the narrative of murder. Wertham's odd incuriosity regarding Irwin's own complex explanations of "self" illustrates the degree to which the analyst is himself engaged in the re-creation — through reeducation — of the subject under analysis. For Irwin, killing and dying are parallel strategies of liberation. For the doctor they are merely different manifestations of a ruling pathology: repeated shorts in the circuit of catathymia.

Whose Story?

Irwin gives every indication of knowing the effect upon him of the co-option, particularly by the news media, of his story.[54] Yet these stories, and most particularly the "reasonable" murder story authored by the analyst, establish the conditions of possibility for Irwin's own account.

In an eloquent moment of doubling, Irwin explains the circumstance of his conversion to the genre of true crime. The crime story only came to interest him when *he* became its subject: "I never read these detective-story magazines until I saw my picture in one. When I read in Cleveland that my mother had died, I wanted to end it all then. I wanted to give myself up to Walter Winchell, but I didn't have the carfare."[55] The significant core of this passage is Irwin's sense of himself as a *story*. Naturally he wishes to direct the progress of the tale, whether that be toward closure (death) or, better still, syndication (Walter Winchell). There is quite some distance between Cleveland (where, reading of his mother's death, he, too, wants to die) and Chicago, where his surrender results in the Hearst papers scoop, converting the saleable property of Robert Irwin into a proliferation of bylines. The end of the journey for Irwin (Cleve-

land to Chicago) is not death, but fame. The story is what counts, and it cannot end too soon.

If we consider Irwin's selfless reason for seeking out the Hearst press (that he wanted to use the fee to "help his two brothers; one who was in jail and the other he thought was a dope addict") to be sincere,[56] then, arguably, we must do away with the spectre of Herostratus altogether. But that would be a little premature. The Herostratus complex itself needs to be reread. The desire for glory, or fame, is not the core concept of the complex: it is the will to become a story. It is this that explains Irwin's metaphorical journey from Cleveland to Chicago—from death to syndication. The money that Irwin obtained from his story went toward continuing his "work on visualization."[57] Although the ultimate aim of "visualization" was to lose himself in the divine, in practice it was a device to improve his mimetic capabilities—to refine recollection to the point where he could effectively reconstruct the object of reference in its complex entirety. Thus he wished to move from the re-creation of the two-dimensional artifact (i.e., to recall to mind exactly a photograph or painting) to the ability to rerun movies mentally and, finally, to the re-creation of whole objects and scenes. This movement out from the "flat" dimensional perspective to the appearance and then the reality of depth is a significant one. It represents to Irwin that "living memory" is not just representative but—through "visualization"—actually constructive. Irwin confused mimesis with creation, believing, for instance, that his killings had merely "borrowed" the lives of the Gedeons, and that his "visualizing" powers would redeem them.[58] For Irwin, description *could* be converted into the thing itself—thus his choice to journey not toward death, but to syndication.

In the final chapter of *The Show of Violence* Wertham ponders the meaning of murder in contemporary society. Murder represents a two-way mirror—allowing access to the most intimate workings of the individual and of "human nature"[59] while also exposing the dominant moral and ideological structures of society ("Tell me what murders are committed and what is done about them and I'll tell you what society you live in").[60] Murder assumes a metaphorical status.

In the various case studies of *The Show of Violence* murder is symptomatic both of individual and social pathology. While Irwin's individual pathology was a focal point of the doctor's analysis, Wertham did not neglect to blame a society sick with endemic unemployment and bureaucratic indifference. Wertham accepted, without qualification, Irwin's own petulant defense: "You know, I'm an unfortunate young fellow who tried to get on in the world and couldn't."[61] By its willful indifference, society reinscribes the closed circuit of the catathymic crisis, refusing to develop and reward those talents which might have forestalled the onset of that crisis. Irwin could find no job and could not support the pursuit of his sculpture; consequently, the depressive cycle (aggravated by insufficient or misguided institutional supervision) led inexorably to a crisis.

Wertham's identification of the need (and thus the right) to work and the necessity of self-expression can be taken as evidence of the degree to which his *Weltanschauung* was informed by the humanism of European democratic socialism, rather than that of American liberalism.[62] Irrespective of this evidence, his interrogation of the interdependence of individual and social pathology that gives rise to murder is a humanistic and positivistic one. It is founded upon the belief that murder — as a social and psychological phenomenon — tells the story of "human nature," albeit a nature which is historically determined.

Like most explanations of human nature, we find this to be a gendered account. The human capital of Robert Irwin, squandered by depression America with such violent results, is inescapably masculine. It is worthwhile here to make a comparison of Wertham's analysis of Irwin with that of his final case study: a "modern Medea" whom Wertham called, simply, "Mary."[63] The doctor became involved with Mary's case, like Irwin's, during the depression when he was called by the court to provide a psychological assessment of the prisoner. Mary was facing a charge of first-degree murder, and the enmity of her community, for slitting the throat of her seven-year-old daughter and partially burning the body. She unsuccessfully tried to dispose of her younger son by slitting his throat, but he survived and was taken into care. Wertham found Mary to be of "lower than average intelligence," and eventually he successfully argued to the court that her charge be reduced because of "diminished responsibility." The judge, seizing upon what, for many experts, still remains a convenient description for the violence of mothers toward their children,[64] accepted this advice and added his own two bits worth on Mary's lack of volition to do wrong.

Wertham saw Mary's crime as the result of social injustice (her inability to afford sufficient child care; indifference on the part of the child welfare authorities to whom she went for help) and personal weakness (Mary's "borderline intelligence" proved insufficient for her to think her way out of the problem of the children, while also contributing to her selfishness, suggestibility, and hedonism). In contrast to Wertham's conception of the needs that were denied Irwin by society — rights constructed as ungendered and universal — the needs denied Mary are determined by her sex, as his use of her mythic precursor makes clear: "Medea expresses, in a case where the consequences are of extreme horror, a struggle for women's rights which are not in conflict with motherhood but [are] a demand for the fulfillment of motherhood without all the unjust sacrifices of individual self-expression."[65] Wertham interprets Mary's murderous act through the prism of a narrow reading of the tragedy of Medea. What might an alternative reading offer? We should consider Medea's choice of victims as both strategic *and* determined. What prompts her to kill her children (her husband's heirs) is not jealousy as such, but her inability to attain the status of citizen-wife. It is her position as *foreigner* that provokes her to attack the status of her husband in the figure of his children (who stand to accede to the realm of power from which she is excluded). As a foreigner, she cannot figure as a wife (only mistress), and murder becomes merely a radical reenactment of what is an already existing social sanction. If we move the focus of the Medea myth from that of her identity as a wronged woman and mother to that of a disenfranchised outsider, an alternative reading for Mary's murder of her daughter appears, and with it quite a different social critique.

In her own testimony, and that of her immigrant boyfriend,[66] Mary appears to fulfill the tasks of motherhood adequately, but without (in Wertham's view) great enthusiasm. The doctor notes that her sole moment of animation in interviews was when she talked about how she loved to dance, and the lack of her opportunities for doing so. On a minimal benefit, supplemented by the equally meager earnings of her laborer boyfriend, Mary could not afford alternative care for her son and daughter. Her life was ruled by her child-care responsibilities. For Wertham, then, the conditions in which Mary found herself (without state support in a depression economy) were not conducive to her properly assuming the duties of motherhood. In a just society, Mary could presumably reap the joys of motherhood. But there is little evidence in Wertham's account of her early marriage that the children were either wanted or planned.[67] It is not, therefore, merely a matter of reconciling the secondary need for "individual self-expression" with the "fulfillment" of that more "fundamental" identity of motherhood. The doctor colludes with the very construct he derides by prioritizing his patient's role as mother, naturalizing motherhood per se. Just as a strict social and familial hierarchy determined the fate of Medea by forbidding her a place within that system,[68] Mary's fate is determined by the insistence of her culture not just that she *mother*, but that she *be* a mother.

Mary sought to shake off that obligation. Faithful to the anecdotal wisdom of dreams, Wertham relates a dream scenario told him by Mary: "Some girl was starting to run away from home and she just seemed to say, 'Well, I won't be coming back.' The girl was running away. They had a rope and tangled her and caught her by the feet, and she fell down. A crowd started to gather and people came for her and took her back home."[69] Wertham reads the dream merely as wish fulfillment: her desire for escape. But the nightmare elements of the dream invite a closer reading. Unlike the clearly defined "I" that is the predatory subject in Irwin's dream of the angel, Mary dreams of "some girl": a subject that is simultaneously object and other. The subject of Mary's dream of escape is chased by a faceless "they" and brought to heel before "a crowd." She is roped like straying cattle, signifying her value to others as lost property. And the place to which she is returned is "home": her place of imprisonment, not the private sanctum of happy domesticity. If this is a dream of escape, it is also eloquent testimony to its impossibility.

Wertham's discussion of Mary demonstrates the false unity of the concept of human nature and, likewise, the uncomplicated fallacy of human frailty that leads to murder. Within the supposedly unified category of the "human," sexual difference marks out the subspecies of "woman": difference visible *only* in and as Woman. That difference bespeaks the vigor of a century-old conceptualization of women's biological nature as in itself pathological — as *other than* the human norm, implicitly male.[70]

Dr. Wertham's "narratives of crime" describe a "magic of murder" that is both spectacle and sign.[71] The use of mythic narrative to structure the stories of murder contained in his case studies produces meanings in excess of his intent (to demonstrate the ability of forensic psychiatry to predict, qualitatively, dangerousness). The raw data of violence are re-authored by the expert to make sense out of chaos: to take the social meaning out of an individual act. The interpretive act of reauthoring the murder narrative is what establishes authority in the tale of murder. The process of interpretation is a thing in itself, distinct from the reason for which the tale is told, distinct even from its subject. In later chapters, I shall be examining the degree to which the ostensible subject of the tale can disappear, even when his or her reconstruction is the core project of the tale's author.[72] That reauthoring act is particularly explicit in the case of Dr. Wertham (as distinct from the "case of Robert Irwin"). In forensic psychiatry the "original pact" of analysis is broken by a structure that bestows upon the analyst the authority of judge.

The Cannibal State:

Murder and Execution in *Star Wormwood*

"His father would nuzzle his neck and say that he would eat him. Roger would cry delightedly that he couldn't. Father replied that he could but he wouldn't, and when this had gone on a satisfying length of time, Roger would clinch the argument: 'You couldn't. I'm too big. Part of me would stick out.'"[73] The parable of the "eating game" is an allusion to the circumstances of the crime for which Roger Haike is executed: his eating of the arm of the young woman he has accidentally killed.[74] More impor-tant, the parable of the "eating game" foreshadows the social critique leveled by the liberal judge. Although he deplores the hypocrisy of a taboo against cannibalism in a society where we daily "eat our neighbors in spirit or in mind," Bok primarily aims his metaphor at the punitive state.[75] The juridical game of capital sentencing leads the state to devour its children.[76] Bok suggests it was Roger Haike's "unique fate to starve or be eaten."[77]

In common with both Wright's *Native Son* and Motley's *Knock on Any Door*, Bok's work has a concern with the failure of the state, and its institu-tions, to minister to the rights and needs of its marginal citizens. Yet Bok's treatise has more in common with Wertham's *The Show of Violence* than with the works discussed in the previous chapter. Although the factual basis of Bok's work is less overt than Wertham's, its truth claims are not. Like Wertham, Bok is an apostle of the science of mind, and his project is founded upon his confidence in the expertise of forensic psychiatry — a confidence that mirrors his own, albeit self-critical, professionalism.

With a classically liberal concern for balancing the rights and obligations of the citizen with the interests of the rule of law, Bok uses the devoured child as a sign of the fundamentally inequitable basis of the social contract. In a secular world, the state — though lacking both the omnipotence and omniscience of God and the symbolic authority of the monarch — still has the power of life and death over its subjects. The state's failure either to maintain the compassion of conscience necessary to rule (in the liberal mind) or to plumb accurately the conscience of its citizens is most clearly exposed in its juridical and punitive functions. Bok seeks to dramatize the cost of such a rule of law for America in its second "century of progress." The novel structure of the treatise pairs prose narrative with analytic commentary; the analytic power of social criticism supposedly demystifies the lyrical fiction of the murder narrative. The persistence of the mystery, however, seems to be a *function* of the narrative of murder. The fiction and "commentary" of Bok's *Star Wormwood* read *against* one another, not as companion pieces. The different fates of these two texts within one attest eloquently to the overwhelmingly symbolic power of punishment — and of capital punishment in particular.

Over the past century and a half, more than two-thirds of American states have legislatively allowed for, and carried out, the death penalty by a variety of means.[78] Legal homicide has been interpreted by its proponents as a strategy for deterrence, punishment and, by its more acute supporters, as a mechanism to control the potentially anarchic effects of private vengeance.[79] The self-evidence of such ideas is continually questioned by the opponents of capital punishment. Whatever the methodological acrobatics of its defenders, for instance, evidence proving conclusively that effectiveness of the death penalty as deterrence just cannot be found.[80] The siege upon the system of legal homicide (culminating in a five-year federal ban on the practice in the late 1960s and early '70s) seems to have been rhetorically effective but materially impotent. The death penalty remains very much a part not just of judicial and penal administration but of American culture at large. It is the importance of capital punishment as a political phenomenon, as a social practice, and as a *symbolic event*, that ensures its maintenance. Indeed, we have witnessed a revival of faith in its benefits since the early 1980s[81] — *despite a marked decrease in urban homicide rates in the past four to five years.*[82] The persistence of capital punishment is best explained by the seductiveness, in the American context, of the concept of just and fitting punishment. Its revival, however, is attributable to more immediate trends in stricter law-and-order legislation and the significant explosion in prison populations. The "tough on crime" approach lends itself to expedience. One could characterize (my apologies for the reductionism) that line of thought: there are too many criminals, and too many nonviolent criminals, in American prisons, so why not make room at the extreme end (rather than attending to the problem of jail terms for minor offenses) by obliterating the most violent offenders. While that might be the logistics of the revival, its symbolic core is, however, quite another matter.

The idea of meeting force with force finds its enunciation in law, in military strategy, in political rhetoric, and in the language of the marketplace. Just as the law of self-defense allows for the use of lethal force in situations where one entertains the *reasonable belief* that one's life is in peril, and where one has "no duty to retreat," the idea of defense of the social body by deployment of the most extreme sanction has a ring of equitable justice about it.[83] The relative ascendance over the past thirty years of the "problem of crime" in the hierarchy of public concerns has only made the doctrine of justifiable homicide, and its equivalent in judicial homicide, a more acceptable response.[84]

One aim of this book is a weighing of the relationship between murder and execution as cultural signs.[85] The fascination with closure in the murder narrative is probably most clearly visible in representations of capital homicide. When the life of the murderer is at stake, the anticipation of his/her death provides a dramatic counterweight to the tale of murder itself. Opponents of the death penalty have argued that there is no ethical distinction between homicide and state-sponsored execution, and that the old biblical adage of "a life for a life" cannot ever, in practicality, represent parity or a just exchange.[86] Yet the balance between a life (or more) maliciously taken and the taking of the life of the killer is an idea that continues to fascinate Americans, a fascination that partly accounts for the longevity of the death penalty. Ironically, that "balance" is treated as a *necessary fiction* both by the legislatures administering capital punishment[87] and by the public at large.[88]

Curtis Bok's story of Roger Haike is very loosely based upon that of a young man executed for the murder of a woman in Pennsylvania in 1931. Roger's story is simple but suspiciously interpretable, as his jury discovers. Undernourished for most of his early life, the leaner years of the Depression throw Roger into a state of insatiable hunger. He learns how to snare rabbits from his only friend, a taciturn boy like himself, bearing a similar last name, Joe Hake. Roger, who minds his own business, does not know that Joe has been having an incestuous affair with his younger sister, Angela, Joe's "well-formed" and "evil" seducer.[89] Unfortunately, this secret eventually unravels into Roger's life when Joe, sick of the tyranny of his sister's sexual demands, revenges himself upon her by not withdrawing at ejaculation. In a fury, Angela flees the house, determined to exact her own revenge upon men in general.[90] Coincidentally, she runs to the school and finds Roger, who has just begun work there as a caretaker. She surprises him as he is about to retrieve a rabbit he has been roasting (against the rules) in the furnace; alarmed, he drops his precious meal into the coals to burn. Seeing her opportunity for revenge, Angela threatens to tell the school authorities what he has done. To convince her otherwise, Roger — always short on words — takes hold of her "in order to stop her from leaving and prevent her from talking or making noise." This intervention only increases Angela's fury, as "the last thing she could abide was constriction of any kind." She begins to scream, and Roger, who hates loud or sudden noise, loses "all control except the will to stop" that "dreadful noise."[91] He throttles her and then, while trying to shake some sense into her, accidentally breaks her neck. When he realizes that her sudden silence is not a sign of acquiescence, but a more permanent capitulation, he panics and tries to shove her body into the furnace. It will not all fit, so when the head and shoulders have partially burned he tries to wedge the corpse in farther, burning himself in the process. He licks at the wound and finds some of the girl's cooked flesh in his mouth. That savor revives his hunger and he numbly gnaws away at the partially cooked arm. Horrified by what he has found himself doing, he vomits and flees, giving no further thought to the concealment of the crime. Significantly, the "evidence" left behind him includes the semen in Angela's body, remnant of her brother's recent revenge upon her. This final trace will clinch the monstrosity of the case against Roger, as he is indicted for rape-murder.

When Roger languishes in jail, the appearance of his lawyer evinces in him a wistful faith in the figure of a protector: part liege, part mother, part father:[92] "A memory from his childhood made him cry out: 'Are you going to take care of me?' "[93] Roger is a child involved in an adult game, the rules of which he does not know.[94] The benevolent state is represented by the figures of lawyer and psychiatrist: the Good Mother, the Good Father. While Roger is riding the train to the state penitentiary, he considers his need to have his lawyer as witness to the execution: "He wanted Morris. He wanted to keep hold of him to the end, as if he were thread and continuity, the only thing that could abide and make a final, rounded experience, short and twisted as it was. He needed continuity: otherwise he would be lost and broken."[95] This "continuity" is wrapped in cultural meanings of the maternal. The lawyer as mother represents nurturance, sustenance, and understanding. But it is the figure of Dr. Danby, the psychiatrist, that comes to represent a *generative* paternity.

Despite the defeating experience that is his lot in the murder trial, Roger undergoes a certain regeneration through the necessity of explaining himself, *of making himself heard.* That regeneration is a move from out of silence to articulacy. What is more, that movement represents the progress toward a potentially greater humanity: "Had Roger lived to maturity, he might have seen that his fumbling between noise and quiet was the ancient battleground of man."[96] But where, finally, does Roger's newly discovered voice come from?

Facing conviction for rape-murder and the monolithic hatred of media and community, Roger is "sparse of words" at a time when they are indispensable. Although Morris is able to get Roger's story out of him, it seems unlikely that he will be able to get the boy to retell that story to a more hostile audience in court. Morris also wants *more* to the story: not what the boy cannot speak, but what *he does not know.* Eliciting that supplementary story becomes the responsibility of Dr. Danby,[97] the alienist:

Danby hypnotized him, got what he wanted, woke Roger up, and told him what he had said. It was then not difficult for Roger to accept what he was told he had said and soon to say it again in his own words.[98]

Roger's voice, then, comes from his unconscious, albeit by way of the authority of the alienist. This ambiguity becomes more apparent as Roger, after sentencing, contemplates his progress to speech:

For months he had wrestled with the strange problems of his case. . . . He had had to become articulate, which was against his nature, and he had said more words than he knew existed. They had done him no good.[99]

Leaving aside for a moment that vital knowledge of the failure of speech, let us concentrate on the paradoxical project of Roger's articulacy. How can he utter "more words than he knew existed"? This is not merely semantical quibbling, but indicates the problematic status to speech when it is gained only through an intermediary voice: that of the psychiatrist. The words that Roger speaks but does not know have a meaning veiled but present; therefore he *speaks in his own voice.* However, the larger project of Bok's treatise works against such a reading by positing as prior and re/generative the healing intervention of the psychiatrist.

While the progress of Roger toward speech speaks of Bok's faith in the "civilizing" precepts of psychiatry, Bok makes even more general claims for the social utility of psychiatry: "The penology of the future is treatment." The occasional divergences of law from justice can be explained by the degree to which law as a system, and legal formalism in particular, reifies fact and makes man immanent, the transparent vessel of lawful or unlawful intent. Bok hopes that the law, like psychiatry, will recognize the mind's opacity, enabling a return to *moral* legal government: "If we let our ideals escape into systems, we are moving toward that dangerous area where a thing and the name of a thing get mixed up."[100] The confusion of the "thing and the name of a thing" demonstrates the law's tendency to valorize "fact." Psychiatry, however, does not dare rely upon that self-evidence:

Freud has set a great wind blowing in man's mind. . . . In the law this is a tough cross-wind, and it is driving the profession to regard facts as icebergs, complete with large underbodies which must be examined.[101]

Although Bok questions the tenets of a formalistic legal positivism, he cannot escape from positivism itself. There *is* a truth to be found, if only by looking more deeply — looking, indeed, for the rational man, that ideal subject of liberal thought:

[T]he importance and effect of free will are becoming less and less as a person's early influences and motivations are revealed. Psychiatry can show their grip upon him to explain his past action and, by helping him to understand his plight, free him from similar pitfalls in the future. As man develops in moral caliber, his choice of the right action will become increasingly automatic. And as psychiatry develops its techniques, it will increasingly help him to clear the path to instinctive choice.[102]

The mind *is* knowable — given the correct and refined instrument of measurement. And man, ultimately, *is* perfectible.

The law as Good Father "bends an attentive ear" to the "difficult problems" of those on the rocky path to perfection.[103] The metaphorical equivalent of Roger's articulacy is law's sensitivity to that still, small voice. The critical edge to the commentary section is blunted by its faith in the regenerative powers of the state and the moral paternity of law. More important, though, Bok's optimism is undermined by the resolution of the story of Roger's move from silence to speech. What, after all, is the net result of those words that had "done him no good"?

Roger's fate is announced in court by the "terrible words" of his jurors convicting him of first-degree murder. Later, during sentencing, the judge reiterates those "dreadful words" of punishment. Despite speaking "more words than he knew existed" in his own defense, the law has the last word. Roger's newly found voice, in the form of his testimony, provides the law with its authority to annihilate the speaker. Bok is at pains to point out the difference between law at its best — "bending a troubled ear" to the knotty problems of the psyche — and the dead letter of the law that produces judgment without moral authority. The law that condemns Roger has a great battery of words, but its heart is silent, a silence manifest in the "remote and bloodless language" of the decision of the state supreme court to refuse certiorari in Roger's case: "it sounded as if someone had taken the case into the desert and left it there." That disconnection is further symbolized by the governor's departure, on the eve of the execution, to go sailing in a yacht with no ship-to-shore telephone.[104] The opposition of silence to speech in *Star Wormwood* produces a meaning in excess of the *logos* of that pairing. Generally figured by Bok as the subordinate and less desirable quality in the pairing, silence comes out "on top" elsewhere. What, after all, is Roger's "nature" but to be taciturn, "sparse of words"? His foray into speech does not save him. Awaiting execution Roger "grew ever more silent":

It was comforting to be quiet and not racked by words and questions . . . and the same continence in language kept him from reading.[105]

Roger's "continence in language" is self-defense: silence holds him together. His reticence overlays *presence*, while the noisy silence of law protects only *absence*.

The principal metaphorical forms of the work converge at the moment of Roger's return to his "natural" silence in prison — a silence ratified by the undemanding, comforting presence of his lawyer, Morris Longa. This figuring of the Law as Mother presents a counterweight to the Law as Father — the psychiatrist's ushering of Roger into the realm of speech.[106] Morris Longa is complicit in Roger's return to reticence:

Morris gave him what solace he could and went away. He didn't try to make an occasion of his coming or to find subjects of conversation, for he realized what it was that Roger got from him and knew it was no dependence on time or words.[107]

Roger gets from the presence of Morris something that has "no dependence on time or words," suggesting Roger's return to the pre-Oedipal Feminine, that space *prior to* speech. Roger is afraid, entering the death chamber, that he has been deserted. He fears that he must approach death alone, and the grief rising in him has the inexpressible want of the infant:

[T]he black door opened to let them enter the death room, and closed behind them. He wanted to call out Morris's name, but his mouth was dry and he could utter no sound. There was no word for him either, and his spirit sank to its lowest point. He had been deserted.[108]

Bok's expression "There was no word for him" means literally that no one greeted the boy, but it also suggests the uselessness of language to Roger: *he neither has the word nor can be called by it.* Here the disobliging instability of the subject before/within language is indicated by the sanctions imposed by the Law as Father upon the Law as Mother. Morris Longa, who arrived too late to see the boy in his cell, is attendant upon the execution. He wants to call out to Roger but is constrained by the rules not to do so. Eventually, however, Morris does speak, *against the rules:* "The rule was silence, and Morris had not dared to speak before, in fear of being excluded or even ejected from the room."[109] As Morris speaks the words "I'm here," he symbolically demolishes the silencing authority of the Law as (Bad) Father. That "I'm here" is a declaration of maternal authority — the power to comfort the inexpressible want of the infant by *presence* alone. But that declaration brings with it the penalty of "exclusion," of "ejection." The Law as Mother is anathema to the Law as Father. It must be cast out for the Law as Father to pose successfully as *Law:* an undifferentiated and objective authority.

The metaphor of the devouring parent — law that consumes not just its subjects but its own heart — is associated with Bok's metaphorical opposition between noise and silence. Bok inadvertently reinscribes the mystery of murder during his analysis of the faults of the system that penalizes it. That mystery returns in the form of metaphor, the troping mechanism that cannot be equaled by Bok's analytic commentary. The problem of silence remains. What is at the heart of silence? What inhabits its depths?

Given this reinscription of the mystery of murder, what must become of Bok's belief that crime, as a "disease of civilization," can be "studied" and remedied? The psychiatrist's ability to explain the "deviation" of the murderous criminal from "mankind's moderate average madness" is an illusive mastery.[110] Roger lives, kills, and dies in a world of speakers who do not mean what they say, where words are powerless to save him. Bok has faith in the power of forensic psychiatry to discriminate between "incorrigibles" and those who can be redeemed by treatment.[111] Although Bok deplores capital punishment, he allows for a category of "incorrigibles" — those whose minds can never be brought to order, whose motives are inscrutable. These are "fit" subjects for execution: "mad dogs" who do not "always snarl and foam at the mouth."[112] That exception to Bok's humanitarian rule testifies to the importance of the symbolic power of execution. Execution offers the satisfaction of (false) closure: the violent answer to the unanswerable question of madness. In Bok's own text the vision of rationality and order is self-defeating. The *precise* vision of psychiatry turns out to be particularly fixed and partial. Like the thick glass of the train window through which Roger can see only at its center — momentarily capturing glimpses of the landscape he is passing — psychiatry provides a view that is both brief and partial, captured at the very moment it is already lost.

Star Wormwood and *The Show of Violence* are texts that claim for themselves an adjudicatory role, weighing the status and value of forensic psychiatry and its impact upon due process and penology. They undergo a kind of slippage, their determined aim deflected by a narrative of murder the direction of which they, finally, cannot control. Wertham's narratives arise from real subjects, his patients under analysis. His retelling of their stories is therefore explicitly interventionist and constructive. His tale mystifies as much as it enlightens, like the mythic narratives he uses to establish his psychotic archetypes. Both Wertham and Bok insist that the "penology of the future is treatment."[113] Their rational projects founder, the mystery of murder reappearing within their own (and their subjects') intricate processes of interrogation and interpretation. The meaning of a particular murderous act is not stable, its instability ensured by the unacknowledged narrative function of classification. The meaning of murder as excess returns in the mobility of metaphor that is the heart of both sociological tracts. For Wertham and Bok, the act of murder becomes a point of reference for the determination of the ethical character of the murderer. Their determination whether that act was consistent with, or a departure from, what is constituted and an *ethical nature* is an important function of the reauthoring act. This book is a critique of authority in the tale of murder generally. Yet it is also, unavoidably, a narrative with its own authoritative terms *and* author. While I have been preoccupied in this chapter with the co-option of the subject of the tale by its interpreter, I will next be discussing the disposition of the subject of the tale of murder when its reauthoring is accomplished not by a single interpreter, but by a chorus of commentators. Along with my return to the issue of the subject, my own status as author also comes under scrutiny — prefatory to the final chapter's critique of the self-reflexive nature of the tale of murder generally.

4. True Crime Romance I:

A Genre Defiled

Love is just an episode in a man's life, but it is the very life of a woman.
Herbert Rosenberg, Defense Attorney

My story is a love story. *Martha Jule Beck*

The retired assistant district attorney of Nassau County, New York, Henry ("Hank") Devine, remembers Martha Jule Beck well, although he met her only once. At the special appeal session convened in the death cells at Sing Sing, he recalls Mrs. Beck's stare as she triumphantly told the assembled lawyers: "[T]here's just one difference between you and me: *I* know when *I'm* going."[1] Hank Devine is still an imposing man, although his stature has diminished under the depredations of old age. His walking cane is placed before him on the polished wooden table of the law library, and the high gloss of that table is accentuated by pale autumnal sunlight. Mr. Devine's voice is boisterous in the quiet. I, too, am excited: able to talk, at last, to one of the principals in a case that has, till now, consisted entirely of depositions, transcripts, and books of evidence. The library in which we sit is not thirty miles away from the cellar in which Ray Fernandez buried Janet Fay's body, wrapped in Martha's pink chenille nightgown.

Mr. Devine seems glad of an opportunity to talk about the "Honeymoon Killers." The case was a sensation in its day, a real circus. Yet his enthusiasm is not tempered by the perspicacity of mind for which he was known in his heyday at the Office of the Nassau County District Attorney. Details slip and recur. Yes, he remembers what Martha looked like: she was a "big girl," maybe "300 pounds or so," and, he tells me with curmudgeonly charm, "not nearly as pretty as you." She decorated her cell with paper chains. She was an "intelligent woman" (meaning she should have known better). But it is the modus operandi of the killers that really fascinates. Devine repeatedly returns to the state in which the body was found, curled up tightly and buried beneath the concrete floor of the cellar in the South Ozone house.[2] "They rolled her in a ball and just dropped her in there." He wonders how many other poor women might have been similarly dealt with: "Who knows how many. . . . [N]ow I don't know . . . but we had people out there in the Midwest . . . and they weren't looking at cornfields." Devine regrets not having taken up the invitation to the execution: it was a pity to have been "in it" but not to have been there at the end.

At the time Henry Devine took up the case for the state on appeal, the facts had long since been established. Those Midwestern cornfields had not yielded any further revelations since the conviction of Martha Beck and Ray Fernandez in August 1949. The appeal process was merely a means of dickering over the details of due process, a due process the end of which was the scheduled execution of the Hearts Killers.[3] That moment when Martha Beck eyed the lawyers and told them she wanted no further appeal proceedings on her behalf showed that she, at least, was inured to the prospect of her imminent death. Both Beck and Fernandez had been scheduled for death since their highly irregular extradition from Michigan (where they'd been arrested for the killing of Delphine Downing[4] and her two-year-old daughter, Rainelle).[5] Mr. Devine recounted the words of the governor of Michigan as he offered up his already infamous wards: "We don't like these laws down here." Michigan, unlike New York, had no death penalty.

Beck and Fernandez had been the center of frantic media activity since their arrest in Grand Rapids. In a spirit of cooperation that benefited everybody but the suspects, the arresting officers in Kent County, Michigan, posed their wards for photographs, passed on their personal letters and, in one particularly sleazy incident, stole a photograph of Martha's two children to give to the press.[6] As the extradition process moved on, stories originally printed in the Grand Rapids press began appearing back East in *Newsday*, the principal Long Island paper. Before long, the notoriety of the accused killers spread beyond those states in which the arrest and trial occurred. Eventually, the pair would come to be known as

"America's Most Hated Murderers," although they held that title neither exclusively nor permanently.[7]

Indeed, the infamy of Beck and Fernandez ensured them a place in the annals of true crime. The crimes of the Lonely Hearts Killers or Honeymoon Killers struck a resonant chord in the culture in which they occurred, and that same culture then became the audience for the re-staged (and rewritten) murder events. The two chapters following will track the emergence of the true crime version of the killings and its authoritative portrait of the killers, offering a critique of the ways in which authority — in a tale for which there could be no definitive truth — was constructed by a framing of the meager "facts" by generic narrative structures. My own moment of hopeful expectation as I set out to interview Hank Devine is eloquent testimony that the author of the tale of murder can become beguiled by the proximity of "fact," by the possibility that one is about to find out (or tell) "what really happened." And yet that optimism, that certainty, can be borne out only by reference to other authorizing narrative strategies (such as those deployed by Wertham and Bok) which can "flesh out" the factitious meaning of murder. In the case of the tale of the Hearts Killers, the reauthoring of the tale is not accomplished by a single author but by the multiple voices of legal authority, the media, and the wider culture which is both source and conduit of the media. In such a circumstance, the search for authority eschews the ahistorical, archetypal, mythological, and metaphorical narrative structures of Wertham and Bok in favor of more readily accessible cultural scripts in the pulp fictions of romance and crime.

The story of the Hearts Killers grew from a morass of conflicting detail — detail which was contained in the confessions leaked by the Kent County detectives and which was later battled over in the testimony of the principals during their forty-four-day trial. Martha Beck, a twenty-nine-year-old nurse from Pensacola, Florida, and Raymond Fernandez, a thirty-four-year-old American of Spanish descent whose occupation on committal for trial was listed as "construction,"[8] were being tried in Nassau County for the murder on 4 January 1949 of Mrs. Janet Fay, a sixty-six-year-old widow to whom Fernandez was then engaged. The couple had been initially arrested in Michigan, where they were being held for the murders of Delphine and Rainelle Downing, whose bodies had been found beneath damp cement in the cellar of Delphine's Grand

Rapids home. The Michigan murders and a couple of other "suspicious" deaths (Fernandez's paramours) never resulted in indictments, and the Downing case was officially closed after the New York conviction of Beck and Fernandez for the Fay murder. Crime writers, not unlike the retired prosecutor Henry Devine, would nevertheless continue to allude to the "many other" unsolved murders of single ladies for which Beck and Fernandez might have been responsible.[9] Once the narrative of murder had been wrested from the restrictive arena of the courts,[10] the murder of Janet Fay became a kind of metaphorical standard for the greater criminal careers of Beck and Fernandez. One body rolled into a ball and buried never seemed quite enough.

Conflicting accounts of Fay's murder arose from out of the initial confessions of the killers, accounts which were later refuted on the stand as being tendered under duress. Even given the contest over those accounts between the defendants themselves, and between prosecution and defense, the cumulative tendency was to bestow upon Martha Beck the primary agency. She was the one who wielded the hammer — whether as a furious but contingent act[11] or in a blackout induced by the stress of obsession for her lover.[12] This tendency of Martha to bear the weight of the crime (giving a double entendre to the media's favored name for her, "Fat Martha") prompted the defense to abandon the insanity plea for Ray Fernandez a third of the way through the trial. His new defense was a bid to reduce the charge to one of accessory after the fact.

The defense's claim of Martha's insanity was a confused one. Herbert Rosenberg, representing both clients (despite the conflicting strategies), tried to impress upon the jury two possible scenarios: the hammering was committed in a "blackout," or, had she been conscious, Beck had no control of her actions and was unable to determine that they were wrong. The burden was upon the prosecution to prove her sane, yet their task was simplified by the defense's apparent confusion of insanity and "abnormality."[13] The prosecutor, Edward Robinson, was quite happy to concede the "abnormality" of the accused. In point of fact, everyone involved in the trial seemed happy to do so — with the notable exception of Beck and Fernandez themselves.

Before the insanity defense was abandoned for Fernandez, Rosenberg got him to tell the court his life story, that testimony being a portrait of violent times that could not have failed to affect the defendant. In Spain,

Fernandez had been indentured by Franco's forces to help administer the execution of Loyalists in his home town. Sometimes those Loyalists were his own friends, and the totality of his experience in the Spanish Civil War had upset his moral sense. Failing to demonstrate the plausibility of this psychological battering, the defense also presented the court with evidence of organic defect: Fernandez had sustained a head injury when a ship's hatch, improperly secured during a storm, fell in on him.[14] Unfortunately, when the insanity plea was abandoned the prosecution (ignoring the evidence of brain injury) turned the story of Fernandez's war experiences against him. He had not been driven insane (in the legal definition) but had merely lost all decent human feeling.[15]

Both defendants were led through their life stories by Rosenberg. The biographical testimony alone takes up hundreds of pages. Both stories were presented in order to establish the human *presence* of the defendants, for, after all, first-degree murder carried with it a mandatory death sentence. Secondly, those stories were meant to picture the helplessness of the defendants before the forces inside them which had propelled them through a chaos of crime toward murder. Picking up on a casual phrase of one of the defense psychiatrists, Rosenberg described Martha Beck as "a slip of the Potter's hand." By the end of the trial, Martha had ended up in exclusive possession, figuratively speaking, of the hammer. Possessing the murder, she also became the sole barometer of that "abnormality" which the defense so vainly tried to code as insanity. Beck's pathology—the abnormality so frequently alluded to—was not criminal, but moral:

[T]here wasn't one criminal tendency shown in her background until she got involved here. But look at her entire background, her dealings with the defendant Fernandez, her love for him, her attending these marriages [to other women, his "marks"], playing strip poker, acting as a witness [to one of Fernandez's marriages to a rival]. Go through that entire background and can you honestly come to the conclusion that she was a normal person?[16]

Yet what *was* the content of that "abnormality"? At the time of the trial, the nature of Fernandez's and, particularly, Beck's abnormality was deemed so offensive by the news media that they neglected to print it. As late as 1961 a respected English writer of true crime, Colin Wilson, observed that "the details of [the] sexual relationship that emerged (both were complete degenerates) were so indecent that they were never published."[17] The media did frequently allude to the "sordid" histories of the defendants in place of those more immediate facts about the sexual relationship that only the court would hear (the press gallery being, in this instance, silent witness).

The discussion of abnormality forms one of the few continuous threads of the trial. That the murder happened was not disputed, but how and why it happened were topics of hot dispute.[18] In this particular case, as well as in the tale of murder more generally, a definitive account continues to be unknowable. Given the lack of a definitive version of the Fay murder, authority in the narrative had to come from another source. The elasticity of the account of murder could be capitalized upon only by the insertion into the narrative of the vital subtext of the murderers' abnormality. In all accounts of the Lonely Hearts Killers, including the trial, it is this shift of emphasis that constructs the tale of murder.

From the time of the arrest till just before the execution there appeared at least eight different accounts of the night of the murder (see Appendix). Six of these were tendered (allegedly) by the suspects, the remaining two were the composite versions offered by prosecution and defense. Although the account of the murder itself is not to be confused with the tale of murder *as a whole*,[19] as the central axis of the tale it holds a particular fascination. In each version it is possible to see the point of entry for the *real* story, for that supposition which is the moment of truth: the revelation of the character of the murderer.

At the conclusion of her statement to Dr. Richard Hoffmann (see Appendix), Martha wrote that she had "never killed anyone in [her] life."[20] The depositions of the Kent County authorities do not agree. In all versions of the killings of Delphine[21] and Rainelle Downing, it is Martha who murders the child, drowning her in a laundry tub.[22] The only other documented death with which the pair was linked is that of Myrtle Young, whom Fernandez married and then sent home, heavily drugged, on a Greyhound bus. When Myrtle Young arrived at her destination, she was dead — although, according to the coroner, the cause of her death was natural and by no means the necessary result of the sleeping pills she'd been given. There was also the question of the suspicious death of a lady in Fernandez's company (prior to his meeting Martha Beck) while the two were traveling in Spain. The prosecution in the Fay trial would allude to an outstanding warrant for Fernandez's arrest there, and would hint at his administering an overdose of digitalis. These accusations were not substantiated.[23] As Jane Thompson died before Ray met Martha Beck, it is inappropriate to list her as one of the possible victims of the Lonely Hearts Killers. Only the deaths of Janet Fay and Delphine and Rainelle Downing can be reliably connected to Beck and Fernandez.

Why and how did three murders earn Beck and Fernandez the title of "America's Most Hated Murderers"? And why did the spurious tally of twenty killings continue to be held to their account?[24] Clues to the construction of the composite, the "authoritative" tale, can be found in the various versions of the Fay murder. Martha's final attempt to fix the blame for the murder onto Fernandez could only have been ineffective. It came too late to challenge the authoritative account. Indeed, it was irrelevant to the murder narrative that Martha Beck may not have actually killed Mrs. Fay. Martha's late but insistent denial of culpability is co-opted by an established narrative that reads Martha's fear of Raymond Fernandez as merely another manifestation of her romantic obsession. The mutuality implicit in the fatal contract of the *folie à deux* will not allow Martha her dissent. The couple were portrayed as murderous lovers, as textbook examples of the phenomenon of *folie à deux*. The infamy of "America's Most Hated Murderers" can therefore be explained by the way in which their tale was received and understood by contemporaries. The story of the Hearts Killers came to be read, both by its initial mediators and by their public, through the generic lens of the romance.

An Unlikely Heroine in a Deviant Genre

Just before his death, Ray Fernandez responded angrily to those who'd so assiduously followed the tale of his and Martha's ill-fated union. "What," he demanded in a letter published by the *Journal American* (8 March 1951) "do the public know about love?"

What the public knew about love was, in fact, a great deal. Like crime, love was something that *happened* to people, not just something read about in the papers. The American public set great store by personal experience, but it was a discourse of romance that formed the conditions of existence for that experience. The public came to know love, like crime, through its mediators. One saw crime in comic books (set in cityscapes where villainy had no apparent social context); one could read about it in a variety of written forms of the crime genre, from the genteel to the hard-boiled, as well as in the daily press and in the columns of *Time* and the photo-essays of *Life;* and one could see crime represented in the crime movie, the women's film and — if one happened to be of the inclination — in French cinema paying homage to American *film noir* (one could also see crime in the Western, where it was framed by a more general lawlessness that, a little like the world of the superhero comic, was a background against which "good" and "bad" stood out in clear relief). People in rural America looked toward the cities as the place where crime "belonged," and, as often as not, those in the city looked, in much the same way, to those neighborhoods in which *they* or *their kind* (their race, their class, their ethnic group) did not live. Crime was something one occasionally saw (or turned away from) and, more often, gossiped about. And, finally, there were those whose interest and experience in what passed for crime was — in one way or another — thorough and immediate. Personal experience, public discourse, and commonsensical knowledge collapse into one another. A recent work analyzing the vital juncture of urban discourse and the crime genre has noted that the diverse ways in which the city was representationally "mapped" rendered

such oppositions as reality/fiction and authentic/fake inapplicable. The "real" city merges with what Robert Warshow has famously called the dangerous, sad city of the imagination. "History," distinct from fiction but still a species of narrative, increasingly appears as one text among many.[25]

This "dangerous, sad city of the imagination" is a city of crime.

Of course, there is not one, but many, generic "species of narrative" (to borrow Ralph Willett's phrase) from out of which that grander narrative species "history" is constructed. Take the daily news, for instance. Although the presentation of news in the contemporary newspapers was structured by genre and its writers were supposed specialists in their areas (the crime writer, the fashion writer, the gossip columnist), the reader could expect to read more than one section of a paper to take in the news. The more important an item of news, the more likely it was to draw in elements of other genres, and thus to draw a greater audience. So it was that Dorothy Kilgallen, normally the film and theatre columnist for the

New York Journal American, was sent off to cover the Hearts Killers when the trial first opened.

The two best-selling pulp genres of the late 1940s and early 1950s were, as today, romance and detective fiction. The immense popularity of the "women's film" (a genre identified as the blending of *film noir* and the romance) amply demonstrates the interdependence of these genres. Certainly their audiences were not mutually exclusive, and it was in the advertising columns of *True Detective Magazine* that Janet Fay found an ad for Mother Dinene's Lonely Hearts Club, her membership in which would prove fatal.[26] In the case of the Lonely Hearts Killers these two powerful pulp genres collided, greatly increasing the reach of the narrative of murder.[27] For a public well primed in both the love story and the tale of murder, the reported testimony of *People* v. *Fernandez* was indeed a rare dish.

Reports of the trial followed the various accounts of the murder, while also dwelling on the biographical detail. The insanity defense, at first deployed for both defendants, soon focused on Martha. The three versions of the murder from her mouth (the two Michigan statements and her testimony on the stand) established her primary position in the murder narrative, while also defining the "abnormality" of the defendants' relationship.[28]

During Martha Beck's four days of testimony, the public vied for a place in the courtroom. The day on which she ran to Fernandez and kissed him repeatedly before being drawn away by the matrons, the judge had to quell a "riotous demonstration . . . when 150 persons, mostly middle-aged women, tried to rush the courtroom." This same capacity audience of women also heard Mrs. Beck tell her attorney, "I loved, do love and will always love" Ray Fernandez.[29] Covering the trial's opening, Dorothy Kilgallen quickly identified Martha as the significant figure in the tale: "she so big and extroverted, he so small and withdrawn." Mrs. Beck was "outwardly the more colorful of the weird and wretched team." Kilgallen wondered at Martha's ability to "remain nerveless through gaudy descriptions of the crime and shocking references to her own part in it." The columnist soon found the physical sign of that unworldliness:

[I]t is her hands that really tell the story of her calm. They lie, one in her lap, one on the table in front of her, absolutely relaxed, palms upturned, the fingers curled a little like a child's in repose. . . . If these are the hands that wielded the ball-pein hammer . . . then someone should take a picture of them for the annals of crime and criminals. They look like hands that would rock a cradle, not hands that would wield a lethal weapon.[30]

A few years later, journalists would rave about the small hands of Barbara Graham, not believing her ability to pistol-whip Mabel Monaghan to death.[31] Unlike the skepticism that the petite frame and good looks of Graham evinced in her supporters, "Fat Martha" provided ample discursive space upon which to project the murder. Her pleas to the press to accurately report her weight (185 lbs.) were ignored, and Kilgallen scoffed at this minor concern of the murderer at being "called a fatty." Yet Martha's weight was *not* an unimportant fact at the trial, where it was treated as the physical manifestation of her mental abnormality by the defense and, by the media, as her *defining characteristic*. Correspondents wrote of her as that "fat, grinning woman of incredible calm."[32] Descriptions of her appearance while testifying tended to make the clothes disappear into her body, a body that overwhelmed any attempt at adornment:

Mrs. Beck was . . . heavy with make-up. Her cheeks were rouged and her lips appeared pendulous under thick layers of lipstick. Mrs. Beck wore a two-strand necklace, almost concealed under the folds of her chin.[33]

This description was the news media's preface to Martha's testimony that she was sexually accosted by her brother at age thirteen, pestered by a lascivious brother-in-law and, for successive years, had to fend off men at home and at work.[34] The record of these sexual tribulations was offered up by the defense not to show reason to mitigate harsh judgment of the defendant[35] — who had herself suffered in life — but as a principal part of the evidence of her insanity. The press headlined their report "Sordid Childhood Told By Martha" and wrote that her mother's refusal to let her date boys "led, according to the witness," to Martha's "incestuous relations with her brother, Dudley."[36] From the very outset, the frame presenting Martha's story of systematic abuse is skewed. The defense argued that moral depredations left her mentally unbalanced, yet the overall impression given in their argument is one of organic defect.[37] Martha produced, and even sought out, her own degradation. The media tended to follow that line of reasoning, while the prosecution, intent on demolishing the insanity defense, simply turned the stories of Martha's victimization into evidence of bad character. Martha's testimony that she had lost one of her jobs when she "slapped hell out of" the doctor who made a pass at her became ammunition for the prosecution. Assistant District Attorney Edward Robinson told the jury:

Is she the poor little innocent girl that they would have her painted here? . . . Is she the one here who wants to take her life every time somebody crosses her? One who has been bounced around when she was a youngster, deprived of everything in life, downtrodden by her mother?

. . . That character, that woman who tells you how she slapped hell out of a doctor — everybody was making a pass at her by the way — she was able to take care of herself; looks pretty healthy as she sits there now.[38]

As the prosecutor indicated the defendant, he was gesturing at "Fat Martha": all of her purported "200 pounds," her murderer's hands, her huge, painted, devouring mouth. The story of her life could not be read outside the vessel that contained it.

Reporting the second day of Martha's testimony, then, the press wrote of her "200 pounds shaking with sobs."[39] Martha's "frustrated romances and sexual abnormalities" were detailed to a press that alluded only vaguely to the detail of those "abnormalities." The *Journal American* told its readers how Martha had been advised by her doctor to "indulge in 'various other forms of intimacy' " (instead of intercourse) with Fernandez, and that same doctor had opined that her "earlier experiences" with her brother were the root cause of all her troubles. The testimony that the press declined to relate — that would by successive writers be described as "sensational" and "degenerate" — was of Dr. Luzon's advice to Martha Beck that she ask for oral sex from Fernandez. Martha claimed never to have experienced an orgasm, and Luzon suggested that cunnilingus might be the means to attain the satisfaction that Fernandez was apparently so anxious to provide:[40]

[The doctor] told me that . . . those measures would bring forth satisfaction when the normal average intercourse would not, and he told me not to look upon those as being ugly or vulgar; that when two people loved each other, that no matter what they did, it was not to be considered abnormal.[41]

Doctor Luzon also suggested to Martha that she enter therapy to try to heal some of the damage caused by abuse. But, against Dr. Luzon's repeated admonitions, both the court and the public did regard that sexual practice — even unnamed — as "abnormal," as "ugly" and "vulgar." The reason for Martha's inability to achieve orgasm would then get lost, once again, in the translation of the psychic into the physical: trauma into misanthropy.[42]

On the second day of testifying, Martha began to detail for the court, the press, and the assembled spectators her various suicide attempts. One of these occurred when she witnessed Fernandez making love to one of the women whom he was trying to bilk of her fortune. The *Journal American* wrote that Mrs. Beck's jealousy impelled her to throw herself in the Connecticut River, "only to be rescued by Fernandez."[43] They clearly implied that such melodrama was quite ridiculous. Yet, one month earlier, a competitor in the *Journal American*'s "How I Got my Man" contest told how she had used the "often ridiculed method of a fake drowning to attract the man of [her] dreams." The correspondent wrote with great satisfaction that she "swam a little way from the shore and then began to clamor and shout. Sure enough Johnny came rushing out."[44] The contest, wrote one of its judges, "proved what we have long suspected. . . . [W]omen, when they want something, know how to use all the clever tricks in the book."[45] Martha's "tricks," although not unusual (excepting that they had apparently led to murder), were wholly disapproved of. What might have been an ordinary litany of self-sacrifice in the pursuit of romance became, in retrospect, a sign of pathology. Martha's "madness" and murderousness overspilled her actual 185 pounds. The media (who were sometimes wrong on her weight by as much as 100 pounds) were unable to detach the romantic script from the body upon which culture dictated it was written. So written, the romantic script folded in upon itself: part romance, part horror story.

The generic requirements of the romance have changed slightly over time. Feminist rereadings of the genre have reclaimed its erotic agency for women, but that is an agency which can still be seen as self-defeating.[46] The position of the female desiring subject vis-à-vis the male object is a critical subject for analysis, but one that is complicated when the failed heroine of the romance becomes a murderer; when the romance itself becomes a tale of murder. The subject positioning of the romantic heroine is important here to the extent that Fernandez's role in the tale of murder was not, and never could have been, the central role. The traditional romance demands that the romantic subject be (or be positioned as) a woman. The penalties of that requirement for Martha Beck were profound indeed.

Put crudely, the generic demands of the pulp romance are simple. The desiring subject should be skilled in one of the ministering occupations: teacher, nurse, governess. These worldly skills are only on loan — they can be redeemed for the domestic role of mother and wife at any time. Working is a way of marking time in the romance. The work that is done by the heroine is mere scene-setting; it does not actually form any part of the action. In the romance the object of desire is either downright threatening or completely disinterested. Once his bad behavior has been curbed or his attention won, the compact of romance ends with marriage — offering a lifetime of love and sexual satisfaction in a monogamous relationship. To take on that life, which is a kind of rebirth, the heroine gives up paid work: her true life's work revealed as her ability to transform, through loving, the love object. In the romance everything is veneer. Surfaces are intricately described: scenic locations, food, clothes. The heart of the romance is its costume: ensemble and accessory.

In many ways the tale of murder told at the trial and through the newspapers conforms to these generic requirements. The "fear of love unfulfilled" that typifies the mechanism of suspense in the romance needs only the slightest change of emphasis to bring with it "the suspense of an unanswered question" more typical of the crime story.[47] The difference between narrators' accounts is generally only one of emphasis, of direction. The tale told by the press centers on Martha; she is its subject. Various elements gain priority in the telling, and others are diminished, precisely because of the demands of the genre. Martha is a registered nurse, and a good one: she works for a while as superintendent of a home for crippled children. She has one child illegitimately and another in a failed marriage. She has a number of failed relationships, and then Raymond Fernandez comes along. He is better to her, more considerate than any man has ever been. She goes to live with him and is then forced to make a choice between keeping him and keeping her children, as his lifestyle and living arrangements forbid such obligations. She chooses Fernandez over the children, whom she hands over into care. Both Fernandez and Martha continue to work at their legitimate occupations (he as laborer, she as nurse),[48] while Raymond pursues his money-spinning "hobby" of entering into romantic liaisons with spinsters. In order to fit in with Fernandez's career, and to be near him, Martha poses as his sister, rather than the lover she is. Yet Martha is jealous and suspicious of ulterior motives in his liaisons, and she attempts suicide on several occasions, feeling herself to be a failure. She can envision no other alternative to Raymond's love. The murders of both Janet Fay and Delphine Downing are ostensibly prompted by jealousy. On the stand, Martha takes most of the blame for the murders, protecting her lover. Once convicted, she continues to write love letters to him and to publicly profess her love. As the execution date approaches, Martha instructs her attorneys to stop pursuing her case for clemency. She wants to die, but she is not executed until her lover is already dead, having preceded her to the chair.[49]

Obviously this summary is not set in the traditional romance mold, but the way in which it was played with by its narrators (including the defendants themselves) yields the essence of the tale of murder as romance. In telling her life story, Martha revealed the significance to her of the romance genre. She told the court about her reading habits:

[W]hen I would read a novel that was very interesting, or that the heroine was going through a very romantic period, I would dream and plan and wonder how it would be if that was in real life and it had happened to me rather than just being fiction. . . . [W]hen I would go to bed at night, rather than being able to relax and go to sleep, I would continue thinking back over how happy the different women in the stories were, and I used to wonder if I would ever be able to have such happiness.

Q. And were you dreaming constantly of being in love?

A. I would say that I was, yes.

Q. And being loved by someone?

A. That is true.[50]

This part of her testimony was condensed by the *Journal American* into one paragraph:

I read Shakespeare, Dumas, Tennyson, Browning and others, and had day dreams about heroes and heroines I read about. I wondered if I would ever be able to fall in love. I dreamed of a family life that was different from the life I had at home. I was attracted by a young man who frequented the library in the summer of 1938. I carried his picture always in my mind.[51]

The difference between the transcript and the media versions of Martha's romantic musings is substantial. While the former suggests a very clear sense of the difference between real life and fiction, the media version turns Martha Beck into an inveterate "dreamer," and an obsessive one at that. The news media's "romance" then, is a situation without context: fiction's defiance of life. Not a story with a subject (Martha Beck) but a *symptom*. In her own testimony, on the other hand, the distance between romantic fantasy and real life is measured by the latter's failures:

Even though I would continue to read the novels and would wonder how it would be to be in love or loved, the affair that I had with my brother would always push itself to the front part of my mind.[52]

Those failures are themselves shaped by the language of romance. Martha speaks of the "affair" with her brother, bestowing a mutuality on the event that it patently lacked. The media had achieved the same effect with their earlier decree on the cause of the abuse: Mrs. Seabrook's refusal to let Martha see boys "led" to her "incestuous relations" with her brother.[53]

Martha established herself not as romantic heroine, but as witness and spectator as she marks out the space of the subject. Vicarious and specular, the romance offers to its reader the chance to be both the subject of the tale *and* its audience. Only as she began to tell her own story would Martha Beck become the romantic subject, doing so in a script not entirely her own.

Martha tells a love story, but the court and the reporters are convened to hear the tale of murder. The defense tries to stress the continuity of the defendant's work record, noting in particular the responsible positions held — more than adequately — by Martha. Full-time work is incompatible with the picture of the pair as con artists, so the many laboring jobs taken up by Fernandez vanish from the retelling of the story.[54] Martha's work goes by the way too, positions sacrificed through inattention and for the greater cause of her love.[55] In fact, she continues to work intermittently, but her work is no longer a *part* of her. The sociability that is the subtext of work (and, in the case of nursing, its very ethics) is found lacking in Martha. Imagine the reaction to her testimony that she had originally wanted to become a mortician:

[T]here were only two funeral homes in the little town where I was born and raised and all of the attendants were men. During that time, two very close friends of mine had died and at the time when I went to the funeral home to see them they were surrounded by men and I couldn't understand the fact that even though a person were dead why a woman would have to be taken care of by a man, and I felt that I . . . might be able to give a little ease to the loved ones by knowing that a woman was taking care of their female loved ones.[56]

In the context of the murder trial, her salvo at the male-dominated death professions seemed evidence of a morbid disposition. The defense brought this out, like much of Martha's life story, purely to the end of proving her "insanity." Work could not exist for Martha. She was denied the dignity of a vocation, both because she was a woman and because she was this particular woman. Her career as a nurse, second choice to a career in embalming, is merely a means for Martha to exercise her desire for power, her warped nurturing instinct. The issue, then, is not work, but the disposition of the worker. The story of Martha's ambition to be a mortician would, predictably, become an important one in the true crime chronicle.

The conceptualization of work in the tale of murder as romance is significant. Two nightmare romances converge here: Martha's love story and the story of predation of the Hearts Killers. Fernandez's real work is his seduction of moneyed spinsters; his ability to select and woo the best prospects on the lists mailed to him by Lonely Hearts clubs. Ray is "the bald-headed, wig-wearing Lothario who lured women to destruction."[57] For Ray, the toupee (and his baldness) become as telling a sign of pathology as Martha's weight. His masculinity is a pose, his seductive skills false promise. The toupee is a necessary tool of his trade; it hides his vulnerability (age, loss of virility). The hairpiece becomes a staple of the media descriptions and, later, of the true crime chronicle of the killers.[58] In point of fact, the trial record reveals that Fernandez purchased the toupee not long before their arrest and wore it only twice.[59] Ray's "work" demands the toupee, not the tools of the builder's trade; so, the toupee stays.

Martha's work becomes the work of the subject of romance gone wrong: she works not to win her man (and make him over), but just to keep him. Fernandez, for Beck, was "one hundred per cent better than any other man."[60] Never mind that she worked as a nurse at St. Luke's and Holy Cross in Chicago while they were there, her real vocation was *keeping Ray*. Keeping Ray entailed, for the press and the accounts to come, a number of sacrifices. After leaving her job and her home state, Martha came to New York to be with Ray, a move that entailed another dispossession: "she abandoned her two children at a Salvation Army mission to become the mistress of Raymond Fernandez."[61] As the romantic subject, Martha was obliged to choose Ray over the children, since their presence disrupted the story of love.[62] The children disappear from the romance, only to reappear in the tale of murder. The defense and the prosecution both need the children — or, rather, that the children be lost. In its final and desperate straits, the defense tried to solicit from one of the state's psychiatrists an admission that a "woman who gave up her children" might be a psychopathic personality.[63] Harkening back to Martha's own explanation that she was "torn between two loves," the prosecution spoke sarcastically of "this awful, terrible decision [where] she had to choose between love for her two children and love for the guy she was going to live with, although she was frigid."[64] Here, then, is the romance as horror story; the order of the romance is inverted. The children are an end, and a promise: arriving too early in the plot, they represent its undoing. Likewise, the desire of the woman should be present but restrained, a foil to the aggressive desire of the male and the force that compels her to make *him* love. Martha's "frigidity" is that desire turned inside out: a black hole into which masculine desire is drawn. Her "frigidity" consumes the maternal instinct.

On the third day of Martha's testifying, the *Journal American* wrote that she had "added a suicide complex" to the "story of frustrated romances and sexual abnormalities."[65] Laboriously, Martha sought to put into context the "at least seven" suicide attempts that she could recall. Not all of these occurred while she was with Fernandez, but most did. The prosecution attacked this testimony with a relentless cynicism. How could a woman, so set on dying, fail so ridiculously in her attempts?[66] Martha's desire to die, like her sexual desire, is not great enough to fill the huge vessel of her body. "Fat, frigid" Martha is a well into which desire and death fall. The tide of affect turns inside Martha's great body: she is implicated in the "sex mania" of her lover, and in the murder of two of his conquests. As the romantic subject in the tale of murder (the two become one) Martha becomes the antithesis of the romantic affect, while retaining the power of the subject.

As the love object/murderer, Raymond is as much afflicted by lack as Martha is by excess. His are the skills of the seducer, not the husband.[67] Martha's "frigidity" is the occasion for refinement of these most illegitimate skills. Fernandez begins to indulge in "abnormal vices": the unproductive sexual practice of oral sex. Both partners in this sexual act are "abnormal," but Martha as instigator and primary beneficiary of its pleasures is somehow worse. Martha experiences her first orgasm during oral sex, yet the prosecution still refers to her "frigidity," defining the illegitimacy of this particular pleasure. Even her orgasm is wrong. When Martha had "the reaction, she would get upset." Fernandez added that "after the abnormal sexual, as you say, well, she would be very quiet. It may last maybe for an hour; maybe sometimes 20 minutes."[68] This fugue state was referred to a number of times throughout the trial as evidence of the peculiarity of Martha's desire. A modern reader might think instead of the flashbacks suffered by survivors of sexual abuse, the flip side of sexual pleasure for many women.

Both defendants were closely questioned regarding their sexual life together. The difference in the nature of their responses is marked. Fernandez sometimes showed a sense of decorum, taking on the shame offered by his own lawyer's description of his "abnormality."[69] Martha, for her part, refused to be shamed, trying to retain the privacy and integrity of the relationship:

Mr. Rosenberg, the love-making . . . that you have described as being abnormal, is something that took place between Mr. Fernandez and I, because we loved each other, and I consider that something practically sacred. . . . For the love that I had for Mr. Fernandez, nothing we did was abnormal.[70]

Although the papers declined to write about the details of the sexual relationship, they were not slow to pick up on Martha's apparent "shamelessness":

The testimony was so lurid that large portions of it were unprintable and the courthouse was jammed daily with spectators fighting for admission. Despite the abnormal background of their relations, Mrs. Beck said her love for Fernandez was so profound she would have stopped breathing if he told her to.[71]

Silenced by the controversial nature of the sexual testimony, the papers fall back upon the tale of Martha's obsessive love. The news media's decorum about the sexual detail of the case did not necessarily mean that the public was ignorant of that content. It was much remarked upon throughout the trial that spectators "fought for admission" daily, and the public galleries were overcrowded. This audience of "middle-aged housewives"[72] is unlikely to have been a silent one, and the judge's admonition at the close of every session that those present should not "form or express an opinion concerning the case or any aspect of it" was directed only to the jurors.

The significance of that quarreling entourage of women is not to be underestimated. Even if they were the same 150 women at every session, the contribution to the case of the spectators' view — their information fragmentary, and probably poorly digested — is considerable. The media are not, after all, the only vehicle for news and information. Gossip and speculation form the very life of the tale of murder. When the disseminating body of that story has any degree of social homogeneity, the narrative will have an enhanced authority, speaking (in all its parts) to the familiar, known, everyday world out of which murder arises.

Those housewives who watched the tale of murder unfold were not an extraordinary audience. Jurists and crime writers alike have frequently reproved that "idle class of women" who delight in murder trials.[73] Many women, working or with other obligations, would have had no time to spend in overheated courtrooms with poor acoustics, straining to hear the generally banal details of crime. In the late 1940s, though, women were being once again pushed out of the work force. The career of "housewife" was becoming more of an honorary position and less of a vocation, thanks to the service of her inanimate helpmates: vacuum cleaners, dishwashers, clothes dryers, smaller and more efficient stoves, washing machines, and refrigerators. The materials of housewifely leisure were many. She was the primary consumer of that quintessential literature of domestic isolation, the romance. From the magazines on the coffee table the word "True" proclaims itself any number of times: *True Romance* side by side with *True Crime Detective*. The middle-class housewife might be tempted to test that "truth," to lift it out of the pages of the magazine. A short walk to the county courthouse was sufficient for this experiment, and yet the witness fronting up to the "reality" of a murder trial would come equipped to read that often boring text, with little or no consistent narrative line, as the more rollicking "truth" of the tabloid or the pulp magazine: *true* crime, *true* romance.

Martha told her love story to a hostile court, and told it in such a way (at the behest of her lawyers) that it became — to everyone but herself — the romance as horror story. Martha, for all who watched, could never have appeared to be the ideal romantic subject. "Fat, dowdy Martha"[74] was a parodic figure: just enough of the discourse of romance survived in the tale of murder to thoroughly condemn her as a woman. Martha herself at one point aptly asked whether she was being "tried for murder, or because I'm fat."[75] She alone was faithful to the tale of romance, and her rendition fell in with the gendering strategy of the discourse of murder. In her final letter to the media, written just hours before she entered the execution chamber, Martha wrote:

What does it matter who is to blame? My story is a love story, but only those tortured with love can understand what I mean. I was pictured as a fat unfeeling woman. True, I am fat, that I cannot deny, but if that is a crime, how many of my sex are guilty? I am not unfeeling, stupid, or moronic. The prison and the death house have only strengthened my feeling for Raymond, and in the history of the world how many crimes have been attributed to love?[76]

This final plea from Martha to read her story as a "love story" should be placed in its proper context. I have argued above that the whole mechanism of the trial and the surrounding media controversy worked to produce a tale of murder in the distorted generic script of the romance. But the story, so to speak, did not end at the conviction of the defendants, on 18 August 1949, for first-degree murder. Throughout their incarceration in the death cells at Sing Sing, Martha and Ray became the objects of even greater scrutiny by news media no longer restricted in their text by the fact-finding mission of a criminal trial. The chronicle of Martha's and Ray's on-again, off-again prison romance became the focus of this new leg in the journey of "fat Martha" and "skinny Raymond" to the chair. The *Journal American* printed their love letters to one another, finding more interest in those epistles than in news of the progress of the couple's appeals through the court hierarchy.

The women who had been the trial's most faithful attendants maintained their interested position as spectators. Some tried to get a more active involvement. The execution, described as though it were a popular new venue, seemed to be a natural step up from the public galleries of the courtroom:

> Prison officials announced that this will be the biggest "execution night" in point of attendance since that of Mrs. Mary Creighton, Long Island "Borgia" who went to her death in 1937.
>
> During recent weeks hundreds of requests for invitations have poured in, many from women, some of whom bluntly stated they'd like to pull the switch themselves on Martha. Women are traditionally barred from executions.[77]

This passage recalls the prurience of the defense during the trial when it proffered Martha's ambition to be a mortician as evidence of her "abnormality." Women die, but their corpses should be handled only by men. The state is not above *executing* women, but is too decorous to allow them to be witnesses to the event. What is particularly notable in this passage is not just the overwhelming presence of women, but the absence of one particular man: Ray Fernandez. The women soliciting invitations aren't offering to pull the switch on *him*. Martha is in every respect the focal point of censure in the tale of murder as romance: she is the failed romantic subject, a failure that reflects as poorly upon her sex as does her conviction for murder. Both failings are inextricably entwined.

"Death House Romance"

Throughout the Sing Sing romance, Ray was censured (along with Martha) for his part in the parody of romance in which they alternately cooed and cursed at one another. Ray's disadvantages as the love object had been established early on in the trial, when his claim to being merely an accessory to murder gave logistical support to the media's portrait of him as weak and vacillating. Fernandez never quite measured up as a Lothario—after all, to the media he was that "*bald-headed* Lothario." The Lothario, even as criminal, had a heroic appeal that Fernandez patently lacked. Throughout the trial of the Hearts Killers, the *Journal American* was busily serializing the story of Sigmund Engel, a late-middle-aged "gentleman" who swindled women of their fortunes through various methods of romantic inducement, including the promise of marriage. Engel remarked upon the "curious fact" that "no woman I courted ever blamed me for a thing — until I stopped courting her. None was impelled to 'blow the whistle on me' through any motive save jealousy."[78] Engel had never murdered any of the women he "courted." Yet what saved his reputation was not so much his restraint in that regard as it was his ability to retain the stature of romantic object, even when his motives were venal. He was, in short, a higher class of crook than Fernandez. No "dime store Don Juan" was Sigmund Engel.

The apogee of the postwar Feminine was also vividly illustrated by the *Journal American* in its photo pages. Beneath the cloyingly cute headline "Bronx Quads by the Basketful," Mrs. Collins proudly displays her multiple progeny: the infants loll in a clothes basket, their mother's smile above them full of healthy white teeth. Waving behind them, flag and standard of the American dream, is a full line of wash. Everything is a startling white.[79] Martha Beck could not be more clearly unlike this paragon of white American motherhood. Her association with the props in this domestic scene was a perverse one: she had drowned, not dandled, a baby in a washtub. Indeed, the governor of New York State, when commissioned for clemency by the couple's lawyers, was extraordinarily aware of the difference between the maternal ideal and the portrait of the maternal that Martha Beck represented. When Rosenberg was petitioning Governor Thomas Dewey for clemency he made a plea that the governor "remember the children!" (meaning Martha's two children). Dewey apparently replied scornfully that he *did* remember the children (a two-year-old drowned in tub of water), denying the plea as he did so. However, it would be naive to assume that the governor acted solely upon sound information. This anecdote, recalled by Henry Devine, can only really demonstrate the *currency of the story*, and all the ideas about Martha's monstrous femininity which that story embodies. Its factual reliability is of secondary importance.[80] Martha Beck, in very signal ways, represents the nadir of the postwar American Feminine.

In the death house the currency of love, to the American public, must have seemed a curious and corrupt one. The letters between Beck and Fernandez published by the *Journal American* mixed ordinary props of courting, like flowers, with less prosaic symbols. Martha wrote that "if I have to go to the electric chair to prove my love — I'll go." The letters were not consistently affectionate, as both parties — acting on the unreliable information of prison rumors — recriminated the other alternately for their part in the crime or their lack of romantic attention. The crime and the romance appeared once again entwined. The papers speculated upon the wearing aspect of a relationship within which emotions vacillated between jealous remonstrance and declarations of undying love. As the execution watch became more focused, reporters tried to discover which of the condemned lovers was threatening to break. The appeals process suggested that Fernandez was employing the maximum in legal strategy to turn aside his sentence, while Martha had merely fired her lawyer. Martha would profit from any successful appeal on Fernandez's part, but the media scorned her stoicism as much as they did the vehemence of Fernandez's pleas for clemency. Perhaps they were not surprised that she refused to struggle for what they saw as a "life spent wallowing in enough abnormalities and crime to set any psychiatrist's jaw ajar." The papers also noted that "in all the 21 months that she has been in solitary [Martha] hasn't had a single visitor," in contrast to Fernandez's regular visits from his three sisters. This lack of filial feeling was underscored by the revelation that Martha hadn't written once to her brother, Dudley, "a Pensacola policeman."[81] What kind of a sister was this who wouldn't write to the brother who raped her twice when she was thirteen and then, when finally exposed, spoke rarely to her thereafter?[82] For the daughter to be filial means: be good, submit, be selfless. Martha, in prison, is held to account for her lack of filial obligation, just as she was mocked by the prosecutor who said she wanted to "throw off the yoke of motherhood" and that she couldn't "very well stand the restraint of the mother."[83] Martha became "promiscuous" supposedly to escape and punish her mother. That "promiscuity," conceded by her own defense at the trial, became a threat both to the ideology of the family and to the literal family. Martha's own reading of the romantic promise, that she "dreamed of a family life better than [her] own" with herself at the center as wife and mother, is obscured by the portrait of the failed romantic subject: the bad daughter, the unmarried mother, "frigid."

Martha resumed her place as the focus of press attention as the execution date approached. The provenance of the crime lay with Martha, even as the press reported that "of the two, Fernandez now was . . . the stronger . . . in surprising contrast to his weak, wishy-washy, reluctant attitude when Martha, on their sprees of murder, taunted him for being spineless."[84]

Raymond declared that he would die like the man nobody thought he was. But he was wrong about that. Execution commentators noted the prison's departure from convention when Martha, the only woman of the four condemned to die that night,[85] was taken last to the chair. The paper coming out on the eve of the execution had promised that "according to prison protocol, it will be Martha who will die first, under the rule that the weakest must have the swiftest end."[86] The weaker turned out to be "wishy-washy" Raymond Fernandez, who followed Richard Power to the chair. Fernandez was not perceptibly more shaken than Martha, but the decision to execute her last would cap a script that had called for her to take the lead role in the crime. Fernandez "walked to eternity in an unspectacular manner except that he was unafraid."[87] His last minutes showed a controlled reserve: as he seated himself in the chair, witnesses saw him reach down "to preserve the crease in his trousers as he sat." This ease could not save him in the eyes of the press. Fernandez died as the man *they* thought he was: the "mail order Romeo," primping to the end.

The order of execution was the final billing of Beck and Fernandez, putting the seal upon Martha's preeminence in the role of murderer. She entered the death room and the witness "thought at once of the nightmarish dreams, as a child, when an ogress appeared to instill terror." The following lengthy description of her execution was, as ever, full of allusions to her weight — as if it were the last, best evidence of the crime for which she was dying:

You looked at this grotesque figure as it walked through the door, her head bobbing from side to side, porcine, her eyes beaded in layers of fat. Then you looked at the voluptuous mouth turned upward in a half smile. You looked at her ankles, slim for the mountainous burden they carried, and at her hands, slender and tapering and incongruous to the flaccid flesh above her elbows.[88]

There is a lot of looking going on here. Unlike the description of Fernandez's death, a simple third-person narrative, Leon Racht here forces the reader to watch Martha with his eyes: the child's eyes, beholding an ogress. Racht told how Martha was "so big she had to wriggle to squeeze herself into" the chair. Then he returned, as Dorothy Kilgallen had when the trial opened, to the metaphor of those "incongruously" delicate hands:

You looked at the slim hands and while pity tore at your soul, you remembered then that those same tapered, red-laquered fingers had done to death women and a baby. You thought of those hands wielding the death-dealing hammer. . . . And you thought of the same hands forcing two-year-old Rainelle into a tub of muddy water to drown her after her widowed mother had been murdered.

The killer's hands "curled" and then "relaxed from the force of the current." When she was pronounced dead, her fingers were the same bright red as her nail lacquer. Unwilling to let go of what he seemed to perceive as the mark of the harlot, Racht observed in closing that the dead woman's "lipstick contrasted sickeningly with the whiteness of death."

Even the death of Beck and Fernandez in the chair was not the final scene in the drama of the Hearts Killers. The following day's paper, covering the scene of execution, passed on to the reader the last words of the condemned and the farewell letters they exchanged. Martha's last statement, in which she wrote that her story was a "love story," was not printed complete; the press declined to reproduce her accusations that they had portrayed her as "unfeeling, stupid and moronic" and had made ridiculous assumptions based upon her weight alone.[89] The *Journal American* did publish in its entirety Ray's "last note," which was a meditation on the nature of romantic love: "the most potent force in the world." Also published, transcribed, *and* photographically reproduced, was Martha's poem, "Memo to Ray," an innocuous piece of doggerel professing her love for Ray. The inclusion of this photograph was consistent with the obsessive attentiveness of the press to the physical traces or symbols of Martha's criminality. At the outset of the trial, a reporter had observed that Martha wrote "left-handed, quickly, with her tongue between her lips."[90] The photo of Martha's last poem is meant to reveal, in its *form*, something that the content cannot convey. In much the same way, the press looked not to her testimony (or even the testimony of others) for the truth of Martha Beck, but to the *word made flesh* — the "obese" form, the "fat" body of the ogress.

The in-depth coverage of the trial by the *Journal American*, among other tabloids, established a pattern of misinformation invaluable for the promotion of the tale of murder to the canon of true crime. Trial testimony was embellished, an interpretive flourish that became increasingly bold as time passed. The staple elements of the tale of the Honeymoon Killers began to appear during the execution watch, when the press reminded its readers of the crime the couple were condemned for. In that summary, the detailed testimony of the trial began to carry a new burden of "fact" and inference about the killers. The crime was apparently both the result of an injudicious mixing of fates (*folie à deux*) and the consequence of unnatural passions (principally those of the "woman who loved too much"). One article introduced both readings in concert. Discussing the crossing of paths that led the couple to the threshold of the death chamber, Racht wrote:

Had not the spidery, vulturine Fernandez picked Martha's name from a list of 200 he bought for $2 from a matrimonial agency, she, and perhaps even he, would not be sitting in doom's shadow today.[91]

Racht makes the unusual suggestion that Fernandez was more predisposed to the fate of murderer than Martha — although this conclusion should be read in the context of Racht's coverage of Fernandez's final plea for clemency (as opposed to Martha's silence). Ray's path to murder is, finally, a good deal less interesting than the trail of feminine desire that crosses it. As *Time* observed, "[L]ittle Ray's gift was his undoing, he attracted his own nemesis, Mrs. Martha Jule Beck."[92] Racht did a recap on the character of that nemesis. Martha and the children came to New York to be with Ray, but their reunion was hampered by the presence of the children. Martha's solution was soon forthcoming:

"I left them at the Salvation Army," she said, blithely. "They'll never find me. Come, make love to me honey, we're alone."

The callous cruelty of this unnatural mother would have revolted the ordinary man. It only appeared to fascinate the warped Don Juan. He was in Martha's web now. And little did he dream he would strangle in it.[93]

Martha's "blithe" sexual invitation to Fernandez after abandoning her children had nothing to support it in fact, but it was a portrait that went well with the paper's previous descriptions of Martha's "iceberg calm" and "sordid" past. The portrait of Martha as the unnatural mother was a serviceable one. Detailing the demise of Deliphine [*sic*] Downing and her daughter Rainelle, Racht combined elements of the unnatural mother and the failed nurse to play up the degree to which Martha's "feminine instincts" had been corrupted. After Ray had arrived to finish off Delphine with a shotgun blast to the head, "little Rainelle . . . cried constantly for two days." Martha finally suggested they "put her down with her mother" and they drowned the child "in a washtub full of water."[94] Just two days later, the same writer changed the story of Rainelle's death to even better represent Martha as the doppelganger of the all-American mother: "Mrs. Beck . . . admitted she held the Downing woman's 20 month old daughter by its feet while immersing its head in the muddy water in the murdered woman's grave."[95]

Racht's was a brief account of the crimes, but it was sufficient to indicate the direction of the tale, and to place the lead players in their appropriate poses. The tale left more than one question unanswered, but it required—in a sense—precisely that uncertainty. The *Journal American* pointedly wondered (as would retired Assistant District Attorney "Hank" Devine some forty years later) "how many others there might have been."[96] Uncertainty might suggest an end to speculation, and its futility, but *not knowing* in the tale of murder is the very engine of narration.

For a while Martha Beck and Ray Fernandez were "America's Most Hated Murderers" because, individually and as a couple, they had become parodies of the postwar American romance. There was nothing spectacular or outrageous in the method or number of their killings: the papers carried daily reports of a huge number and variety of murders that rivaled, or even excelled, the brutality of Beck's and Fernandez's crimes.[97] But the combination of the choice of victims, the fraud that led to their deaths, and the supposed character of the killers was enough to seriously unsettle a public who watched the unhappy convergence of the romance and the tale of murder.

One early commentator, Wenzell Brown, attacked what he saw as the root cause of Beck's and Fernandez's crimes: the romance industry of the Lonely Hearts clubs. Although the killers were dead, "no lessons seem to have been learned. . . . Even the Lonely Hearts clubs continue to advertise unmolested, and the roots of evil—neglect and indifference—remain untouched."[98] For Brown, the Lonely Hearts clubs formed a predatory ground for unscrupulous men who would take advantage of a demographics of marriage that left a great many women spinsters or widows.[99] These women were likely to become the victims of their own dreams of romance, for in Brown's analysis women dreamed while men merely schemed:

The women that fell under [Fernandez's] spell were for the most part, a sorry array. Most of them were elderly and unattractive. Some were grossly stout, one was badly deformed. They were mostly women whom an average man would not give a second glance — women who had been passed by life and who were grasping desperately at any vestige of romance.[100]

On the other hand, the few men who joined such clubs were, in Brown's opinion, either psychopaths, degenerates, fortune hunters, or criminals.[101] In his discussion of the trial, Brown expanded his analysis of vulnerable, silly women schooled in romantic dreams:

Who came to witness the trial? Perhaps there were a few serious students, interested in the processes of law. But in large they were plump, middle-aged or elderly women seeking vicarious thrills. . . . These were the type of silly, over-sexed, frustrated females upon whom Raymond Fernandez had fed his vanity.[102]

With that supposition, the crimes came full circle: the spectators become the victims, among whose number one of the murderers could, herself, theoretically be located.[103] Certainly Brown makes harsh and ill-informed judgments about the women who seek mates through Lonely Hearts clubs, but he is dead-on in his analysis of the vulnerability of these women to their romantic dreams. What Brown cannot fathom, however, is the substance of those dreams in a culture that puts a high valence on the romance. So credible was that dream of romance that Martha Beck, murderer, died for it.

5. True Crime Romance II:

Portentous Meetings

The outsider's view remains hazy, cinematic, exaggerated, formed by cop-operas and a chaos of statistics. To the outsider, American murder seems as vehement and anarchic as American free enterprise, or American neurosis, or American profanity. . . . But sometimes, and far more worryingly in a way, shapes and bearings do emerge from the turmoil and portents are suddenly visible among all the blood. *Martin Amis*

What has always seemed to me of paramount interest . . . is contained not in the word "Who?" but in the word "Why?" *Marie Belloc Lowndes*

Two years after the deaths of Martha Beck and Raymond Fernandez another couple was executed, by lethal gas, in Missouri. A member of the press attending the execution sketched the scene for the papers. Beneath the curious gaze of the spectators a man and a woman sit strapped into the twin chairs of the death chamber. The prurient artist has drawn Bonnie Heady and Gus Hall awaiting death in nothing but their underwear, thereby committing fraud upon a public reasonably familiar with the formal modesty of the execution routine: the condemned dressed to show as little of the mess of their extinction as possible (black trousers for men, the dun-colored prison frock for women). This fanciful portrait accentuates one of the central motifs in the tale of murder shared by Heady and Hall, Beck and Fernandez, as well as innumerable others: the murderous couple as lovers.

The psychiatric category of the *folie à deux* has contributed a great deal to the repertoire of the true crime tale of murder. In the previous chapter I showed how contemporary accounts of the Hearts Killers cast their tale as a romance (albeit a romance gone wrong, its lovers having become parodic figures). As the tale of the Hearts Killers percolated through the cultural conduits of the news media it came, by and by, to the attention of non-American readers. The English narrators found the Hearts Killers after the murderous lovers had themselves died, no longer available to trouble the script of the drama with their niggling voices. That tale, written as a romance through the powerful and complex workings of a set of references particular to American culture, was integrated into a wider generic structure by the English commentators who adopted it. While the murderous careers of Beck and Fernandez seemed to those outsiders to be exotic and thoroughly American, they were also received as part of a wider Western culture: one of love and its excesses; of madness, obsession, cruelty, and the *folie à deux*. This second stage in the scoring of the drama of the Hearts Killers was significant in that it was these English accounts (along with Wenzell Brown's) that would inspire the final (and most influential of all) American tale of the Honeymoon Killers: namely, Leonard Castle's 1970 film of that name.

Folie à Deux

The elision of "insanity" and "abnormality" that occurred in the legal and psychiatric arguments condemning Beck and Fernandez was not coincidental — it was, in fact, encumbent upon the concept of *folie à deux*. Few successful defenses have been mounted on the basis of *folie à deux*, one of those few being Clarence Darrow's famous plea for mitigation of sentence in the trial of Richard Loeb and Nathan Leopold, whose 1924 murder of young Bobby Franks for "thrills" had so scandalized the American public. The beauty of Darrow's strategy was that, by pleading the boys guilty, he could produce psychiatric evidence of their "abnormality" (rather than their insanity) to mitigate sentence, thereby avoiding altogether the knotty problem of arguing their innocence.[1] Other advocates who followed the strategy tended to forget this vital point and would argue for the lives of their clients on the basis of their "abnormality," when the jury was charged only with weighing evidence of "insanity." The slippage between "abnormality" and "insanity" was literally and rhetorically dangerous, providing the space for the *folie à deux* to come unstuck from its psychiatric context. So abstracted, *folie à deux* became a descriptive and explanatory narrative structure in the tale of murder.

The psychiatric definition of *folie à deux* is itself pretty loose. One proponent of the type explained its possibilities: "*Folie à deux* or communicated insanity . . . is induced by a stronger character, the inducer, upon the weaker, the inducee (*folie imposée*) but delusions may occur simultaneously by reciprocal influence in predisposed associated individuals (*folie simultanée*)."[2] Whether *folie imposée* or *folie simultanée*, "communicated insanity" suggests a portentous moment of meeting between individuals whose monstrous natures are not necessarily created in the forge of that union, but activated. The *folie à deux* allows the search for murder's origin to backtrack a "predisposition" to psychosis, while also portraying a murderousness that belongs not to a single individual but to the third entity — the lovers — that, contradictorily, stands between, unites, and separates the actual lovers.

Just a year after the double execution of the Hearts Killers, the first extensive study of the case came out in print.[3] Its title promised to deliver the "unpublished facts" behind the case, and the author, Wenzell Brown, had been busy in the newspaper archives. (Like much crime journalism of the era, Brown's work is woefully short of cited sources. The factual basis of his revelations must therefore remain largely untested.) Despite his reliance on newspaper reports, Brown was quick to chastise the papers for their simple-minded assessment of the murderers:

> The tabloids vied with one another in printing sensational stories. . . . [S]trangely enough, none of the newspaper stories equaled reality in its grotesque detail. If Martha Beck had been the stony, emotionless and fully vicious creature of newspaper accounts, she would be of little interest. Similarly, if Ray Fernandez had been simply a small-time gigolo, a craven coward dominated by a masculine woman, he too would be worthy only of passing clinical attention.[4]

Brown began to redraw the murderers to fit the space cut out for them by an inaccurate but sensationalizing press. His revelations about Martha Beck were few, but his attention to the detail of her "difference" and its implications was indeed tireless. His portrait of Fernandez also went substantially deeper into its subject than had the former commentators. He revealed, for instance, that Ray had become a practitioner in voodoo when he was imprisoned in Florida in the early 1940s.[5] While Martha's predisposition to murder came from her misanthropism, Ray's originated with the head injury that left his mind idle and his moods uncertain. Brown seemed reasonably sure that Martha would not have taken to murder had she not met Ray, and Ray would never have followed the murderous path so far if not for Martha.[6] Like Leon Racht, Brown hinted that the couples' crimes were the result of *folie à deux:* "each somehow brought out the latent evil in the other and magnified it until it burst forth in the form of insensate brutality."[7]

By introducing the spectre of the *folie à deux*, Brown was able to retain his focus on the murderous dispositions of both parties (their "latent evil") while also bringing in the fatal scene of murder: the criminal industry of their partnership. Biology and fate combine: chance and predestiny. Both elements are essential to the polished narrative of murder. The history of the murderers provides for the origin of the act and its fundamental (rather than immediate) motive, while the meeting/melding of the principals sets the scene for the actual murders. Only then can the narrative proceed tidily, made distinctive by its sense of portent. Its moral is to be gleaned from the structural peaks of the tale of murder: the murder's foretelling, its occurrence, and its echo in the execution of the principals. The moral of the story lies in the diminution of mystery, in the conjured solution to the question repeatedly asked of murder: "Why?" The answer pretends confidence, but is querulous and paradoxical: the murder happens *because* of the murderer. And even that answer is a trick. *There is no murderer until the murder.* Although the tale of murder should not be confused with that other exemplary crime story, the detective mystery, both share the doubling structure of the "open" story of the investigation and the "hidden" story of the crime: "the initial crime on which the tale of detection is predicated is *an end as well as a beginning*."[8] In the true crime genre, the tale of detection very often takes the form not of the chronicle of police attempts to identify and capture the murderer (although that is an integral part of the genre), but of the revelation of an undetected psychology in the life of the murderer. It is therefore the psychologist who is the detecting hero of the piece.[9] It is not the identification of the killer that provides *jouissance* in the true crime tale (as it does in detective fiction), but the ascription of an intelligible motive for the crime.

The tale of the Honeymoon Killers enters the canon of true crime as one of portent and metaphor. The discursive obligation on Martha to embody the bulk of the story's violence is more insistent in the developed tale. Thus, the "glandular disorder" responsible for Martha's obesity and exaggerated sexual drive was "not a mental state but a physical one over which she had no control."[10] Brown's apparent kindness in excusing her moral blame is a red herring. So much of what Martha is and does is of the body. That which is not corporeal is entirely banished. There is no moral stature in the misanthropic figure of the murderess.

Brown, with the leisure not allowed the newspaper reporter to construct a detailed history of the subject, tells, for the first time, the tale of murder's origin. "Fat Martha" does not just appear in (and as) the text: we see her grow. Brown draws this figure out of the past — a fat child, sexually abused, whose "ovarian-pituitary disorder" made different both her appearance and the uncontrollable desires it so poorly masked. The writer, believing he has found the subject he has just created, wonders why no one could have predicted there would be trouble with Martha Beck:

Martha . . . had a . . . glandular disorder which made itself visible when she was a young child. Her physical development into womanhood at the age of nine did not escape the loungers who hung about the Milton drug store. It should have been obvious to any trained person who came in touch with the monstrously fat child that certain psychological mutilations were inevitable.[11]

Brown is not saying that murder would be the final outcome of those "certain psychological mutilations"; he would not be so crude. The teleological imperative of the tale of murder is such that the most innocuous signs indicate the conclusion to the action, the final and identifying mark of the murderer. That "monstrously fat child" is a murderer because she will become one. Brown goes beyond picturing Martha's moral state mired in the vast territory of her body. Her body itself has a shadow, its excess baggage. Her fat is fate:

As Martha grew older, some of her outward problems diminished. While she remained excessively stout, she also grew taller. No longer was she the sex-ridden little monstrosity of her elementary school days. . . . Martha's tortured need for sex gratification, however, did not lessen. The glandular disorder worked her body with the most violent sex urges. . . . The nature of her original sexual experience filled her with horror, but it could not subdue the craving within her. Fear and desire vied with each other and kept her in a constant state of agitation.[12]

The layers of fat are simultaneously a mask to her true nature, its sign, and a mere shadow of the monstrosity that is Martha Beck. Like the prosecution in the trial, Brown reads Martha's alleged "frigidity" as the result of desire's excess, not its lack. On the foundation of her childhood rape he can therefore logically build a history of promiscuity that culminates in her liaison with Fernandez. The sexual scene of their literal and figurative coming together is initial evidence of the *folie à deux* as murder's origin:

[F]or the first time in her life Martha obtained full sexual gratification. Fernandez, schooled in the ways of sex, introduced Martha to erotic practices of which she had no knowledge. Her response was so violent, so uninhibited, that even Fernandez was frightened. . . . The big nurse gave herself to the Spaniard with fierce, almost animalistic abandon. She wept, sobbed that she should remain with him forever, even begged to be beaten.[13]

Ray's attention closes the circuit of desire for Martha. As she experiences sexual fulfillment for the first time, the hidden essence of her monstrosity and its shadow territory outside the body suddenly unite, drawn once again into the body's lineaments.

The *folie à deux* calls for the collision of two flawed personalities to be immediate and decisive. At the moment of collision, the psychological (or physical) flaws that previously marked out only an uncertain difference now mark out its refinement: the two as one, as murderer. Brown collapses the order of events that came out in the trial (and invents others entirely) in order to make the meeting of Fernandez and Beck sufficiently fatal. To that end, he must bring forward Martha's discovery of orgasmic pleasure and make it the result not of a doctor's advice, but of Fernandez's particular sexual skills.[14] All of the elements of her obsession are foreshadowed in that initial union: the declaration of eternal love; her masochism. Also present is the surrender, or seduction, of Fernandez's will, and the clue to Martha's dominance. He is frightened and flattered by her passion.

Portents of Pathology

Brown's reconstruction of Martha Beck establishes a second error necessary to the structure of portent in the tale of murder. Martha testified at
her trial that she had initially chosen to become a mortician; forbidden
this choice by her mother, she went on to train as a nurse instead. Brown,
however, has Martha's first job be that of assistant to a local funeral
director:

At last a job came along. It was a frightful, gruesome job that might well have
shattered the nerves of a well-adjusted and hardened woman. A local mortician
hired her to wash, embalm, and prepare for burial the female corpses which were
brought to his establishment.[15]

Martha's only contact with the mortician's trade, in fact (apart from her
thwarted desire to enter this male-dominated field), was her friendship
with the couple who ran the Milton funeral home, the Baggetts. Mr.
Baggett drove the ambulance for the hospital where Martha worked.
Brown creates the fiction of Martha's first job as undertaker's assistant,
then joins that story to the actual chronology of her sudden exposure to
romance literature. The image of a young woman wedded to the romance
tale while working with the dead presents, for Brown, a more accurate
prototype for Martha's pathology than does that same woman reading
the romance novels in the library of the "Women's Club" where she
worked:[16] "The thought of the huge, highly emotional fat girl trying to
shut out the scenes and scents of the dead by dreaming of passion and
romance is grisly beyond words."[17] The portentous quality of this early
collision of love and death is underscored by Brown: "years later when
she had killed two women and a child she recalled these days" in the
mortician's service.[18] The implied irony is that Martha's caring for the
female bodies of the dead, her intimacy with them, became the greater
intimacy of the murderer with the corpse of her victim.

The finishing stroke to this portrait of the pathological origins of Martha Beck is Brown's insistence on her promiscuity. Martha was long at the
mercy of the desires engendered in her by a "pituitary-ovarian deficiency";[19] yet, because of her "abnormal bodily structure," she was somehow unable to satisfy that desire. Brown takes up the tone of Martha's
mother's chiding voice as he repeats her charges against the daughter that

True Crime Romance II   113

shamed the Seabrook clan. Martha, for instance, is said to have been dismissed from the maternity hospital where she was working in 1944 because men had been "coming to her room" and she had been "running around all the time."[20] In fact, Martha resigned her position at the Pensacola Maternity Hospital in order to have an illegitimate child, whose arrival she had duly warned the board of directors about. The board suggested that she take a leave of absence and return to them (their implication being that the baby would be adopted). She refused that offer precisely because she wanted to keep the child.[21] Yet Martha's own story of this fatherless first child — controversial enough in 1949 — is not sufficient for the portrayal of her promiscuity. It is necessary, instead, that she be *found out*, that her desires be exposed as duplicitous. That duplicity — arising as much from her inability to satisfy her desires; from the tension of a bodily condition that heightens her libido and a body that will not allow her satisfaction — disappears at the moment of her union with Fernandez. Discovering desire commits Martha both to keeping it and to owning up to it. Thus she moves from being secretly promiscuous to reveling in her abnormality. That brazen quality is the final portent of Martha's pathology. Murder is the result of the emotional largesse of the sexual obsessive, a grand gesture in the sexual repertoire of the erotomaniac. Thus, Brown wondered at the prurience of the jurors who convicted Beck. Did they not see the whole picture of the deranged sexuality hidden beneath her mere vulgarity?

Afterward, individual jurors said that they were swayed by the coarse language, the exhibitionism of the defendants. But would a normal man or woman deliberately use the expressions, the vulgar speech, the obscenities employed by Martha Beck when she knew her life was at stake?[22]

Brown has plumbed the depths beneath the tabloids' shallow sketch of the "stony, emotionless and fully vicious creature" that is Martha Beck. The "real" murderer is the one whose origins are clear. The function of portent in the tale of murder is to make the murderer big enough to contain the displaced questions of murder. *To write "Why?" back into the story is to write the story backwards: to arrive at the murderer at the tale's outset.*

In Brown's text, Ray Fernandez occupies a position of surrogate dominance. His black moods, the result of a brain injury, predispose him to violence, and yet he is a more feckless villain than Martha. Once again, it is his questionable stature as a Lothario that is the basis of his pathology. Brown reports that Ray's attachment to voodoo allowed him to believe he could hypnotize women. The writer gives little credence to that gift, allowing instead that Ray had power over women who tended to be "silly, over-sexed, frustrated" and, of course, middle-aged.[23] Such women, for Brown, are pitifully gullible. Fernandez's powers of persuasion need not have been great, his charms only skin deep. Much of that which is Ray slides around on the surface, unlike the layered mystery of Martha's pathology. Given this shallowness, the structure of portent is less pronounced for the tale of murder in which Ray is object. We are, for instance, given intimations of the weakness that will bond him to Martha — one of those women he, as seducer, is meant to be manipulating. Brown tells us that Ray apparently had a fondness for "big women" at the brothel he frequented in New Orleans, Sammie's Bowery Follies.[24] Being weak, he is attracted by the substance of these women, a solidity that marks not strength but vulnerability in a culture that punishes ugliness. Ray is seduced by his own power to seduce. His ability to bring Martha to orgasm for the first time "enslaves" him to her desire, because it is imperative that *he* be desired. His vanity is his downfall. Brown pictures Ray purchasing the ubiquitous toupee on his own account just after his release from jail in Florida.[25] Ray's narcissism in the tale of murder means that he is a subject that refuses the position of subject: his gaze is directed inward. His vanity, his weakness, the suggestibility demonstrated by his belief in voodoo — all point toward the erasure of his place as murderous subject in the text. Ray's murderousness is supplementary in character. Essentially, the structure of portent for Ray tends to strengthen the complete tale of murder as a *folie à deux*.

The murder of Janet Fay occurs more or less at the middle of the book, and is closely followed by an account of the Downing murders.[26] This places the event of murder as the pivot between the unraveling of origins in the first part of the text and, in the final section, the fated end of judgment and execution. Brown's willy-nilly distortions of Martha's biography cannot alter his uncanny faith in her, and his reliance upon her, as subject in the tale of murder. Brown's account of the Fay murder is a peculiar blend of the eight versions I have identified in the Appendix. It most clearly resembles that of the defense — leaving out any evidence of premeditation, yet offering the motive (and explanation) that is so singularly lacking in any account tendered by the actual murderers. Ray asks Martha why she did it, and she replies: "I don't know. I saw her making up to you and I just couldn't stand it. Everything went black and the next thing I knew she was dead."[27] This piece of dialogue echoes Martha's lawyer, Herbert Rosenberg, telling the jury on summation "how" (i.e., "why") the murder happened. There is a tension here between the unanswerable and unanswered question of how/why the murder occurred (a moment of aphasia in the narrative literally marked by Martha's "amnesia") and the teleological imperative of the murderer's invention. The event of murder is foreshadowed by the structure of portent because it cannot be clearly limned at the moment of its occurrence.[28] The contradiction, therefore, is that the murderer *must* precede the murder itself. Martha's view of the murder structures Brown's account because she, necessarily, is the subject of the tale of murder. While she does not "remember" the murder, and by her own account did not mean to kill, the irony is that her word gains authority in the text because it is the word of the murderer.

Martha's presence at the murder is a slippery one. She has no conscious presence, and yet so much of the tale of her murderous origin is a story of the body, not the psyche. There is a bitter irony in Martha's amnesia. Ray's absence at the moment of the murder is literal, but once he returns to the room he ceases, in a way, to be there. His presence has less substance than Martha's. While he reacts hysterically, she is grounded in the bloody practicalities:

Fernandez tried to lift the body and, when he did so, blood gushed from the wound. Martha, with her hospital training and her experience in the mortuary, suddenly became calm and collected. "We've got to stop the bleeding," she told Ray, "or it will drip through the floor to the ceiling below."

Fernandez grabbed up a scarf from the table and shaped it into a tourniquet. . . . He was sobbing now and his hands were trembling so that he dropped everything he touched. Martha, on the other hand, had regained her composure.[29]

She is "collected," while he drops everything he touches. It is that very immanence, that being whole in the face of murder, which marks out Martha as the murderer. Despite the subcategory of the *folie simultanée*, the *folie à deux* generally structures a dominant partner in the fatal pairing.[30] The interdependence of both partners in the concoction of the chemistry that leads to murder is a defining characteristic of the *folie à deux*, but it is also one that must be elided. Martha's dominance in the tale of murder is complete, so much so that her presence sometimes overwhelms the plotting of the tale as *folie à deux*. Ray's presence provides the necessary stage for the murder, but it is Martha who occupies the spotlight.

"A Typically American Crime"

In the years after their deaths, "America's Most Hated Murderers" did indeed take their place in the canon of true crime, a place assured them by Brown's attention to detail in his reconstruction of their characters, if not of the case. Brown's reauthoring of the contemporary tale of the Hearts Killers became the casting-off place for English commentaries that began, if they did not complete, the journey of Beck's and Fernandez's tale of murder into the canon of true crime. The couple's crimes must have seemed, to the English, a telltale combination of peculiarly American excess: commercial greed, obsessive romance, and routine violence. The Hearts Killers were therefore quickly adopted as exemplary figures of American criminality by a number of English commentators.

It is appropriate to deal with these accounts here because they had a profound influence on the shape of a B-grade film version of the crimes that would attain cult status: *The Honeymoon Killers*. It is appropriate to take up the English treatment of the "doings" of the Hearts Killers because, as it has already been noted, the sources for authority in the tale of murder are diverse, and tales of murder (however particular their historical and cultural codings) are by nature intertextual.

There is material enough for a whole other work on the fascination that American murder holds for English true crime writers. Even the most reductive of these tours of Yankee murderousness offers an understanding — albeit a simplistic one — that crime is culturally constructed. Five of the most "obvious" elements of that particularity are commonly identified:

1. the wide availability of guns
2. the history and culture of organized crime (the Mafia, gangs, drug lords, etc.)

3. the racial and regional demographics of crime

4. the identification of the "serial killer" by and in American jurisdictions (although there is a respectable European antecedent in the "mass killer")

5. the continued existence of the state's power to kill its killers

These "factors" — so identified — are simplistic as well as mystifying, not equal to analyses of the complex phenomena that define "murder" at any one time in the United States. (True crime, as a genre, is notoriously conventional in what it counts as murder, and its power to plumb a culture's construction of its crimes of violence is consequently limited.)

During the late 1950s, three English accounts came out in quick succession,[31] each claiming for the Hearts Killers the dubious honor of being two of the most famous or notorious murderers of the century.[32] H. Montgomery Hyde, a prolific writer of crime and espionage nonfiction, wrote an account that (like many of his works) reproduced the accusatory tone and content of previous studies while still appearing to reserve judgment.[33] His restraint and apparent fidelity to the facts are belied, however, by his assertion that the "case caused a sensation throughout America. Besides focusing attention on the scandal of the Lonely Hearts Club, it brought up the whole question of crime and abnormality."[34] "Crime and abnormality" had been a burning question for a century or so before the Honeymoon Killers appeared. Neither it, nor they, were anything new. For Montgomery Hyde, like other commentators, "abnormality" had its silent partner in the term "sexuality." Not only is "sexuality" sublimated in the term "abnormality," but it is encoded in the romance — a genre that trades on carnal as well as material pleasures. Montgomery Hyde's acceptance of the pair as exemplary murderers explains at least partly the fascination that the two would continue to exert for the next decade. The case of the Honeymoon Killers, in the guise of the *folie à deux*, should still be read — bifocally — through the lens of the romance and crime genres.

David Rowan's account was a relatively terse one, heavily reliant upon news reports and, tellingly, upon Brown's work. Alone of all the in-depth portraits of Beck and Fernandez, culminating in the film version of their exploits,[35] Rowan's resists the temptation to refine the sensationalist and mythic aspects of the case. His account refuses to occupy the position of the murderer as subject, and is accordingly less inclined to stress the dominance of Martha Beck. Without her looming presence in the text, Rowan's tale of murder demonstrates the "How?" and not the "Why?" of those infamous killings. The chronicle flirts briefly with Ray's sensibilities (his vanity, to be exact),[36] but ultimately stands outside both antagonists — content to survey the two as objects. For all of that, Rowan is glaringly wrong on a few of his facts and happily confuses the chronology of Beck's and Fernandez's initial romance.[37] Still, his account more closely resembles the "facts" of the case than any other since the brief write-up in *Time*. Rowan is not, however, entirely immune to the importance of the case constructed by the media, and reauthored by Brown, in which descriptive and analytic excess restages the event of murder in the much larger and more appealing venue of the murderer's mind. For Rowan, like the trial jury itself, "the whole flavour of the case suggested something far uglier than criminal unbalance."[38] That ugliness indicates the much proclaimed degeneracy of the couple, while also gesturing toward the significance of the romantic text in the tale of murder.

Rowan's story is in two parts, comprising the crime and the trial and then the long wait in the death house. It may be Rowan's status as an outsider, as intellectual "tourist," that leads him to section off the story of Beck's and Fernandez's continuing romance in the death house. The "tourist" is much more likely to perceive elements of culture as "artifacts," as discrete objects, remote from a context that he or she is not privy to. In such circumstances the "artifact" can become invested with all kinds of meaning — at once perplexing, mysterious, and eerily familiar.[39] Rowan may, on the other hand, simply have wanted to keep a strict sense for scene and chronology. His decision to include a second chapter on the years in Sing Sing is, at any rate, an interesting one. Rowan justified this structure:

After the conviction of the pair, most people would have remembered only the salient facts of the murders. The couples' characters would have become blurred — unpleasant, but indefinite.

. . . Yet it might have been anticipated that Fernandez and Mrs. Beck would prove exceptions. Their personalities could not, would not be ignored. With each new killing they had boasted of their love for one another. From now on, they flaunted the boast even louder, in a manner which was to add an entire new section to their story.[40]

The time in the death cells is not a mere postscript, but the final act that reveals the larger meaning of the drama. Quite apart from the keen interest shown in how a condemned prisoner is "taking it," the execution sequence in the tale of murder provides the scene for those portentous clues to be more fully played out.

In the quote just above, Rowan suggests that Beck and Fernandez made a spectacle of themselves with their continuing mutual obsession. They called attention to themselves at a time when the public normally would cease (at least until execution night) to be interested in their story. That unregeneracy of character proves to Rowan the case for the couple's pride of place in the true crime canon. They are there of their own accord — because their very peculiarity demands it. But say we look at that continued notoriety another way. Beck and Fernandez did maintain their relationship at a high emotional pitch, creating, on at least one occasion, problems for the prison administration.[41] At such times, they could not help but attract the attention of the press. Still, it is not as if the news media were steadfastly looking the other way. Rowan's "entire new section" to the story is based upon copies of the letters between Beck and Fernandez that were passed by prison censors *directly to the press*. That material became saleable precisely because it fitted in with the already existing script on the Hearts Killers: the public still wanted to read a romance.

It is worthwhile here to consider the different publicity given to (or, more pointedly, withheld from) another couple incarcerated in Sing Sing just a few months after the executions of Beck and Fernandez. Ethel and Julius Rosenberg were indisputably notorious: "atom bomb spies" who had supposedly sacrificed their parental role for that of communist conspirator. The news media consistently ignored the Rosenbergs because their story ran counter to the generic grain of Cold War discourse.[42] It was owing entirely to their own efforts and to the bravado of one left-liberal newspaper that the Rosenbergs' story began to be heard at all. Atom bomb spies were arguably no less interesting and complex than murderers to the American public in 1951, but Ethel and Julius Rosenberg never figured in the press as anything other than stereotypical communist dupes, certainly not as parents or lovers. Their primary loyalty was instead to the shibboleth of communism. Those agitating for clemency on the Rosenbergs' behalf stressed the romantic, domestic, and familial connections denied by a press that remorselessly wrote the story of the Rosenbergs in the spy genre.[43] The spy as lover seemed not as potent a cultural text as the murder as *folie à deux:* the tale of the murderous lovers.[44]

The story of the last months of Beck and Fernandez in Sing Sing is told as one of love's, rather than justice's, vicissitudes. Here the structure of portent is bolstered by a continued emphasis on the couples' romance and, in particular, on Martha's fervor. Rowan's "The Death House" ends, typically, as he tells how the prison authorities decided to take Martha last to the chair, where she "died with a faint smile on her lips."[45] That "faint smile," in Rowan's as in others' readings, was not the nervous rictus of someone about to die under the gaze of a packed audience,[46] but the smile of a woman who dies knowing herself loved.

The tale of the "death house romance" is integral to the elevation of Beck and Fernandez to the canon of true crime. Only the tale of murder become romance can justify Rowan's observation that, despite widespread disapproval of capital punishment, "not a single voice — for possibly the only time in record — was raised in public protest against the decision to execute them." Rowan is logically unable to account for this singular lack of public sympathy, despite his contention that Beck and Fernandez were "termed 'America's Most Hated Killers' with good reason." The "three brutal murders that were admitted . . . and the many more that were feared" were not sufficient explanation, but are all that remains if the murder is read outside the romantic script that is its true context.[47]

In the Canon of True Crime
The Honeymoon Killers

Apart from Paul Buck's *The Honeymoon Killers,* which has recently been reprinted in the prestigious Blue Murder series, Bruce Sanders's essay on Beck and Fernandez is one of the few in print today.[48] It is also one of the longest.[49] Sanders described Beck and Fernandez as "the most incredible lovers in the twentieth century, people belonging to a nightmare, living characters no novelist or playwright could employ in a plot with any presence of reality." Then he cautioned, "and yet they were real enough, horribly so."[50] In his brief introduction to the volume in which "The

Incredible Lovers" first appeared, Sanders makes one of the most frequently heard boasts of the true crime writer:

[These] stories are more compelling than any fiction, more illuminating than pages of criminological statistics or columns of figures arrived at by commissions and committees with no brief to evaluate instincts and emotions, but only acts and deeds.

And to what end these most elucidating tales of murder? Not merely entertainment, which would be too base a motive for the unraveling of such mystery. The problem of murder limned in the narrative should provide a key to its own solution:

The violence recorded provides a problem in human relations that appears insoluble. Yet it is a problem that must be faced and tackled, and it cannot be tackled adequately or successfully unless it is understood. Towards this end these narratives are presented as human documents.[51]

The tale of the murder literally stands in for the "columns of figures," the reports of commissions and committees of inquiry. The murderer is at last admitted as a sign. This bold claim is made in the authoritative voice of true crime and, in Sanders's case, at a certain historical moment. The controversy over the exercise of the death penalty in England (prompted by the execution of Derek Bentley for killing a policeman, and of Ruth Ellis for shooting her lover) was still a heated one when Sanders was writing. The legislative changes of the mid-1950s were less a step toward abolition than they were insurance that every test would be made of the deservedness of the convicted to hang.[52] Sanders's concern was to provide a profile of true wickedness to aid Her Majesty in deciding whom to eliminate lawfully. In this way, the ethical project of the work — however appalling its basis in "fact" — is not dissimilar to that of more respected authorities like Fredric Wertham and Judge Curtis Bok (see Chapter Three above). It matters little that Sanders's profiles are drawn from criminal history in the West generally, because that is supposedly all to the good in providing a larger picture. The characteristics of a particular murder and murderer might be culturally determined, but the problem of murder itself is a "universal" one. As in the classic detective story, the meaning of murder and its mere scenery should not become confused. Neither the waving date palms nor the ornate interior of the first-class carriage is any indication of the "Who?" and "Why?" of murder. The act of murder does, however, supposedly expose a truth about the banal world in which the killings occur: "like a searchlight it throws a sudden glare on what just before and soon afterward appears as the common gray surface of life."[53] This epiphanous quality is not found in the detective mystery, but it is one of the distinctive elements of the true crime genre.

In Sanders's vision of the Hearts Killers the portent of plot is bolstered by the signifying power of the prop. Ray's infamous toupee is a vital element of the scene of murder: it is, after all, Delphine's discovery of Ray's baldness that is the catalyst to the killings. The death of the Downings is the place from which the backwards narrative drift begins. Thus, rather than using Fay's murder as the casting-off point in the search for murder's origin, Sanders takes the last murder first.[54] Vanity, signified by the toupee, is the cause of Ray's immediate downfall. Sanders also establishes early the status of romance in the text, now an overt parody of love. Here begins to sound the cruelly ironic tone that will inform all of the following accounts. While vanity is what makes a killer of Fernandez, it is the love of a "silly, frustrated female" (in Brown's phrase) that provides the necessary victim. Rainelle's blissful ignorance of the "love . . . unfolding like a tropic bloom in her mother's bemused brain" marks her out as the sole undeserving victim: the girl child not yet affected by the feminine disorder of romance. Fernandez kills Delphine when she blurts out, in horrified shock, that he's old. Martha is written out entirely from this account of Delphine's shooting,[55] but her responsibility is inscribed as more than that of a mere accessory by the way in which she comforts and absolves her lover:

"Martha," he said, a choking sob in his voice, "she saw me without the toupee, and said I was old. . . . [Y]ou don't think I'm old — not too old?"
. . . Her weighty arms opened and he went into them gratefully. . . . "Never mind, darling boy, we'll fix things, like we always have."[56]

Martha's "composure" and Ray's "hysteria" infantilizes Ray in the face of the monstrous maternal figure that is Martha. She is the place within which murder gestates. Before killing the child,

she patted him, walked to the door. "Just you dig a hole in the cellar, honey, and make it deep enough for the both of them."

... She always seemed to know what to do when something had to be done. And there was always something to be done. Like now.[57]

The Feminine is a figure of such monstrosity here that we find the order of genesis reversed. Ray is discursively emasculated when he is told to dig the grave (the womb) for her to fill.

In Sanders's account, Martha is always in control; she always has the upper hand in the partnership. She dominates, but also nurtures. Ray's fealty to Martha is too complete, forcing Sanders to explain the couple's apprehension in Michigan as the result of mistakes made in the first — and much earlier — murder of Fay.[58] Martha had not, at the time of the first murder, perfected her technique of dominance, nor had Ray released his will to her. The Fay murder creates, for Sanders, the true character of the murderers and the murder as *folie à deux*.

Sanders's Martha is fast-talking, foulmouthed, smug, and doting.[59] Her affectionate terms for Ray are literally or tonally diminutives: "Ray boy"; "Ray darling"; "darling boy." When she is angry, her language combines the shrill quality of the shrew and the authoritative bluster of the nurse. Thus, when she arrives on the doorstep of the lover who has supposedly just jilted her, and is asked what in God's name she is doing there, she replies: "Can't you see? . . . Moving in, buster."[60] Martha's tonal range runs from the barked command to the breathy reassurance, while Ray's is typified by the wheedling tones of the flatterer and the whine of the coward.

Sanders's dialogue has the feel of the hard-boiled crime thriller, that particularly American incarnation of the crime story.[61] This resonance is accentuated by the propensity of the (English) writer to read the murders as foreign and, therefore, as gesturing to some endemic American violence. Sanders's fascination with the misanthropism of his characters, with their seediness, is an homage to the hard-boiled genre. His text lacks, however, the most important figure of that genre: the detective, that cynical logician witnessing the decay of his moral and physical environment. The writer of the generic true crime tale cannot take the place of the detective in such "fiction," because he or she — outside the text — cannot dispense the necessary justice. Yet the writer must try, however unsuccessfully, to assume that position. His or her employment of the empty forms of the hard-boiled detective story — a crime story sans detective — tends unwittingly to turn the irony of portent into parody and black humor. Although Sanders closely follows Brown's interpretation of Martha's murderous character, his campy *noir* changes the direction of criticism. Instead of providing a lesson in the origin of murder (Lonely Hearts clubs, naive authorities, etc.), contextual detail creates the conditions for satire. Discussing the period in which Martha supposedly worked in the mortuary and became an avid fan of the romance, Sanders wrote: "Martha Seabrook became a person living two lives. One with the dead who were finished living. The other with the living who had never lived."[62] The snappy patter of the detective mystery turns Martha's pathology into a couple of good throwaway lines. Yet those lines profess an intimate knowledge — as if the writer, like the detective, was saying beneath his breath, "I've got your number, babe."

Once Martha becomes Ray's mistress,[63] her life takes on the "semblance of a grotesque but intensely exciting charade."[64] The love story becomes the *folie à deux* as black comedy. Sanders bestows upon Martha a seeming delight for evil, and unplumbed depths of *ressentiment*. Beneath the bravado of her hard-talking banter lurks a vulnerable and obsessive woman, from out of whom murder originates. When Ray tells Martha what his "real" work is, she is not shocked but, on the contrary, intrigued. She suggests they "work together":

> She had suddenly seen an opportunity for hitting back at her own sex, for squaring the overdue account for all the humiliation and misery she had suffered from the years of tender girlhood.[65]

Martha warns Ray that he "better let" her in on how he "operates," adding that he should not "make it sound too good" for she "could get awful jealous." Sanders reads his character straight out of the hard-boiled genre, and yet the figure that mouths this warning is not the curvaceous blonde who so often takes the role of the *femme fatale* in *noir* — she who manipulates, awarding "love" while plotting murder. Martha is a gross parody of that figure. The embodiment of the traditional *femme fatale* role by "Fat Martha," the ogress,[66] creates the black humor of this particular tale of murder. The seductive, cooing lines are read much too clearly as warning rather than as invitation. Ray's inability to see the monstrous figure of his lover, so apparent to the reader, makes for a parody of the modern tale of seduction that is the *noir.* The role of *femme fatale* in certain hard-boiled fiction and in *film noir* (exemplified by Barbara Stanwyck's role in Chandler and Wilder's *Double Indemnity*) marks out an inversion of the nineteenth-century tale of seduction that I have briefly analyzed in Chapter One above. In the modern version of the tale, it is the male figure whose loss of innocence heralds death as he becomes prey to the *femme fatale*. Martha's decision to wreak her vengeance on the women whose normality mocks her — rather than the men who have shunned, abused, or failed her — is Sanders's move away from the *noir*. The true crime writer, unlike the hard-boiled crime writer, is obliged to account for Martha's murderous career.[67]

Sanders's revisioning of the tale of murder as black comedy was a persuasive one. "The Incredible Lovers" provided the lead for the final and most famous account of Beck's and Fernandez's murderous careers. The film *The Honeymoon Killers* (and its later novelization by Paul Buck) developed Sanders's portrait of Martha violently defending her object of obsessive love. Both also elaborated upon the image of Brown's and Sanders's "silly, oversexed, frustrated" and vulnerable older women who became (through Ray) Martha's prey.

Reclaimed by the low-budget, gritty realism of the 1960s crime movie, Sanders's unwitting homage to (or rather parody of) the hard-boiled detective genre is returned to its rightful place.[68] *The Honeymoon Killers* is black comedy of the cruelest kind and an unwittingly self-reflexive tale of murder. For, although written as a romance, *The Honeymoon Killers* ends up mocking the cultural script that demands it should be so written.

While homicide statistics in the 1960s (in contrast to statistics on property crimes and sex crimes) appeared to be relatively stable, *perceptions* about the violence endemic to American society had undergone a change since the postwar period. Fredric Wertham, who in the late 1940s warned that the "individual act of murder exists against a background of victimization of many people,"[69] would have been gratified by the critical legal realism of the "new criminologists,"[70] by the spate of commissions charged with investigating the roots of crime in poverty,[71] and by the doomed "Great Society" of Lyndon B. Johnson. "Crime" had acquired a bevy of new meanings in the America of the late 1960s. Although Richard M. Nixon cruised into the presidency on the tail of his promised law-and-order legislation, this apparent rallying to the party of order should be viewed in the context of the struggle by African American communities for civil rights, the rise of the New Left and the women's move-ment, the expansion of civil liberties sanctioned and enshrined by the rulings of Justice Earl Warren's Supreme Court, and widespread re-sistance to the investment of American troops in Vietnam. The concept of a "criminal society" had been politicized: it no longer merely defined that "underclass" so long beloved by sociologists. The politicization of the term "crime" and the tendency for the "criminal" disenfranchised to turn their oppressors into objects of moral scrutiny — reversing the usual order of surveillance — was bound to affect fictional representations of crime.[72] Such changes are certainly discernible in the final working of Beck's and Fernandez's tale of murder, and yet it would be dangerous to overemphasize the critical or revolutionary status of those changes. Re-silient indeed are the moral strategies contained by the "backwards narra-tive" in which the psychiatrist (or his representative) is detective. Like a bad penny, the murderer comes back: not as she is, but as she is con-structed by a discourse of murder in which she is both genesis and end.

6. True Crime Romance III:

The Honeymoon Killers

Some of the truth has never emerged and never will be known. Therefore both the film and the novel have taken the liberty of fictionalizing probable scenes. We trust these are just as likely to have taken place as anything recorded.
Paul Buck

Shirley Stoller looks like she might have been a few pounds shy of Martha's average weight. The film version of Martha Beck is a good deal grimmer, in general, than was the woman that even hostile reporters called "fat, *smiling* Martha." The smile of nervous reflex that was sometimes caught by press photographers throughout the trial is replaced, in Stoller's Martha, by the pout (and by a sly, assessing squint). There is also a divergence between the screen version of Martha in *The Honeymoon Killers* and the character in the novelization. That distinction is the outcome not merely of the demands of medium, but of larger structural differences between the two works. The satiric elements of the plot are clearer in the film than in the novel, and yet the novel evinces a more critical awareness of the romance as part of its narrative strategy. This distance between the film and the book is evidence that the novelization is a good deal more than just a descriptive summary of the film. Paul Buck's fascination with Beck and Fernandez led him to do further research in creating the novel, rather than relying on the film script alone.[1] His novelization changed the plot line in places and greatly enhanced Martha's internal monologues. Both the screenplay by Leonard Castle (who took over the movie's direction) and the novel by Buck show considerable investment in the character of Martha, an investment that is unsurprising given the development of the tale of the Hearts Killers in the true crime canon.

The brevity of the film (108 min.) is compensated for by Buck's inclusion of a coda to the novel, covering the period that Beck and Fernandez spent in prison. The coda and the appendix (a commentary on the necessary fictions of film and novel) are both subtitled "fact." That classification sections off the story of Ray's and Martha's fate at the hands of the authorities as somehow qualitatively different from the tale of murder proper. Buck cannot end the novelization at the point where the film leaves off, and he feels it necessary to add a commentary because the true crime fiction — by the sheer impetus of narrative — has the authority of "truth," yet there is another "truth" called "fact." After all, this is a real life story, and the scenes invented are "as likely to have taken place as anything recorded." The "real" — because of the strategic nature of the material upon which the "facts" rest — is ultimately unknowable. In this vacuum of reliable information, the tale of murder retains its inviolability. Buck is torn between his impulse to serve a "truth" and his duty to retell an already well-formed story.

Buck — like those before him — is driven to explain the murderers, particularly Martha Beck. Whereas Wenzell Brown tried, however inadequately, to provide a structural context for the Hearts Killers' crimes in an unregulated romance industry, Buck attempts a rudimentary critique of the moral climate and the gender order in postwar America in order to explain the availability of Ray's marks, Martha's obsessional behavior, and the sensationalizing reaction of the press to the murders. Despite the occasional insight, Buck fails to make much of an advance on Brown's analysis. He, too, reproduces apocrypha as "fact," and his recontextualization unwittingly follows the mythologizing tendency of former accounts. The story as told travels a familiar path and yet Buck, cogitating on what actually may have happened on the night that Janet Fay was murdered, makes a most surprising observation:

Since both [Ray and Martha] were able to supply fairly acceptable reasons for their innocence, the following question could be asked. *Although it is only a very remote and unlikely possibility, could there have been a third person present?*[2]

This "third person" is a phantom presence, considering that Buck has just told a story throughout which a distinctly corporeal Mrs. Beck has wielded hammers, drugged helpless old ladies, and drowned innocent babes. Buck makes this preposterous suggestion because of his belief that the "facts," however shaky their demeanor, really can stand outside the story. He himself has seen the "facts," he has read the transcript, and yet he is guilty of telling a new version of the same old story of the Hearts Killers. The insertion of the "third person" is a metaphorical expression of the double bind he, as narrator and supposed historian, has found himself in. The "third person" is the silent (because guilty) witness to *what really happened*, one whose presence does not actively disprove the story, but represents the means by which all troublesome excess can be excised. As a historian, Buck has failed adequately to explain both why Martha did what she did and why she was treated as she was. But if she was merely keeping (along with her love) that conventional secret of another's guilt, then much that is wrong with the tale of murder is righted. The "third person" is implicated in her crime—and not her brother, mother, psychiatrist, lawyer, judge, press, public, jailors, and executioner. And Buck does not have to upset the established authority of this particular tale of murder with the actual *story* of the "third person." He can have his cake and eat it too.

The Honeymoon Killers has been called by critics "documentary-like" and a "dramatization" of real events.[3] The title that precedes the credits tells the viewer that he or she is about to see an "incredibly shocking drama" and the "most bizarre episode in the annals of American crime." In an era where lower production values (because of the losing contest with television) characterized Hollywood, as well as independent, productions, the reduction in quality was compensated for by the reduction in the costs of making film and the freeing up of the set by the technical revolutions in sound cameras. The 1960s saw the rise of the road movie to a genre, but the increased mobility of the camera affected other, already established, genres as well. Mobility was a production fact but it was also, simultaneously, a textual value. The 1960s crime movie, then, gravitated toward the itinerant gangs that had terrorized the Midwest in the 1920s and 1930s: the Dillinger gang, Bonnie and Clyde, Ma Barker and her boys. Moreover, the increasingly bloody depiction of various bad men's "bad ends" was also characterized by the scenes of flight, pursuit, or just plain "moving on." The car and the road are both integral parts of the modern crime movie, whether of the A or B side of a production package. After all, the programs sold by and large to an equally mobile audience: patrons of the drive-in.

Originally to be directed by Martin Scorcese (who would produce some of the foremost American crime films in an era when audiences and critics both came back to the movies), *The Honeymoon Killers* finally went into production with a director whose experience lay, inscrutably enough, in opera. The film's low production values are evidenced not just by the peculiar lighting, poor sound, and the claustrophobic effect of the interior sets (which actually add to the atmospheric power of the movie) but by the filmmaker's decision to relocate events onto a more contemporary, mid-1960s, scene. Realism would have been a little too expensive to film (the novelization returns events to the late 1940s — but with, nonetheless, only a faint sense of period). The decision to update events has some interesting consequences for the evolution of the tale of the Hearts Killers, whose story, suddenly and inadvertently, moves closer in content to the helter-skelter era of Charles Manson and the "serial killer": a time of drifters, of strangers killing strangers. Although both the film and the novel restage the myths of this tale of murder, they also assume an ironic distance from the America that is the killing ground of the piece. The fact that the film sets the events it depicts in the 1960s only increases the power of the script to dissect the culture that "gave" its victims to the Hearts Killers before demanding the couple's lives in its own act of retribution. *The Honeymoon Killers* is very much a film of the 1960s: a B-grade film made at a time when competition between the movies and television was perhaps at its bitterest. And the film is remorseless in its mimicry of the "ordinary," the domestic, the suburban in American culture (that to which television — according to its critics — supposedly belongs).

The black humor of the film (and, to a lesser extent, the novel) is derived from its grim, monochromatic realization of the details of murder, juxtaposed with a surprising attention to the idiosyncrasies of the main characters, murderer and victim alike. This retelling of the tale of the Hearts Killers is partly the result of the narrative accretion I have described in the chapters above, but it also reflects a discursive shift in the construction of crime in and as American culture. As the "final" version of the tale, it adds new irony to the pride of place given to Beck and Fernandez in the "annals of American crime."

In the closing scene of *The Honeymoon Killers* a matron hands Martha, who is waiting to be led into court, a love letter from Ray. This final exhortation to romance, Ray's desire to "shout his love for [Martha] to the world,"[4] is then transformed into a private declaration of love. Castle's direction underscores the feeling that this is a private moment by having the matron remove herself to the other side of the corridor while Martha "hears" (in voice-over) Ray gently speak the words. By rewriting this most publicized communication (featured in at least three New York daily newspapers) as a *promise* of love, rather than its *postscript*, Leonard Castle puts the final touches to the tale of murder as romantic fantasy. The romance of the Honeymoon Killers is enacted in Martha's obsessive mind, and is played out in (rather than on) her gargantuan form. Because it is a private matter — the record of an obsession — romance becomes a matter of unfulfilled ideals and desperate delusion; the narrative, accordingly, veers between tragedy and farce.

Twelve minutes shy of two hours long, the action in the film is necessarily telescoped. The frame of the film narrows, time and its witnesses are squeezed out, and Martha becomes the alpha and omega of the text. The execution as event disappears from the text, but its meaning retains a shadowy presence. The opening scene shows Martha entering a smoke-filled room, the site of an accidental chemical explosion. Smoke creeps beneath the ceiling as Martha chastises the nurse and male orderly who have, obviously, been using the room for a sexual liaison. "Together . . . you're just as bad as ammonia and chlorine!" Martha tells them. This scene presages a more fatal mix than ammonia and chlorine in the supposed *folie à deux* of Ray and Martha.[5]

The execution figures in this way, tangentially, not merely because the brevity of the film denies it a place. When Buck reinserts the execution in the coda, it is briefly described; he spends more time on the prison days. Pointedly, he writes: "The facts in the coda refrain from comment, as here I do not wish to condone the methods by which the two killers were brought to justice." Elsewhere, discussing the irregular extradition of the couple from Michigan to New York, he opines that "Ray and Martha were flown to New York to be executed. (The trial was regarded as a subsidiary.)"[6] While his disapproval of 1950s due process is overt, the film — owing, at least in part, to its having "updated" the crimes — avoids the judicial and punitive issues. We leave Martha as she is about to go to her first day in court, although the ending could have been served just as well had she read the letter in the death house.

This disavowal of the fate of the couple is a sign of the times that produced both texts. The 68 percent of people who apparently favored the death penalty in 1953 had become just 51 percent by 1960.[7] By 1970 there would be a five-year functional moratorium on executions throughout the United States. The fascination with killing evinced by the rapaciously violent crime movie of the 1960s is therefore complicated by a tendency toward moral self-searching. The violence of social retribution is examined in such diverse texts as *In Cold Blood, Bonnie and Clyde, To Kill a Mockingbird*, and *Town without Pity* (to name but a few). This impulse to eulogize *and* critique was not restricted to the crime genre but surfaced, to varying degrees, in the modern Western and in the war film. The relative liberalism of the times, exemplified by the moratorium on executions, may have given rise to a nostalgia for the kind of rapacious violence that supposedly warranted summary or formal execution (the denouement of *Bonnie and Clyde* springs to mind here). Even if "death stood condemned" statutorily speaking, the specular nature of violent death was on the up and up.

Fragments of Fact

The film *The Honeymoon Killers* has a different kind of explanatory power from that of all the previous written accounts. The search for origins necessarily works along synchronic rather than diachronic lines (if we except the movement of "screen time" in the film). And yet Castle shows a surprising commitment to documenting the evidence of the murder of Fay and (to a lesser extent) the Downings. The displacement of the killings historically is made up for in part by Castle's inclusion of these traceries of fact — although perhaps not enough to warrant calling the film a "docudrama." Such ephemeral traces of the murders' origins might have been lost on an audience ignorant about the accounts of a case tried twenty years before. Tony Lo Bianco's Ray has a crescent-shaped scar on his forehead, a relic of the shipboard accident that had supposedly injured Ray's brain. We see this clearly but can impute no history to it. The scar is just *there* — Ray does not even rub his forehead in moments of stress or anger to draw our attention to it. In other words, the scar exists not for the benefit of the audience, but *for the record*. There are other references to the "real story" of the murderers: a disc of tunes from the South Sea islands is dragged out the night of Ray's and Martha's first date. Ray was born in Hawaii, after all, although from the script we know him only as a Spaniard. Later in the film the couple are shown entering the Kenmore Hotel in Manhattan, which was, indeed, the place where they stayed while Ray first wooed Janet Fay.[8]

Film, like any other medium, is by nature intertextual. Any work could be expected to carry its freight of more or less decipherable references to other texts, and yet it is interesting to examine what, for *The Honeymoon Killers*, are the points of reference. We are fed glimpses of past "real lives": marks on the body, places visited. This fidelity to the "real" story is integral to the true crime text, regardless of whether or not it plays to an audience of fans whose heads are crammed with the trivia of famous killings. Even if Castle did not think his audience would pick up such references, *he* perhaps needed to insert them: from those scattered relics of fact comes the authority of the tale. These few things are at least tangible, while all else must remain ineffable: "events as likely to have taken place as anything recorded." The narrative authority of the tale of murder is derived from practically everything but the "facts" of the case. And yet that *excess* depends upon such disparate threads of evidence: the hammer, the hotel room, the Lonely Hearts column, Ray's scarred head.

In both the film and novelization of *The Honeymoon Killers*, traces of the "real" dialogue between the murderers, and between the couple and their victims, appear. The various accounts of the Fay murder that came out at the trial — a most detailed and probing inquisition, establishing the killers' reputations — reappear scattered throughout the entire murderous career of Beck and Fernandez as portrayed in the film. Thus, one of the couple's earlier alleged victims mouths many of the lines Martha attributed to Janet Fay. Myrtle Young, who dies from an overdose on a Greyhound bus en route to Arkansas, is forced into her fatal drug stupor by Martha, who resents the older women's repeated importunings of Ray for sex. She watches through the door while Myrtle pulls one breast from out of her nightdress, asking Ray whether he'd "like some sugar." This scene is but one of several that utilize Martha's controversial testimony of the night of the Fay murder, when Martha saw, supposedly, Janet Fay put a "shrivelled old breast" to Ray's mouth, cooing "Don't oo want some sugar, honeychile?"[9] This moment, and the conversation between Myrtle and Martha when the former is trying to establish whether Ray can "screw or not," deploys a discredited "truth"[10] to establish the integrity of the murderer's character and, therefore, the authority of the tale of murder.

Authority in the tale of murder comes from the deployment of "facts" — fragments of the "true" story — as narrative building blocks. Thus a great deal is attached to those fragments of the trial record that do make it into the film. The redeployed dialogue tells us about the speakers and their relationship to one another. If one of the victims in the film mouths words attributed to one of the *actual* victims, the figure of the victim is established: *the kind of woman who dies*. The women who die and the woman who kills in *The Honeymoon Killers* are almost interchangeable. It is this likeness that creates a self-critical dimension in the film, although it is never able to rise above irony to an actual critique of the American romantic ideal.

The filmmaker's decision to replace Martha's children in the story with a partly senile mother is a significant one. The scene of desertion is underscored when it becomes one of filial failure. Yet the register of that betrayal — and its meaning — is altered. Because of her vulnerability and her dependence, Martha's aged mother is an adequate stand-in for the figure of the deserted children. And yet there is an element of shrewishness in the mother. She, unlike the children, cannot be entirely innocent. The slippage between murderer and victim is accentuated by the function of Martha's mother in the text. As her daughter abandons her into care, heading for New York and her fake marriage to Fernandez, the elderly Mrs. Beck yells:

You're digging my grave because you're killing me by leaving me here. . . . God damn you! God damn you! I hope you end up like this. I hope someone does this to you!

This "curse" demonstrates several of the workings of portent (as irony) in the film. The solitary tear that tracks the curve of Martha's cheek as she walks away beneath her mother's window demonstrates that she feels guilt and sorrow, but she cannot avert the course of her love. And, indeed, someone does "do this" to her: she is finally betrayed by Fernandez's willingness to make a joke of her love by lying to her about his sexual activity. "One more to fleece. One more to fuck, one more to kill, kill, kill," Martha moans in one of the final scenes.[11] Discursively, Martha's mother is the couple's first victim. She is charmed by Ray when her daughter first meets her beau. "The Latin from Manhattan," the elderly Mrs. Beck simpers. She even offers to dance with the younger man.

Just prior to the actual murder of Fay, Ray told Martha to "keep that woman quiet, no matter how it is."[12] Choosing to follow instead the outline of Martha Beck's revised statement (see Appendix) the essential piece of dialogue during Fay's killing in the film is Ray's whisper to Martha as he refuses the hammer: "If you love me you'll do it."[13] In two other vital sequences in the film — one the metaphorical murder of Martha's mother, the other the literal killing of the Downings — the character of Ray echoes the missing line. He tells Martha over the phone that she cannot even think of bringing her mother with her to New York. "Get rid of her . . . choke her . . . I don't care what the hell you do with her, but you can't bring her up here!" he yells. Later, Ray is similarly short about the disposal of little Rainelle Downing. When Martha is wondering what to do with the child, he tells her to "put a pillow over her face . . . smother her . . . I don't care what you do as long as you get rid of her!" This reliance on the resonance of both of the murderers' actual testimony (the two early statements which formed the basis of the prosecution's case) tends to make the responsibility for the killings more clearly shared. And yet, the ubiquity of Ray's dismissal of the victims into his lover's hands for disposal, his challenge that Martha do that vital "something," describes her position as besotted supplicant. Like the other women in the film, only more so, Martha wants to please Ray. In *The Honeymoon Killers* the women are virtually of a kind in their outrageousness, their crassness, their foolishness, and their naive vulnerability. This flattening of the differences between killer and killed indicates the importance, in this text at least, of the "Who?" in murder, as much as the "Why?"

Disposable Dames

Wenzell Brown's analysis of the evils of the romance industry and his derisive asides about the "silly and oversexed" women who populate the

Lonely Hearts clubs are developed to interesting effect in the film. Regardless of whether they die or not, the spinsters whom Ray cons are marked for death in a culture within which they have become, quite simply, redundant. That redundancy is symbolized in the text by the complete mystification of these women by fashion. Janet Fay, who was in real life a dressmaker, becomes, in the film, a maker of hats. Janet's hats are the most ludicrous contraptions. She is energetically off the mark in her fashion sense, a failure observed by the film's audience, who laugh *with* the murderers as they bluff her along, full of praise for her talent.[14] With such talent Janet could just "rake in the money." It is by holding out the promise of helping her invest in a hat shop that Martha and Ray are able to convince Janet to withdraw her life's savings. Just as she believes she is still marriageable, Janet also thinks she is a maker of fine and fashionable hats. Yet she, and her handiwork, are both a far cry from "marketable."

The first of Ray's victims, Doris Acker, also had a penchant for unfortunate hats; in one scene she wears a huge, feathery assembly. But her redundancy in the consumer culture of desire is signaled by quite another form of naivete. Like the widow Downing later in the film, Doris is enthusiastic in her patriotism. While soaking in the bath, preparatory to a good scrub, she sings "America the Beautiful." With Doris conveniently out of the way, Ray and Martha rifle through her suitcase and, accompanied by a boisterous chorus of "Battle Hymn of the Republic," we see Ray counting a wad of the stolen cash. As Doris launches into the following verses, we see the shadows of Martha and Ray making love in the next room. Doris's old-style patriotic enthusiasm is juxtaposed with a more cynical view of the American dream: the pursuit of happiness in the form of money and sex.

Ray and Martha are certainly playing the market, the rhythm of their lives derived from the demands both of the product they're exploiting and its economic circuit. At the start of the film, Ray hurries away from Martha (who has just lent him $100) with the excuse that he must return to New York for the working week's start of banking hours. Later, the couple dawdle through a car trip, only to arrive in Queens after the banks have closed. Although the crimes have been updated to the 1960s, the economic world in which they occur is almost an anachronism: an America in which cash counts for a great deal, where issuing banks must endorse their checks, and where a closed bank or the wrong branch means an unclinchable deal. The pace of the film, and the lives it portrays, are set by cash counted, bank hours, and the constant traveling from town to town to cash checks at regional banks. Money—rather than being an intangible, mobile, and disposable standard—carries with it a sense of place and time. Both the crime and the victims are anachronisms in the increased mobility of a changed postwar America.

Ray and Martha almost transcend the inertia of their victims by extorting profit from their very redundancy. The method of their criminal career reveals a cynical reading of the simpler values they mimic and exploit. Thus, Ray and Martha fall in happily with Delphine Downing's patriotic lessons, her celebration of Lincoln's birthday, and her constant commemoration of the lesser-known anniversaries of American history. But Ray's knowledge of what America is, and what it means, is more idiosyncratic. Martha complains, "If we stay here much longer she'll have me sewing flags like Betsy Ross!" Ray is baffled. "Who's Betsy Ross?" he asks. He understands perfectly the need for a woman getting on in years to find a second husband, or to wrap an illegitimate pregnancy in respectability. He understands the continued trustingness of women who put their money into the hands of their husbands. The good old value system of Christian Middle America is what allows Fernandez the profit of his sport. *The Honeymoon Killers* describes one set of American values falling prey to another, more cynical version.

And yet, the newly acquired value system is not entirely different. The connection between the mawkishly innocent world of the spinsters and widows and that of their exploiters is Martha herself. I have been careful above to stress the preeminence, in the film, of Fernandez's direction of the crime: his cynicism is more or less complete and, accordingly, his profit from the crimes is greater. Even in his failed endeavor to swindle Evelyn Long—the only woman in the film represented as "normal"—Ray profits from what obviously are enjoyable sexual relations with the young widow. Because Evelyn Long is able to step out of the value system that decrees she should not have sex with a man to whom she is not married (and if she does, she ought to feel guilty about it) it is Martha who suffers. Throughout the film it is Martha, as much as any of the other of Fernandez's victims, who clings to a notion of fidelity and true love. Martha is just another version of the monstrously ridiculous woman who has become redundant to the American dream of romance as it is, day by day, so halfheartedly lived. In its willingness to lampoon such women, the film is stating a de facto belief in the system that passes them over, that so rigidly classifies attractiveness and sociability.

Buck wrote in his coda that each of Fernandez's victims "had a certain willingness to be led to her fate." This malleability came from "their refusal to come to terms with their unattractiveness and their sexual dwindlings." Romance with Ray, therefore, was a means to sustain a delusion. Martha, no less than the paramours fleeced by her lover, was bound to accept the conditions of a romance that she has not earned. Such a deal could be read as cynical, but Buck turns away from the concept of a conscious acceptance by these unwanted women of the un-favorable terms of the romantic contract. Martha Beck had "come to terms" with the fact that she "could never have appeared less than ugly." She had enveloped herself "in a protective dream world where everything was perfect for her" — where she invented a war hero husband and the vital social life that, in reality, she lacked. Buck wrote regretfully of the ungenerous court and jury that failed to recognize "that Martha's life was a complete fusion of truth and fantasy."[15] The strategic nature of "cop-ing" becomes, in Martha's case, the pathology of delusion. "Many women must live in the fantasies of romance stories," but Martha was not content with such vicarious living. The point at which she crossed over from exigency to madness was when she started to manufacture the romantic script *herself.* Martha "managed to convince not only friends but business acquaintances" of the existence of her hero husband, Joe Carmen, father to her first child.[16] Women, therefore, can be expected to hold onto the unreal hopes peddled to them by romance culture, and to make do with their lot in whatever way they can; but to exploit the script for their own purposes is going too far. However, it is not quite clear how Martha is different from those other women who embroider the nature of their romance with Ray for friends and relatives.[17] That she is driven to murder cannot be the difference, because something must precede the murder to explain it. Once again, the old conundrum of the tale of murder's origin appears.

When she is peremptorily dismissed from the hospital where she is matron, we see Shirley Stoller's Martha have it out with the superinten-dent. In a fury, she tells him: "I'm not so sure Hitler wasn't right about you people." Martha's anti-Semitism is possibly meant to gesture toward her Southern parochialism, but it also shows the kind of temperament that will accept any ammunition into its large armory of contempt. Martha's insult should be read in the visual context of the scene: behind her on the office wall is a poster of a pretty nurse, smiling, with a finger to her lips. The legend beneath reads, "Shhhhh!" Martha is not the sort whose face will ever don an educational poster; not the kind of woman upon whom the controlling charm of the coquette will sit well. In a culture that enforces propriety most particularly upon those within it who would give anything for the opportunities the desirable get, Martha's impropriety is pure *ressentiment*.

Marie Belloc Lowndes's fascination with the "Why?" of murder seems a little incurious. In the developed tale of the Hearts Killers in the true crime canon, the "Who?" and the "Why?" of murder become figuratively inseparable. The structure of portent in the tale of murder works in such a way as to prefigure an ending that is, simultaneously, the beginning of the tale. The ironic mode functions wholly upon the foregrounding of the outcome. Portent, in the tale of murder, is a form of trickery. For the character of the murderer is not merely an actor in the narrative: the narrative figure becomes the very event of murder itself. The *folie à deux* makes a single chemistry of two distinct actors in the murderous couple: one *completes*, rather than compliments, the other. In the development of the tale of the Hearts Killers, the importance of the narrative structure of the *folie à deux* was such that it was the necessary link between the contemporary versions of the crimes, read by onlookers as a parodic romance, and the later narratives of those English commentators who embraced the murders as both exemplary *American* crimes and *universal* evidence of romantic excess. The transmutation of the tale of the Hearts Killers into satiric form was a consequence of these earlier developments, the legacy of the *folie à deux*, and a cultural shift in narrative authority generally. The continuing tendency of the tale of murder to focus on the murderers and to adopt him/her as subject seems to beget by the 1960s a less authoritative script than that spoken by Wertham's Irwin, or the lawyer who speaks for Roger in *Star Wormwood*. The uncertainty and self-reflexive nature of the new script does not exert itself, however, as fully formed critique but as irony, as parody, as a joke. Martha, as subject, remains the surface beneath which the mystery of murder waits, barely contained in even her gargantuan form. The Hearts Killers were the perfect subjects for film because so much of their story is about veneer, about surface: from the supposedly expanding girth of Martha, to Ray's toupee, to the layer of concrete that would not harden over the Downings' graves. Where the search for murder's origin tracks through the murderer's psyche even much of that which is psychological is rendered visible (and intelligible to the layperson) by its register upon the body of the murderer. The *visceral text* is a tale of murder told on the body.

Part II
The Killed

It's a funny old world . . .

and a man's lucky if he gets out of it alive.

W. C. Fields

7. Killing Grounds

No one made vows, or lit candles: it was, eventually, just another TV news spot concerning the trials of a friendly but disastrously underdeveloped area.
James Baldwin (on the Atlanta Child Killings)

I went mourning without the sun: I stood up,
and I cried in the congregation.
I am a brother to dragons, and a companion to owls.
My skin is black upon me,
and my bones are burned with heat.
My harp also is turned to mourning,
and my organ into the voice of them that weep.
Job 30:28–31

The politicization of the term "crime" in the 1960s shifted certain narratives of murder onto a more critical territory, a territory for which the sites of greatest contest would be race and gender. James Baldwin, Kate Millett and Ann Imbrie explore in different ways that contested ground, and their critical discourses on murder challenge, with varying results, the generic conventions of the tale of murder. These writers seek to place the killed at the center of their narratives: those to whom, inevitably, all answerable questions must be directed, despite the fact that they are deaf, dumb, irreconcilably gone. In these texts the dead are listened to and spoken to, and the reader takes up a place beside them — not vicariously, as in the generic tale, where one is positioned by the murderer, but sharing the fragility of those routinely made vulnerable, the *chosen* victims.

In the recent bumper crop of American miniseries based on actual murders, the banal *and* the outrageous have been chosen to represent American violence. Serial killers and women convicted of conspiracy to commit murder seem particularly in vogue, although television dramas with a social conscience might go so far as to explore the prosaics of murder in an "unequal" society. Many cases of domestic homicide have recently made it to the small screen, crimes made infamous by the use of the battered women's syndrome as a defense. This, says the apostolic voice of prime-time television, is the "problem" of murder in America. *This*, it must also admit, *is entertainment.*

Murder as television drama deals with typicality and atypicality, with everyday violence and "monstrous" cruelty. Serial killers account for very few of the victims of murder per capita in the United States, but they make popular representational fare. The curiosity evinced by the public about this supposedly new category of murderer has itself made the "psycho" or "serial" killer the bogeyman of murder. Women who kill are, in any and all cases, statistically unrepresentative of murder in America.[1] Popular culture's fetishization of the woman murderer — whether as a psychotic killer,[2] a woman pushed too far by male violence, or a plotting neurotic — ironically indicates the relative safety of society from female violence. The woman murderer is both alterior and exotic.[3]

As distinct from its representations in popular culture, a sociological analysis of murder gives rise to a different image of American violence. Like most "objective" empirical evidence, homicide statistics claim to make an accurate diagnosis of the ailing constitution of the American polity. The rate of homicide in America is many times that of its European counterparts: 10 per 100,000 inhabitants, rather than the 1.1 per 100,000 in England.[4] People usually are killed by intimates or acquaintances, although American statistics indicate an increasing rate of killings by strangers in the United States.[5] Homicide rates in urban and rural areas are not necessarily higher and lower, respectively, but there is a higher rate *overall* in the southern states.[6] A comprehensive study made in the 1960s on homicide as a cause of death found that people between the ages of twenty-five and forty-four were the most likely both to die by violence and to kill. Among that vulnerable group, "blacks and Chicanos" were identified as ten times more likely to die as victims of homicide. "Homicide," the study concluded vaguely, "remains a leading cause of death in certain segments of the population."[7] More than twenty-five years later, the federal Centers for Disease Control in Atlanta, Georgia, brought that statement back into stark focus. In the last years of Ronald

Reagan's presidency, the homicide rate among young African American men had risen in 1 in 1,000.[8] It now stands at 10 per 1,000. Nowadays "one out of every 21 black men can expect to be murdered. This is a death rate double that of American servicemen during the war [WWII]."[9] In 1992 46,000 African Americans between the ages of fifteen and twenty-four died by homicide. In the same period and age group, the figure for whites was 32,000. Given that African Americans represent only 12.5 percent of the total population, 46,000 represents a grossly dispropor-tionate rate.[10] A black male of any age is seven times more likely than his white peer to die as a victim of homicide.[11] Indeed, homicide has become *the* major cause of death among African American male youth.[12]

The reality of American murder so frequently taken from such statistics as these can be both reactionary and paranoid. White political pundits who deploy the terms "race" and "ethnicity" as if they themselves had none look at the scourge of "street crime" and behold a vast sea of poor black and nonwhite faces. The very concept of "street crime" takes its structural sense from the social and cultural category of the "under-class" — a grouping that differentiates its inhabitants by their alterity alone and, singularly, by their relative poverty. The underclass as other has no color in its *overt* theorization, but it is definitely nonwhite if white is taken to mean the affluent, orderly, middle-class male that is the unproblemat-ized citizen upon whose existence the rule of law is founded. In such a con-text, those "shocking" homicide rates take on the dimensions of an epi-demic: something carried by and among the Third World poor among us; something that has always, since time immemorial, afflicted the poor. *That is just the way it is.* Thus James Baldwin's recollection of a traditional affir-mation of black faith: "I ain't got to do nothing but stay black, and die!" translates, without its air of resignation, to the context of a racist America that slaughters, with mind-numbing regularity, its black children.[13]

The high rate of murder by and of young African American men seems to be treated by the institutions of American justice as historically contin-uous with that apocryphal definition of murder from the "Old" South: "If a nigger kills a white, that's murder; if a white kills a nigger that's justifi-able homicide; *if a nigger kills another nigger that's just one less nigger.*" Judicial and correctional systems work far below the standard of the constitutional ideal that has been devised and revised throughout the history of the Republic, and sanctioned or extended with varying degrees of success by the U.S. Supreme Court. This failure of the functional realities of "equal justice" and equal protection before the law is eloquently illustrated by the fate recently of antidiscrimination and affirmative action legislation before the Court. Holding to its concept of liberal individualism, and in a return to strict formalism in its legal reasoning, the Court has lately rendered majority decisions that refuse to engage with the problem of institutionalized racism.[14] No longer does "equality of opportunity" imply the need for remedial policy. "Equality of opportunity" increasingly registers as a thing best attained by "race neutrality" — by "strict scrutiny" and suspicion of all racial classification, whatever its purpose. Even in areas of the judicial system where overwhelming evidence has indicated an unacceptable degree of arbitrariness and racial bias, such inequality has been dismissed as representing the predictable anomalies of an imperfect system.

In 1986, George McCleskey, a prisoner on death row in Georgia, petitioned the U.S. Supreme Court with a claim that the Georgia capital statutes were "applied in a racially discriminatory fashion."[15] In support of his claim, McCleskey's lawyers laid before the Court extensive research indicating that defendants charged with killing white persons were ten times more likely than those charged with killing nonwhites to get the death sentence.[16] Although the race of the victim was the most significant indicator of the likelihood of a capital indictment, the race of the defendant was also a determinant.[17] The Court was not impressed by the claim that Georgia had violated the Fourteenth Amendment (equal protection), but did give some weight to the Eighth Amendment violation (cruel and unusual punishment). By placing on McCleskey the burden that he must prove that he, *as an individual*, had been discriminated against, the Court turned away from the concept of social, or collective, injury to that of individual disability.[18] The law *is* an ass, it would seem. Or so the present state of American jurisprudence regarding "equal protection" would indicate. Thus, although the Fourteenth Amendment specifically prohibits "punishments based on arbitrary or unreasonable classifications such as race or color," Florida's state supreme court, upheld by the U.S. Supreme Court, found constitutional a

statute punishing adultery and fornication [that imposes] *a different punishment when committed by a black and a white person from that where the offenders are of the same race* . . . since whatever discrimination there may be in the punishment prescribed is directed against the offense designated and not against a person of any particular color or race . . . since the punishment of each offending person, whether white or black, is the same.[19]

That ability of the law to hold as distinct the offense and its offenders is eloquent testimony to the law's obliviousness to history, to context, and — here I paraphrase — to the ever-*present* effects of *past* discrimination. By refusing to take account of McCleskey's Fourteenth Amendment claim, the majority decision emptied the politics out of the term "discrimi-nation" — leaving it the empty vessel it has, perhaps, always been.

While a discussion of the arbitrariness of the death penalty might seem to be something of a side issue, it is not. The decay of ethical reasoning evident in the Supreme Court's refusal to weigh historical evidence and sociological data is, in and of itself, a grim trend. Its ultimate result is a strengthening of the position of the white male subject as citizen and legal standard. The failure of McCleskey's argument — a failure fatal to the claimant — is proof that the judicial machine, like the culture that runs it, does not care if there is "one less nigger."[20] The tenacity of racism comes from its institutional structure, and the secure foundations of that struc-ture in a discourse of alterity. The history of American racism is not a history of conspiracy. It is the history of ordinary people, living ordinary, even "patriotic," lives: people who are white or act white and who live in a world where *that is just the way it is.* These are "The People" that the U.S. Constitution was designed to protect. Yet there are those who are prac-tically other to that constitution, those who have been struggling to get into history or, even harder, struggling to make that history unrecogniz-able. America's "occupied country," that "friendly but disastrously under-developed area" Baldwin wrote so bitterly of,[21] is Harlem, Watts, Cren-shaw Heights, or — and perhaps even particularly — the Atlanta of the child murders.

On the Seriality of the "Atlanta Killings"

James Baldwin visited Atlanta in early 1982 to cover the trial of Wayne Williams, who had been indicted for the final two of the twenty-eight murders popularly known as the "Atlanta Child Killings." Like the English writer Martin Amis, who was in Atlanta just before Williams's arrest, Baldwin was unsettled by the willingness of the prosecutors and news media to attach the twenty-eight deaths to one killer, making them thereby seem somehow extraordinary. "*The* killings in Atlanta" assumed the status not of category but of title: an honorific term that followed Williams's name as if he could explain it, and it him. Both Amis and Baldwin knew that the killing or disappearance of poor, black children in American cities (or, indeed, rural areas) was neither unusual nor generally remarked upon by the authorities:[22]

[T]he missing, menaced, murdered children were menaced by color and locality: they were — visibly — Black, which in this republic, is a kind of doom, and actually poor — which condition elicits from the land of opportunity . . . a judgment as merciless as it is defensive.[23]

What made these black children so suddenly precious to the authorities was the "pattern" discerned in the deaths as bodies turned up in rivers, by roadsides, in vacant lots. This "pattern" was a dubious sort of connection for Baldwin, who could see little in common between the murders. The children were killed in different ways, their bodies found in different places, and they were not all boys (two girls died); they were not even all children. The two murders for which Williams was indicted were of "grown men," although Baldwin was told that these two were "*perceived* as children" because they were "retarded."[24] For Baldwin, what were called the Atlanta Child Killings and assigned a murderer to author them had, in the actual crimes, no intelligible unity.[25] He did not comment, as did Amis, on the compressed time frame of the disappearances, or on their "alarming" frequency.[26] Unlike Amis, who deployed the concept of the "pattern" even after he'd wondered at the lie at the heart of the term Atlanta Child Killings, Baldwin could not discern in the relation of the murders to one another (or even to their supposed author) this famous and convenient "pattern." In a masterful critique of the catch-22 logic of prosecutorial reasoning, Baldwin argued that the concept of the "pattern" allowed the district attorney to charge the defendant with the very crimes that did not fit the pattern, and to wrap up the other twenty-six, less anomalous, murders. The accused provided the lens through which a "pattern" could be discerned in court; a link was established that would implicate Williams in the other murders. Under such close scrutiny, the behavior of the defendant could give credence to any "pattern":

He may have been observed, standing on a street corner, or in an alleyway, or his kitchen or someone else's kitchen, or a bar, or a toilet, talking to a boy or a girl or a man or a cat or a woman or your wife or his sister or himself: *there is nothing that won't, under pressure, establish a "pattern," and, once one begins looking for a "pattern," this "pattern" will prove anything you want it to prove.*[27]

Baldwin's comment could just as well refer to the whole portentous structure of the tale of murder. For Baldwin there *is* a "pattern," but it is not to be found in the topology of the crimes. What "pattern" there is comes from the place and time of the murders: the city of Atlanta, the State of Georgia, the United States of America:

The cowardice of this time and place — this era — is nowhere more clearly revealed than in the perpetual attempt to make the public and social disaster the result, or the issue, of a single demented creature or, perhaps, half a dozen such creatures.[28]

An "era" is never merely a period. The term contains the resonance of Fernand Braudel's *mentalité* and Michel Foucault's *épistème*. The time and the place cannot be separated. The *time* of murder and the *place* of murder is a city (or many cities: Washington or New York or Baltimore would do) with a large and ghettoized African American and/or nonwhite population beginning to be administered by blacks and people of color. The city, containing a "valuable chunk of real estate" in the ghetto that the state will eventually seek to reclaim, is thereby given over to the care of its interim occupants. "Thus . . . whatever happens in the city becomes the responsibility of those corralled there."[29] In Atlanta in 1982 the place *is* the time in a very real sense. Atlanta cannot quite abandon its past and its identity as that exemplary city of the reconstructed South. Its literal transfiguration in the 1860s had only partly, and much more lately, been followed by a remaking of race relations there — forcefully integrated in the 1960s and boasting a majority-black administration since the 1970s. Knowledge of those gains in the African American community is marred by an easily awakened sense of racial threat.[30]

The murderer is black, the murdered are black, the police commissioner and the mayor and the trial judge are black.[31] The community that organized to draw attention to the murders was itself black. Indeed, the FBI turned up—a dubious kind of cavalry—only after the disappearance of the thirteenth victim, who was from out of state. It is not necessary for Baldwin to preface this entrance with the bureau's own rationale for it: jurisdiction made the murders their business. Thirteen-year-old Clifford Jones was not, like the previous victims, one of the Atlanta poor. He was from out of town, out of state and, quite simply, not *out of mind* to the authorities as the other lost children had been. The crossing of jurisdictional boundaries defines the locus of power, and the interests of the powerful. In Baldwin's analysis, "jurisdiction" is not an empty legal term but is the border sign of a territory where citizenship is still restricted.

It is unlikely that a fan of true crime, educated in reading an unselfcritical genre, would find intelligible *The Evidence of Things Not Seen.* Why is a book that should be about Wayne Williams, the murderer, and what happened to his victims, in fact a polemic against endemic racism? What kind of reporting is this? After all, Baldwin admits that he attended only one week of the trial, and that he could not speak directly about the murders to some of those most intimately affected by them.[32] His investigation of the actual legal strategy in the prosecution of Williams is musing rather than analytically critical. And yet it is this strategy, these "failures" on the part of the reporter, that establish his right to speak and to report. Baldwin writes in the preface to his work: "*My soul is witness.*" This "witnessing" is based upon and bounded by an authority that is tangential (in quite different ways to that of the conventional narrative of murder) to the "facts" from which the narrative of murder is commonly constructed. To say his soul is witness is to speak out of and for history; to speak about social injury, rather than an incidental and idiosyncratic violence. His reading of murder works against the generic preferences of true crime; indeed, his is a *counternarrative* of murder.

Baldwin problematizes the position of subject in an overtly political way. Unlike the ethical agendas of the clinical and juridical "experts" whose reauthorings of the murder narrative I examine in Chapter Three above, Baldwin's ethics is a critique of a liberalism and democracy that aims at social control. His treatise is quite unlike the generic tale of true crime, within which authority is inscribed through reference to the pathologized figure of the murderer, whose "truth" (and the meaning given to murder, therefore) is to be found in his or her difference and *indif-*

ference to context.[33] True crime attempts to align the reader with the storyteller who unravels the matted fabric of supposition and speculation that is at the heart of the murderer's silence.[34] As the jury that rules on the "facts" is allied with the judge who rules on the "law," the assumed alliance of reader and writer in true crime is one of arbitration, of power. This is not to say, of course, that readers of true crime are *literally* law-abiding, Republican-voting supporters of the death penalty. Indeed, true crime has been implicated a good number of times in the very murderousness that it thrives on portraying.[35]

The counternarrative of murder is characterized in part by the way in which authority within the text is provided by a larger discursive context: by the refusal of the author to give up a position (and a history) or to allow his reader similarly to surrender an ineluctably social subjectivity. Baldwin refuses to invest the murderer with authority or to build the story from out of the murderer's psychic history and visceral trail.[36] In *The Evidence of Things Not Seen* the unproven guilt of Wayne Williams is but part proof of the text's status as a counternarrative of murder. The degree of his guilt is less important than the extent to which the putative murderer finds collaborators in the community, the state, and the Republic:

The author of the crime is what he is — he knows it, can make no more demands, nor is anything more demanded of him. But he who collaborates is doomed.[37]

This refusal to treat the murderer as the clarifying lens of murder is symptomatic of a more general suspicion about easy answers, about "authority" in general — a suspicion that is at the heart of the rise, from the 1960s, of a culturally endorsed, politically critical narrative form. The aesthetics of that overtly political form in a "postmodern" age is, accordingly, different. The supposed inscrutability of Wayne Williams that Baldwin describes is not merely a function of his cool demeanor in court, nor is it the impenetrable mystery of "true evil." Williams forms a kind of dead spot in Baldwin's text because he is written not as the *A*uthor of his act, but as its *a*uthor: small "a." Unlike that earlier and more confident age which sought, in its discourse of murder, the amplification and clarification of the act's meaning in the murderer's psyche, Baldwin is compelled to understand that the conduit of Williams's mind leads straight back to the malls, vacant lots, and riversides of the Atlanta so familiar to its poor.

Certainly Baldwin writes about Williams,[38] or, rather, what was said about Williams in an attempt to explain him: that he was hopelessly spoiled, that he was homosexual, or that he had been abused by his father.[39] Such explanations are, at the very least, insufficient. "The world," writes Baldwin, "is catastrophic with spoiled children." As to the accusation of abuse, "even if it were true, it is a universal not to say daily event, and has nothing to do whatever with the slaughter of the children of Atlanta."[40] *Nothing to do whatever!* Not with killings in Atlanta or Harlem or Oswego or Wichita Falls. The questions asked of Williams in court in an attempt to get at the measure of his pathology are not just irrelevant there, in the context of any or all of the killings he has done, but are irrelevant and insufficient in so many other cases where similar questions are asked.

Baldwin's skepticism here is reminiscent of work that stresses the gender blindness of legal and criminological discourses on sexual murder. The world is certainly "catastrophic" with abused children, most of whom are female. These women do not necessarily grow up to become abusers themselves, and they are extremely unlikely to become murderers.[41] The propositions advanced by lawyers and psychiatrists fail to fit the enormity, or perhaps the banality, of the facts of murder in an extraordinarily racist *and* gender-riven world. Feminist critiques of male violence arguably cannot do their theoretical work if extracted from an analysis of related systems of discursive violence, particularly that of race.[42] Baldwin's treatise on the violence of the racist Republic refuses to make the murderer a scapegoat, and that refusal is a significant strategy common both to certain feminist critiques of male violence and to critiques of the violence of endemic racism. Both arguably aim toward the deconstruction of hierarchies of difference that are structurally encoded, codings symbolically upheld by the individualizing and biologistic discourses of criminology and forensic psychology.

At the conclusion of the work, Baldwin suggests that "Wayne Williams must be added to the list of Atlanta's slaughtered black children." This symbolic listing of Williams with the dead is the definitive turn in Baldwin's critique of the true *A*uthorship of the Atlanta Child Killings. Williams, of course, is not literally condemned—having escaped the imposition of the death penalty. But the point at issue is his *dismissal*, and with it the dismissal of the case of the twenty-eight dead (reduced so cunningly by the stirring of the judicial mix to its essence of two). Williams has been tidied up with all the other loose ends of the case (carpet fibers and all). The black police commissioner who oversaw the manhunt receives a phone call from Houston and accepts the commissionership there, and everyone is quick to "defend" the commissioner's decision to move. But what Baldwin hears in this bluster is not a commendation of Commissioner Lee Brown's talents, but applause for the "case itself, and the verdict." Brown, like so much else in that problematic case, "was moved on up, and, above all, out."[43] This "dismissal" is the logical end to a case in which the race of the principals has been everywhere obvious but never actually seen. It is also a logical end to a case of child killings where the killings will continue, although their author is imprisoned. Unlike feminist criminologists like Deborah Cameron and Elizabeth Frazer, who advocate a return of responsibility to the murderer for his actions (in acting out the fetish of misogyny), Baldwin is resolute in his indictment of the "collaborators." Williams, after all, is another black "child," whereas the murderers that Cameron and Frazer study are white men.

On one level, Baldwin's refusal to lay upon Williams the meaning of the murders reflects the sermonlike qualities of the piece. But he is not preaching forgiveness, as such, when so much of the treatise is formed by sheer fury. Williams is not absolved of responsibility for his actions — although, as Baldwin disavows the verdict, the degree of harm the "murderer" has caused remains unresolved. For Baldwin the meaning of the Atlanta Child Killings lies in the anxious need of the authorities to aggregate, contain, and explain them. Baldwin's reaction to the verdict was a "steady, chilled wonder" at the "relief" of those so "anxious to accuse and condemn" Williams. When the committee formed by Yusef Bell's mother began to organize in order to publicize the crimes in Atlanta

that whistle forced Authority to enter, control, and close a case concerning slaughtered Black children, most of them males, a banality with which (and I am witness) they had never, previously, been remotely concerned.[44]

"Authority" with a capital "A." It would be misleading to analyze Baldwin's displacement of meaning — from Williams, as "author" of the crimes, to the "Authorities," who explained him — as merely characteristic of that brand of liberalism from which there arose in the 1960s and 1970s a theorization of crime that emphasized social, rather than individual, causation. Certainly Baldwin's analysis has much in common with this liberal tenet of faith, but the fury of the piece is the measure of its difference. Liberalism in America is strongly implicated in the "collaboration," in the rationalizations of "Authority," that called the Atlanta Child Killings "serial" and dismissed them with the disposal of the body of the murderer.[45] These are "yesterday's Liberals, the Negro's friends, who have now become the Neoconservatives."[46] Liberalism's beautifully naive equation concerning the causation of crime (poverty = crime) was merely a glance in the right direction, whereas Baldwin made the reader stare, long and hard, into the heart of the Republic.

The Evidence of Things Not Seen is but one of Baldwin's written salvos in a long-drawn-out battle with his nation of birth. Twenty years before visiting Atlanta to cover Williams's trial, Baldwin wrote an essay in which he first used the epigraph for the later *Evidence of Things Not Seen*. Referring to a play he was then staging, Baldwin wrote that one of the characters, a murdered child,

is all the ruined children that I have watched all my life being destroyed on streets up and down this nation, being destroyed as we sit here, and being destroyed in silence. This boy, is, somehow, my subject, my torment, too. And I think he must also be yours. I've begun to be obsessed more and more by a line that comes from William Blake. It says, "A dog starved at his master's grave [*sic*] / Predicts the ruin of the State."[47]

Baldwin's misquote made something of a conundrum out of what, by the 1980s, had become an ominous statement indeed: "A dog starved at his master's gate / predicts the ruin of the State." The old liberals who had become Reagan's New Conservatives knew well enough the threat of the "starved dog" at the gate, a threat that supposedly justified the trend toward mandatory and determinate sentencing, greater police powers and, among other things, the "war against drugs." Hard-line policy stemmed from a polarizing conceptual and actual framework: the insider/outsider of the "anthropologist/informant" binary that defines the relationship of sociologist and criminal (or, more prosaically, the apartment guard and the tenant whose security he/she ensures). American advisers on crime and criminality have over the past decade been returning to the concept of an "underclass" as the proper focus of social research. By its very definition, and regardless of the means by which its composition is identified, the "underclass" is an outgroup that requires — through welfare most of all — containment and control.[48] For Baldwin, this was the Horatio Alger line of sociological reasoning: "the problem is not 'race' but 'class' — meaning: those who find themselves on the bottom belong there."[49]

It is in the context of such social, criminological, and juridical thinking that Baldwin's text must be read. His choice of ground for one of the last skirmishes in a lifelong battle against the duplicity of the (white) American Dream was hardly arbitrary. The story of the "menaced boy," as opposed to that of the "Negro problem," finds its fullness in Baldwin's last visit to Atlanta.[50] "The menaced boy" is no figment of the imagination when a young African American man is seven times more likely than a white to die by violence.[51] The tale of the "menaced boy" inadvertently told by the federal Centers for Disease Control in Atlanta echoes Baldwin's tale. That coincidence is the tale of murder where murder, by its statistical nature, becomes a matter of race.

The Gendering of Race in *The Evidence of Things Not Seen*

The tale of the "menaced boy" is also, unavoidably, a gendered one. There *are* analytic sympathies between the feminist discourse on sexual and domestic murder and Baldwin's analysis of the violence of the White Republic. However, one of the most unremarked upon anomalies of the "pattern" to the Atlanta Child Killings was the presence of two female victims among the total accounted to Williams. And what of the still-unsolved murders of thirty-eight girls and women (of whom four were white) killed over the same years and found in the same general areas as Williams's alleged victims?[52] What a silence surrounds these others — beaten, stabbed, shot, and left for dead in one of the city's many desolate spaces. The women and girls who did not "fit the pattern" were perhaps the most obvious evidence of its fallaciousness — evidence that Baldwin nonetheless ignored. It is the story of the "menaced boy" that compels him. His preoccupation is understandable, certainly, given the vulnerability of the young African American man to a continuum of violence. And yet, that vulnerability — masked by bare statistical fact — is structured by a complex conceptualization of African American "manhood."

Perhaps one of the most problematic components of Baldwin's analysis is his concept of a "manhood" historically denied African American men. His conceptualization of "manhood" is an elision of the literal black man and the black subject who is forced to attain the status of subject by the contorting and impossible process of becoming white (that which defines the position of subject). And yet there is no thing, no being, that is *white:* "they were many colors, but they were not White." To assume manhood, and the position of social subject, was to emulate what "was, at once, a menacing, overwhelming, inescapable Presence and an echoing, intolerable absence." And worse, one was "forced to imitate a people for whom you know — which is the price of your performance and survival — you do not exist." This "series of paradoxes" is the defining condition, ontologically and metaphysically, of being black in modern America, the condition of being s/Subject. The concept maintains a gender even in the face of the open and ungendered metaphysical status of the subject. This contradiction is not, of course, the double bind of subjectivity that Baldwin seeks to convey. His parable of "becoming White" explains the means by which color (or the ineluctable position for the African American of that which is "not-becoming-White") defines the "community [that] could always bury its differences long enough to make certain that the Black could not rise to a place of sufficient recognition or threaten the structure of the labor union or the city or the state."[53]

This definition of the exclusionary power of a White Republic that elevates and "whitens" every "color" but black is itself reliant upon the process by which Baldwin argues that subordination has historically been accomplished: the metaphorical (and sometimes literal) emasculation of black men.[54] In a brief analysis of that particular devastation of African American manhood called "sorriness," Baldwin pictures the imminent and literal threat to the black man that comes when he "declares himself a man." "Sorriness" stems from the overprotectiveness of women who try to save their sons, brothers, or husbands by making them hide the black manhood that is so threatening and incomprehensible to white men — who are, indeed, quite willing to destroy the object of their derision. "All of our mothers, and all our women, live with this small, doom-laden bell in the skull, silent, waiting, or resounding, every hour of the day."[55] And those women are caught both ways: spiritually killing their sons by unwitting complicity with the White Republic's emasculating hatred, or, in "making them men," seeing them punished for that affront to white manhood (and white women's virtue).[56] Racial terror therefore makes black women and their men complicitous in their own holocaust: "Brother may never grow up — in which case, the community has become an accomplice to the Republic."[57]

The "emasculation" of the black man is a central mechanism of the maintenance of white supremacy because it helps to ensure that African Americans, alone of all "immigrants" to the United States, have the least upward social mobility of any section of society. The "dilemma" of American manhood is its disorganization.[58] The "legend and the reality of the masculine force and role" is such that black men, less pragmatic than their women, continue to "dream"; to push the limits of "being Black" in the "republic that imagines itself White" to the point, often, of their humiliation or destruction. And the black male "*really* cannot bear [humiliation], it obliterates him." This particular fragility of the black male means that he, unlike women who "manage . . . to stunning and unforeseeable effect, to surmount being defined by others," is destroyed by his very strength and hope:

[W]hen a man cannot feed his women or his children, he finds it, literally, impossible to face them. The song says, Now, when a woman gets the blues, Lord / She hangs her head and cries / But when a man gets the blues, Lord / He grabs a train *and rides.*[59]

"He grabs a train and rides." Here, then, is but one of the metaphorical inscriptions of the literal diaspora that is, for Baldwin, the African American "experience."

In a country where the "family" or male wage still dominates, as does a matrix of powerful masculinist discourses of independence, success, and mobility, the subversion of African American "manhood" is an issue still to be reckoned with. Baldwin is not advancing an entirely uncritical definition of masculinity, nor does he assume a "real" — meaning essential — masculinity. Indeed, the "Republic has absolutely no image, or standard, of masculinity to which any man, Black or White, can honorably aspire."[60] A feminist critique of his position on the black American dilemma of "sorriness" would have to reckon with the changing conditions of the construction of masculinity as opposed to the relative continuity of a *prescribed* and *proscribed* black manhood.[61] But it would also question, as Hazel Carby did,[62] a construction of the category of black women as "women" in a way that deprives them of any useful historical definition other than their position vis-à-vis their imperiled men.[63]

Baldwin's conceptualization of African American manhood shares much with a masculinist homosocial ideal that has been associated with black militants and activists since the 1960s, and yet it is also qualitatively different.[64] Baldwin, like many black activists, spoke for and from the place of the urban, northern black man. And yet this "manhood" is under question if held to the terms so unequivocally stated by Amiri Baraka (LeRoi Jones) when he quipped that "white men are trained to be fags."[65] Toward the end of his life, Baldwin was finally able to write about the terrors of the "American idea of masculinity" in that "hall of mirrors" of race and *sexuality*. Early in his life, Baldwin had fallen in love with a man at a time when he was still committed to becoming a pastor in the black church. The collision of these two (seemingly) mutually exclusive passions — each itself an impossible faith to risk or retain for a young, poor black man in Harlem — destroyed for him forever "all of the American categories of male and female, straight or not, black or white."[66]

The repetition of the metaphor of the mirror throughout Baldwin's criticism is a significant one. Identity is never clear or singular for Baldwin, but is a fragmented, distorting, or multiple "reflection" of all the various incarnations of being: class, "color," gender, and sexuality. The mirror is as unreliable as the eye of the beholder. We are both made and weighed as we "move in the vast and claustrophobic gallery of Others, on up or down the line, to the eye of one's enemy or one's friend or one's lover."[67]

"Having no balls" meant, for Baldwin, both more and less than it did for the "much man" — however and wherever that figure existed. As a "faggot" or a "pussy" he had no "balls," and yet men and women would still seek out the "big black dick" that was the mythological standard of a feared and desired black manhood.[68] It is the presumption of others, and a history of myth, that distills the lives of those who live in the "real" world; that marks out the space of the subject. Baldwin is correct to assume the very real and dangerous effect of the great American dreams of whiteness and masculinity upon those in the "gallery of Others." He does not credit those things as *true*, but simply as ineluctable.

In his exposition on the investigation and (false) closure of the case of the Atlanta Child Killings, Baldwin's concept of that *qualified* difference — the trick of the mirror — is a crucial one. The essay "Here Be Dragons" is contemporary to *The Evidence of Things Not Seen*. Both conclude with a similar injunction. While Baldwin ends the latter work with a plea for Americans to realize the imperative of *community*,[69] he also gestures toward the androgyny and indeterminacy that structures both subject and community: "[E]ach of us, helplessly and forever, contains the other — male in female, female in male, white in black and black in white. We are a part of each other." It is the denial of the fact that we are all *implicated*, one with another, that finally explains the horror and cowardice of the Atlanta Child Killings. The "pattern" that resulted in the promotion of the murders from the work of a quite prosaic violence to that of a single "evil" individual was constructed from a tortured, and inconsistent, use of the concept of difference. All the victims were black — a definition that was arbitrary inasmuch as it was based only upon the fact that they were not *white*. And the "children" were supposedly alike — just that, *children* — despite their different ages, sex, class, or means of death. In this way an aggregate was created. A group was defined by their difference *from* others (including other murder victims who, arbitrarily, did not make the "pattern") and was constructed as an "entity" by the conflation of discrete characteristics into constituent "parts."

Baldwin's allusion to a radical concept of *implication* — whether as androgyny or the literal mix of black and white blood so sternly denied by the very differentiating power of the terms "ethnicity" and "race" — is the final measure of the text's powerful ethical quality. His analysis of the social context of the so-called Atlanta Child Killings can be identified as a counternarrative of murder by its refusal to found its narrative generically in the subject of the murderer. Indeed, Baldwin's refiguring of the concept of "community," and his refusal to credit the discursive processes of differentiation and discrimination that the White Republic so ruthlessly deploys, make *impossible* the use of the murderer as "Author." The singular and determined space of the murderer as subject simply cannot exist, however undeniable his *literal* existence. As counternarrator of the murder tale, Baldwin fractures the subject of the generic tale of murder, finding in that rift quite a different authority.

When the U.S. Supreme Court refused to give its support to George McCleskey's claim that the rights guaranteed by the Fourteenth Amendment had been denied him, the Court voted *for* the legal subject and *against* the man. Arguments are still made in accredited law journals, and before courts of appeal and last resort, that—essentially—the life of a white person is valued more highly than the life of a nonwhite. Statistical evidence, suggesting generally that the severity of punishment is linked to the race of the victim, is perhaps the most persuasive proof of that dictum. The high value placed on the lives of white middle-class property owners is the flip side of a system that cares less for those who have less: people of color, the poor, and children and women (where they are unprotected by referred status). The Court, in its wisdom, looked to an equal standard for all individuals in the fictitious "citizen" and failed utterly to see the social aggregate in an obviously unequal society. Formal legal reasoning asks that discrimination be proved, directly, in each instance, as issuing from the *immediate* context of the "aggravating" situation and to *immediate* effect upon the claimant. The looming term "immediate" stands outside any intelligible social context. Legal formalism stands in direct opposition to Baldwin's concept of implication and community. It denies events their history, and people their place in that history. Legal reasoning is, in and of itself, an aestheticizing discourse. Its resurgence in recent decisionmaking suggests that uncritical discourses of murder—arising not just in the courts but in criminological thinking, the news media, and society at large—will dominate, rather than those ethical counternarratives that may contest them. Counternarratives of murder are marginal and yet they, perhaps alone, attempt to make unfamiliar the actual (meaning political) banality of murder. That sense of unfamiliarity is produced by a refusal to employ the common generic conventions of the murder narrative.

8. Ghosts

I have given my life to ghosts in the closet, ghosts under the bed,
ghosts in the basement, ghosts in the boxes I have carried with me all
summer. I am transient now in my own life, stopping over wherever I am,
living only in the story I have to tell.
Ann E. Imbrie

What we take life to be is what our lives become.
James Baldwin

In America today one of the most morally (if not legally) taboo of crimes is
the killing of a child by its caregiver. The vitriol heaped upon mothers
who kill their children in the United States is not muted, as it is in the
United Kingdom, by a category of infanticide that not only recognizes
mitigating circumstances but describes in itself a crime *distinct* from
murder.[1] There is no such distinction made in the United States. And yet
there remains in American homicide law a sense if not of attenuated
responsibility for such crimes, then of the lesser degree of harm they pose
to "society at large" (that great — if obtuse — legal standard of the common good). The milder penalties attached to infanticide in Britain find an
American parallel in the refusal of state legislators to attach to family or
intimate killings the kinds of legal sanctions imposed for the killing of
strangers. While torture-murder, or murder by hire, or murder for financial gain all fit the criteria of aggravating circumstances and qualify as capital crimes, parental abuse killings or other "domestic" crimes elicit death
sentences only where other "aggravating" factors are present.[2] The lower
value placed upon the lives of those killed within literal or de facto families
is demonstrated by the reluctance to upgrade penalties for parental abuse
and wife killings, despite increasing public opprobrium for such crimes.

Kate Millett's contention that "when a woman does it to you it's different" says more, in both cultural and legal terms, than even she intended.[3]

Critiques of a "progressive," liberal cultural order that professes merely to minister while actually disciplining its citizens necessarily focus upon the construction of hierarchies of difference within that order. The differentiating constructs of race, class, gender, and sexuality work simultaneously and ineluctably on the subject in culture, and yet Baldwin and Millett tend to privilege one or another construct.[4] The following is an analysis of one of these contemporary, explicitly political narratives of murder. Kate Millett's *The Basement*, like James Baldwin's *Evidence of Things Not Seen*, forms part of a larger assault upon the constructive (and destructive) power of the white, capitalist and — as she sees it — *patriarchal* republic.

Millett's critique forms part of a relatively small feminist scholarship dealing with women who kill. Feminist scholarship on murder tends to be divided into two not necessarily distinct branches: those primarily interested in women who kill and those concerned with deadly violence against women.[5] Representing the latter group, Jill Radford opines (perhaps a little mournfully) that the patriarchal phenomenon of "woman killing" has not received the attention it deserves as scholars have rushed to explore the statistically and socially aberrant woman who kills.[6] And yet it would be perilous to assume that the two branches of scholarship are really that distinct. Groundbreaking feminist interrogations of biologism and theories of social conformity (which have structured the criminological, juridical, and penal response to women offenders *and* victims) are essential to both projects, despite the different objects of their enquiry. Those who study women who kill are caught in an uncomfortable double bind, needing to establish the agency of their subject but also qualifying that subjectivity in reference to the reality effects of a discourse within which there is scant choice between the monster and the dupe. Those who study women as victims are more readily able to eschew that difficulty, coming hard up against another in its place: that of the agency of the *victim*. Kate Millett's work on the torture-slaying of Sylvia Likens partakes of both these problematics, and although it was written too early to have the benefit of recent theorizations of what might be called "victim agency,"[7] Millett enters into a curious and complex engagement with killers and killed alike.

Thirteen years after the original publication of her work on the killing of Sylvia Likens by her "primary caregiver" and a group of neighborhood children, Kate Millett explained that *"The Basement* happened to me."[8] Writing this, she was in part simply trying to show the degree to which the case affected her. After all, she had literally been obsessed with what happened to that sixteen-year-old over a couple of months in Indianapolis, during the autumn of 1965. (Sylvia Likens and her sister Jenny had been left in the care of Gertrude Baniewski, a divorced mother of seven, by their parents, who were traveling "carnies." The already poor household found it difficult integrating the two new dependents, and the stress apparently led to Baniewski abusing Sylvia, either herself or vicariously through one of the children she had instructed to aid in "disciplining" Sylvia. Over a period of months the abuse escalated to the point where Sylvia was locked in the cellar and was prevented from eating, drinking, or using the toilet. Gertrude and/or the children would torture her with beatings, burnings, and scalding baths. Sylvia eventually died from an accumulation of wounds, and her death came to light at a point when Baniewski was still dithering through a plan to pass off the girl's death as accidental.) It took Millett nine years to reduce the enormity of her horror to a single text. And yet the author performed a deft inversion of chronology and meaning in that short sentence: she named the crime by *her* book title. The scene of murder haunting her those ten years did not become *The Basement* until she wrote it.

A Structural Critique of Patriarchal Violence

The Basement is a complex and perhaps contradictory text. It can be read as a stringently ethical narrative and a reauthoring of the murder, a project that has, therefore, something in common with the texts examined in Chapter Three above. Through the text, Millett alternately occupies the characters — the subject positions — of murderer, accomplice, victim, and the many implicated witnesses to the girl's death. Reviewers have characterized Millett's flow-of-consciousness style as an attempt to "re-create" the crime, calling it evidence of the "psychojournalistic" nature of the text. How like Curtis Bok's prose chapters in *Star Wormwood* is Millett's occupation of the burned, starved, beaten subject that is Sylvia Likens, or her possession by the tired, tranquilized, bored figure of the murderer, Gertrude Baniewski, who made the girl her sport and her redemption? The fictionalizing process is similar, but the political projects underlying the fiction differ signally.

"Life suggests an interest in certain stories," Millett wrote, a quarter century after she had first been "ambushed" by the "chief story" she would ever tell.[9] It is her definition of that "chief story" which marks both the similarities to and the differences between her text and that of the liberal jurist Bok. Within this "chief story" is a compelling pattern, the single fable that explained all, the "shadow at the back of the cave" — the fountainhead of human violence. Within it also, in the very nature of *telling the story*, is catharsis, the place in which "the heart changes . . . utterly." This belief in the project of tragedy and pathetic resolution is the hallmark of a humanism even more ambitious than that which animated Curtis Bok to write his treatise condemning capital punishment. Millett has a belief in the political integrity of her fiction that Bok never had. While this is not to say that Bok was less affronted by "injustice" than Millett, his criticisms were contingent and their object superstructural, rather than structural. Millett's political analysis is indeed structural, even fundamental. The author's faith in her fiction does not reside merely in a hope that it will lay bare the mysteries of the "facts" of the case and provide exclusive entry to the minds of the murderer and the victim. Her faith and her A/authority reside instead within the ideological context of the fiction. That politics of gender cannot be argued, but must be *told* — told as the story of what our lives must necessarily become. (*Our lives:* the author, the victim, the murderer, and the reader who is ranged beside these three. To enter into the text is to be vulnerable, to be *feminine*):

This is not didacticism or the logical highway of a doctoral thesis . . . this is closer to the mysteries, the tragic and symbolic, something finally inexplicable, something endured cathartically. . . . Savagery ongoing but exposed here, clarified, revealed so that it can no longer be lied about or ignored or dissembled or passed off as anything else, as something wicked or just twisted and senseless, a meaningless random event, something local or explicable through abnormal psychology or subject to various interpretations.[10]

Millett's text does inherit something from the sociological tales of murder told by Wertham and Bok, those tales that made the topology of the murderer an interpretive act requiring the "local knowledge" of an anthropologizing expert. The amateur enthusiasm of Bok for forensic psychiatry or the considerable psychotherapeutic expertise of Fredric Wertham overlaid a metaphorical, mythical and, in many ways, historicizing frame on tales of murder that were historically and culturally located. Millett's ethical project refuses the certainty of a disciplinary frame, but it does rely upon a foundation that is essentialist, archetypal, even metahistorical:

This is the chill of an evil essentially collective, social, cultural, even political. It is the site of an old crime, old as the first stone, old as rape and beatings: it is not just murder, it is ritual killing.[11]

Human violence "overwhelmingly understood" is the product of a transhistorical and transsituational encoding of sexual shame, a sexual shame that is an integral mechanism of patriarchy. To retell the story of Sylvia Likens's acceptance of that shame, and her death because of that acceptance, is to expose the archetypical pattern of violence in the patriarchal world. Millett's fiction arises, if you like, not from artifice or style, but from unmediated access to genetic memory. In this way, the author claims a quite novel authority in the tale of murder. A culturally encoded sexual shame makes the author of the text—like both Sylvia Likens and Gertrude Baniewski (whose voices she adopts)—subjects of that same heritage of shame, speakers of a common language. The retelling of the crime is, in some radical way, as forceful an act as the crime itself. The fiction, like the murder, is a "historical event":

The need for liberation from sexual guilt and enslavement implicit in this historical event—for it is that too, not only a fictive puzzle or equation but an actual event more resonant and terrible than anything merely imagined—could transform us all, could burn away millennia [sic] of savagery.[12]

Millett does not, therefore, "merely imagine" the set of circumstances that led to sixteen-year-old Sylvia being branded across her abdomen with the words "I am a prostitute and proud of it." Millett lives and writes the shame that animated those scarring hands, as well as the shame that eventually stopped Sylvia's own will to struggle: "Because I was Sylvia Likens. She was me. She was sixteen. I had been. She was . . . what 'happens' to girls. . . . We all have a story like this and I had found mine."[13]

"What 'Happens' to Girls"

In a more recent work this line of identification is similarly played out, both in the context of the way in which "life suggests an interest in certain stories" and in the elision of the writer and the killed. Ann Imbrie's homage to her dead childhood friend, Lee Snavely, murdered — one among a number of other young women — by a serial killer whose area of predation was the Midwest, is more a reconstruction of the dead girl than an enquiry into either "what happened" or the mind of the killer. The work is also, consummately, a story about similarity, about those slight changes in the path of a life, or the negligible differences between people, that can result in radically different fates. Those two adolescent girls in Ohio went different ways, their trajectory governed, it would seem, by the varying pressures, direction, and failings of family, school, and relationships:

This is what I'm doing now, imagining history from the distortions of a present floor plan, seeing my way into the lives of women, like me and not like me, all of them one way or another on their own, Lee and the others who followed different paths to the same terrifying end.[14]

"Who murdered her was never the mystery," Imbrie writes. The story of the killer, even in Baldwin and Millett, for whom one of their subjects is putative, the other a collaborator, is essential to the text, a part of its wisdom. Yet Gary Taylor, who crosses through Imbrie's text — a man quintessentially on the move, possessor of successive real-estate investments (a house lived in, then discarded) — is never the text's focus, for all of its power to police him, to keep an eye on him. The last sentence in the book is resolute, not at all mysterious: "I have petitioned the state of Washington for the right to be informed of any changes in his status." Which means, "Where is he? When, and under what circumstances, will he get out?" While asking that the author's interest in his case be recognized, Imbrie's "interest," like that of those others who survived his depredations, is a right earned by suffering. She claims an interest in Lee's place, for Lee and yet for herself. She also denies the killer his mystery and, in the act of unraveling Lee Snavely's fate, would seem to be demystifying the life he took. And yet, so much of Imbrie's text is about the mysterious nature of ordinary lives, of the very typicality that sometimes decrees "extraordinary" violence. Like Millett, Imbrie's textual authority is based upon what she shares and shares with the murdered girl: daughter, adolescent girl, rebel. The difference between victim and survivor is slight and, it would seem, circumstantial. Ann Imbrie, like Kate Millett, testifies to a world that she — coincidentally — survived. But, unlike Millett, Imbrie's interest is intimate, *was* actual.

Kate Millett wrote that her years of meditation before actually writing the book were a period through which she "grew strong enough to absorb the meaning which this young girl's death" had for her. Crucially, those years of gestation spanned the golden age of the women's liberation movement, with all its consciousness-raising about sexual violence, its analyses of the systemic nature of patriarchy, and its strange blend of "meat and potatoes" activism with feminist utopianism. Read in that historical context, the story of Sylvia Likens's murder could not help but take on a "symbolic character, a metaphoric power" for Kate Millett. And that story, when Millett finally came to possess it, was told in order "to do things, to save lives." What could be a clearer expression of the intellectual conditions for production of this text than that terribly brave and naive statement? Millett is herself aware of that naivete as she considers the reception of *The Basement* when first it was published. Sylvia's story was one thing, but *The Basement* is also the story of Gertrude Baniewski, whose voice is heard most frequently in the text; whose voice, in fact, leads the whole chorus. "Gertrude was a paradox, a contradiction." Gertrude's story, that of a woman's collaboration with patriarchal violence, was "bad news around the Feminist campfire" back then. And yet, Sylvia could not be told without Gertrude; that is to say, they arise from the same place. Indeed, their voices, taken up by Millett, seem to come to her from a collective memory of pain, of shame. Unlike the "situated" remembering of Baldwin, whose "soul" was "witness" to those voices coming from the cultural and historical particularity of "being Black" in the United States, Millett's "voices" come from a less well defined source. The presentist concerns of both writers must differ where Millett's activism and her authority both rest upon an assumption of an essential knowledge imparted by the heritage of feminine shame. Millett's fear of entering into the mind of Gertrude Baniewski dissipated at the moment she "could dare to realize" that she "already knew all about her. So do we all; the problem is simply admitting it."[15] When we are all so implicated in the workings of patriarchal violence, such access to the "difference" of Gertrude Baniewski decreases it. The place has changed; the time is past; the child is dead — and yet Millett, the author, walks in the bloody skin of their history.

For Millett a common heritage of sexual shame gives the author access to the minds of both the murdered girl and her abuser, an access less mediated than refined by her own particular shame. How much was that heritage of shame the exclusive territory of women and girls, whose vulnerability is its object? Coy Hubbard, Rickie Hobbs, and even Gertrude's own son, John (all of whom participated in the day-to-day torture and victimization of Sylvia Likens), could themselves be shamed, but it was their fear of this possibility that enabled them, so quickly, to take up that shame as their *weapon*. The boys' ability to escape the role of victim is never in doubt in the way that it was, say, for Sylvia's little sister, Jenny. Jenny was often "around" when Sylvia got thrashed with the paddle, or burned with cigarette ends, or was flipped by Coy (who was learning judo); she was also present at the final, and ultimately fatal, group attack on Sylvia.[16] Jenny "helped" in these scenes because her very life depended upon her complicity. She was quite likely to become an alternate or an alternative target should she not cooperate or should she interfere with what was being dished out, so remorselessly, to her sister. She was vulnerable because she, too, was just another foster child in an already overcrowded household.[17] But she was also a girl: archetypically, therefore, a *possible* victim. Millett makes it clear that even Paula Baniewski — who was her mother's "lieutenant" and one of Sylvia's principal abusers — was never entirely free of the threat that she, too, might somehow bear the physical brunt of that sexual shame.

In Millett's re-creation of the torture scene, Paula is impelled to hate by her envy. She was "already heavy with child, with the torpor of her own weight," and "the natural self-dislike of her obesity forced her to look at and compare herself with the slender, the perfect, the beautiful . . . an ideal desired with all the anger hoarded against the unobtainable, the futile, the tantalizing, hung within reach upon another." Paula's jealousy is part and parcel of the shame of being female. Rickie, John, and Coy could never feel that particular fragility, and their feeling for Sylvia (in Millett's reconstruction) is not hatred but *derision*. That distinction suggests the qualitative difference of their relationship from the shame Sylvia embodies: "[H]ow can we imagine a boy in analogous circumstances, based as they are upon a crippling shame dependent upon specific sexual guilt by cultural definition female; modesty and virginity, the question of being a slut or a whore being questions that cannot be raised about him."[18] It can be seen, then, that "the shadow on the cave wall," the "chief story," is largely a portent for women. The shared heritage of shame that founds Millett's narrative authority in this tale of murder allows Millett to take up the position of the murderer in a curiously *surrogate* way, for Gertrude is a "Kapo," a part of the class of victim she, too, has "chosen" to exploit. Gertrude's abuse of Sylvia Likens is the expression of a violence she does not *own*, but merely *leases*.

Elisions

And here it becomes necessary to return to James Baldwin, who shared the vulnerability of being black (and, once, being a boy) with those about whom his elegiac essay *The Evidence of Things Not Seen* was written. Millett writes that "to be Feminine is to die" but does not then suggest the terms by which her own survival was secured. Later, we find out: a university education, a sexual and intellectual subculture to support her, a political movement in second-wave feminism. She remarks upon her own survival only in relation to those others who did not "make it through." Baldwin, however, can find layer upon layer of armor, or the good luck of circumstance and fate, that protected him. After all, "for the State, a nigger is a nigger is a nigger, sometimes Mr. or Mrs. or Dr. Nigger" but a nigger nonetheless. He was not a Southerner, had financial means and an "honorable" vocation but, for all that, was not his own survival dictated by its own exacting toll — virtual exile? *Complicity* is a complicated concept in Baldwin's treatise in a way that it is not in Millett's "theatre," despite his subsuming of the problem of gender (and the status of black womanhood) under the embattled sign of black "manhood." Where Millett finds *collaboration*, ultimately Baldwin finds *implication*. There can be no corollary in Millett's analysis to Baldwin's uncomfortable realization that

underlying the tremendous unwillingness to believe that a Black person could be murdering Black children was the specifically Southern knowledge and experience of how much Black blood is in white veins — and how much White blood is in Black veins.[19]

While the "concept of color," as a principle of differentiation, does beget racial terror, it is *not* a fact of nature but a ruse of power. The distance between Baldwin's analysis of collaboration, implication, and community and Millett's exploration of Gertrude, the "Kapo," and the collaborating victims Jenny and Sylvia Likens is defined by the impermeability of sexual difference in the latter. In patriarchy there can be no corollary to the "Black blood in White veins and White blood in Black veins." And yet, ironically, it is Kate Millett who survives the decree of patriarchy relatively unscathed, her meditation on "the danger of maybe" notwithstanding.[20] Baldwin, however, is conscious that he survived and painfully aware that others did not:

To realize that one is, oneself, and from the moment of one's birth, both subject and object of the human cowardice — for that is what it is . . . of racial terror, demands a ruthless cunning, an impenetrable style, and an ability to carry death, like a bluebird, on the shoulder.[21]

Baldwin's concept of implication is direct, personal, and entirely thoroughgoing. In following through Millett's critique of collaboration I shall show that the grounds of her analysis are both too wide (the uncrossable divide of sexual difference) and too narrow (the unscrutinized race of the principals).

Collaborating Agent/Victim Subject

This issue of complicity for Millett is both a compelling force in the narrative and the rock upon which *empathy* — as the source of authority in the tale — founders. Sylvia fails to save herself and is complicit in her own slow murder. Jenny fails to save her sister. Gertrude fails to see through the shame patriarchy obliges she assume, a shame she must also visit so viciously upon others. But these "failures" speak of complicity with a violence that is "other," that is an "acting out." Millett struggles with the subjectivity of the murdered girl, the one who cooperates herself to death, and finds herself turning more easily to the position of any or all of the abusers:

Sylvia, victim and center of the whole legend—how you escape me, grow shadowy. How I lose touch with you, becoming the others, becoming as I must, Gertrude, becoming Coy, becoming Paula and Rickie.[22]

But is not Millett's occupation of Coy or John or Rickie—given the terms by which her a/Authority is inscribed—a kind of imposture? Although the boys act out a violent script, it is not completely of their own composition. They are children, after all. And the inhabitants of that Indianapolis household are living below the poverty line on an intermittent income derived from the ironing Gertrude takes in, a pittance received from her ex-husband, and the often late support checks from the Likens. These factors combine in subtle ways to make the abusers themselves fragile, though not absolved of responsibility:

[H]ere were people so naive they enacted the beliefs of the larger society, enacted them literally, and by going so "overboard" exposed the brutality of that basis set of assumptions.[23]

The assumption being that woman is guilty of her sex, a guilt before which the adolescent girl stands quite undefended. And is shamed. Gertrude Baniewski argued in court that she was trying to "discipline" Sylvia, who "would not mind [her] at all."[24] The connection between the abuser and the abused is an intimate one. Gertrude is "disciplining" Sylvia, teaching her the meaning of her sex. The point of comparison between Sylvia and Gertrude—between the abuser and the abused—is their relationship to a shared, intrinsic sexual shame. For Millett, Gertrude Baniewski, like her son and Coy and Rickie, assumes a privileged position vis-à-vis the shameful secret that is Sylvia. The power that enables Gertrude to rewrite a violent sexual script—in which and to which she is herself potentially subject[25]—is the power of a complex set of patriarchal institutions and social practices. "Straightening out" Sylvia is both a mission in itself and a lesson for the other children about their own relation to shame:

[T]he boys gotta learn by example. . . . Not just my Johnny but the others that are given me to instruct. To know the real deep seriousness. Because that's what it is finally. Sylvia just plain refuses to be serious about what life is, the hardness, or the mysteries, the will of God, the burdens. Her duty before her is being a woman.[26]

The church that preaches against sin and for the values of family combines with the secular power of the state (in the form of the social worker, that ever-present guardian of the poor) to give Gertrude, as figurative "mother" and head of the household, the authority to "instruct." "Correction" is such an important mission (one undertaken alone by an adult among children) that it takes on a dangerous yet seemingly sacred power:

One does not say: "I will torture the child to death." Torture was surely not a word Gertrude permitted herself. . . . She was "correcting" the child, "disciplining," using a firm hand. All terms that she must have begun with and then lost sight of later.[27]

The concept of the "wayward child" is only intelligible in reference to those moral institutions that dictate filial and community norms, that define belonging. The murder of Sylvia Likens arises, therefore, not from pathology — which is defined as aberrance — but from an overdetermined norm.[28] Thus, even throughout the trial Gertrude was insistent that Sylvia needed correction, and that her actions in administering that correction were justified. Gertrude argued, by inference, that the murder was the result of the children's interference and co-option of her *legitimate* business of correction.[29] In this way, Gertrude appeared merely to have failed to *save* Sylvia, rather than to have destroyed her. The children made an anarchic parody of the adult moral mission.

Gertrude's power to reprove Sylvia was underwritten by those important cultural institutions that intersect with and structure the family. Gertrude's evangelical church, for instance, gave its blessing to the "firm hand." Disciplining Sylvia, for Millett's Gertrude, was "the Lord's work and sacred."[30] Millett, constructing Gertrude's impassioned monologue on her duty to correct Sylvia as an example to the other children, refers to the trial evidence that both Gertrude's pastor and the local welfare authorities took her word as the caregiver of that loosely bonded and sprawling family and just left her to it. On one of his ministering visits, the Reverend Roy Julian sat on the couch, listening sympathetically to Gertrude's tale of woe about the uncontrollable child, while Sylvia — the whole time — was locked in the basement.[31] Gertrude's authority excelled that even of Sylvia's older sister, who, when she came to check on Sylvia and Jenny, was turned away at the door by Gertrude with the words, "I've got permission not to let you see her."[32] This is a curiously vague phrase.

Whose permission does Gertrude have? Of course, one assumes she means Lester, Sylvia's and Jenny's father: the absent grant-all of paternal authority. But behind the phrase, in its very openness, is a matrix of social institutions that guard the privacy and the integrity of the "family" in all its approved incarnations. Gertrude is a woman, the natural mother of her seven children, and the recipient of various welfare, alimony, and child-support checks. She is, therefore, the logical titular head of this family. Even the welfare agencies that supposedly police the integrity of the "family" interfere only under duress, and in very particular circumstances. Gertrude was able to fob off the visiting public-health nurse who wanted to see the children, using the excuse that she could not see Sylvia because she was, as Millett characterized it, "unmanageable, loose" and "hadn't been there for days."[33] The nurse had come to investigate an anonymous report that the Baniewski household harbored a child with "running sores." The interference of the welfare authorities was prompted not by a concern for the children per se, but by a fear of ill health and all its attendant antisocial ramifications. The neighbors who endured Sylvia's screams of pain for weeks before her death also declined to intervene, not willing to ascribe any desperate meaning to that clamor. Another mother's method of chastising her children was not, after all, their business. The nearest neighbors, the Vermillions, nearly rang the police on the last night of Sylvia's life, but not because of her screaming. She had been scraping a shovel on the cellar floor in a last-ditch attempt to attract attention. The Vermillions were ready to call the police only because the noise was keeping them awake; it stopped before they could do so.[34] There is no altruism here. From the church, to the public-health authorities, to the neighbors, the interest or lack of interest shown in the doings of the Baniewski household is structured by a conception of the inviolability of family, however flawed may be its *particular* examples. And yet Millett neglects to situate the family here in one signal way. I cannot help but wonder whether the leeway extended Gertrude Baniewski by her church and the health and welfare authorities would have been so great if she and her charges had not been *white*. Recent scholarship has indicated the much greater vulnerability of African American women and Latinas and the penetrability, more generally, of the poor, nonwhite family (particularly the female-headed sole-parent unit) before the law, welfare, and the health authorities.[35]

In Millett's analysis there is a distinct continuity between Sylvia's failure to save herself, Jenny's collaboration in her sister's torture, and the indifference of outsiders to the actual functioning of the Baniewski household. Sylvia is quickly convinced that she must have *done something* to warrant her continued abuse. Jenny is sure, too, that Sylvia must have transgressed in some way, even if she cannot see how; she also knows she is herself close to the line of that undefinable "bad." And the church, welfare authorities, and neighbors tend to assume in their different ways — knowing children, knowing girls, knowing "poor white trash" — that the child must have done *something wrong.*

As a product of second-wave feminism, it is not surprising that *The Basement* locates the backbone of patriarchal power in the family. A more novel facet of Millett's work is her attention to the elements of sadomasochism she perceived in the torture-slaying. Her forays into the subjectivity of Gertrude Baniewski, the "Kapo," follows a dominant strain in feminist analyses of the murderous violence of women. Gertrude's violence is the product of internalized misogynistic hatred and stems from her own history of being abused. She passes on to her weaker, more vulnerable wards the violence originally dished out to herself. Millett's portrait of the female collaborator, however carefully elaborated, is the cultural and institutional context to Baniewski's "family" and is, in many ways, archetypal. Gertrude, like Wertham's "Mary," could be described as a "modern Medea": "a woman who in the desperate process of asserting her womanhood in a hostile world seems to negate that very womanhood."[36] While the social situation is limned critically here, the concept of "womanhood" is, contradictorily, taken for granted. In Millett's analysis, Gertrude's disciplining of Sylvia signals the seriousness with which she takes her role as mother and, therefore, her identity as woman. Gertrude's need to instill in Sylvia a sense of shame indicates her desire not just to make "a woman" out of the girl, but to prove that she, herself, is a woman who knows her place. The heritage of sexual shame reconstructed and reinscribed through Gertrude's abuse of Sylvia may have its *context* in the particular constructive powers of class and family in contemporary American culture, but its *origins* are ancient.

Millett's portrait of the female collaborator is a vivid one. How like or unlike various other stereotypical or archetypal figures of female murderousness was Gertrude Baniewski? Her autonomy in the household — an adult among children — makes her a distinctive case. She was a woman who killed a child, a fact that need not be statistically extraordinary. That fact does, however, signal the likely reading of her act as *reprehensible*, given pervasive cultural beliefs about the nurturing role of women. The position of Gertrude Baniewski is a peculiar one: located somewhere between stereotypical vulnerability — i.e., a woman who takes out the violence leveled against her on others — and fully conscious and independent agency, whose violence stems from obscure sources. If it is held to be untenable (as it was by the trial jury) that Gertrude did not know what was going on in the house, then it is certain she provided the impetus for the systematic torture of Sylvia Likens. It is this guilt, and the very degree of Gertrude's murderous agency, that is the central focus of the explanatory strategies of Millett's fiction. (The "problem" of Myra Hindley for feminist analysis is instructive here. Ian Brady has conventionally been portrayed as the more evil and instrumental figure in their partnership, Hindley's slavishness to his whims being composed of a combination of naivete, sexual obsession, and fear. Hindley, as collaborator, is at least partly absolved. That scenario has largely been accepted by feminists, who rightly reject the other predominant explanatory strategy, which thoroughly demonizes Hindley as a figure of the Monstrous Feminine. The problem with cleaving to the former strategy is that a conceptualization of Hindley as collaborator — and, therefore, victim as well as abuser — denies her the fundamental agency that feminism, as a system of revisionist thought, seeks to bestow upon the subject in history.)[37]

Sylvia does not become the speaking subject in the fiction until it is two-thirds complete. She is the blockage around which the flow of narrative eddies. And the source of that flow is the murderer herself, Gertrude Baniewski. The writer's immersion in her subjectivity is testimony to the degree to which Gertrude's position as collaborator is supposedly available to every woman under the hegemonic decree of patriarchy: "Gertrude's screaming still echoing in my mind, but she is easier to know, to hear again in every fight one ever had. One's own bullying yell not that hard to summon. But you are harder, Sylvia, the figure bowed before Gertrude is harder to be."[38]

It would seem to be easier for Millett to inhabit the position of the abuser than that of the victim. Yet Millett writes that one can "get far with Gertrude but not the whole way. Finally it baffles." This point of bafflement is *not* reached in the narrative reconstruction of the crime, so much of which issues from the murderer's internal monologues. In analytic terms, that bafflement — the dropping-off point of meaning in the murder — is ideological. To "go the whole way" with Gertrude would be to assume the position of an agent of patriarchy, the murderer, rather than the subject of patriarchy, who is both collaborator and victim. Thus, although Millett narrates the scene of torture to its ugly completion (from the murderer's standpoint), the analysis that accompanies the narration must outstrip and abandon Gertrude. Gertrude becomes merely the figure of the collaborator. This reinscription of the mystery of murder occurs in Millett's description of the insidious cultural encodings of patriarchy that make of Gertrude a murderer: "Gertrude acted out of faith, convictions, beliefs, convoluted notions, ideological rather than material, forces in the mind, inscrutable, mysterious." Sylvia's murder comprises an aggregate of conditions only secondarily material: poverty, unemployment, depression, illness, all of which are part and parcel of Gertrude's life. That materiality is merely an *effect* of those fundamental "ideological forces" about which Millett writes above. The shame that defines being feminine is acted out in specific cultural and institutional settings but is, in itself, somehow archetypal. Even here the ghosts of mythical archetypes appear: Medea and, explicitly, Herostratus: "And Gertrude [because she is the author of this monstrosity] is like the man of ambition who burned the Temple of Ephesus in order to become immortal?"[39] The violent order of the world that Millett critiques ranges out from the Baniewski household, through Africa, where clitorodectomy is still practiced, back through the Holocaust, even into the imaginary Africa of Kurtz's atrocities in Joseph Conrad's *Heart of Darkness*. To range so widely in search of "the nature of pain, of cruelty" is to lose sight of the overcrowded household on a New York street without appearing to have turned away at all. Millett looks *through* the autopsy portrait of Sylvia's battered face, her lips chewed half away, to find not Sylvia's story, but "the fountainhead of human violence" itself.

The Basement plots the murder of Sylvia Likens as sadomasochistic ritual, a ritual undertaken in the normality of the domestic situation. Its props are rope, the paddle, a lit cigarette; even more banal objects such as stacks of ironing, a blaring TV, the bath, the litter of pop bottles in the cellar.[40] It is in the wake of the exposition of Gertrude's sadism that Sylvia's voice finally enters the fiction. The scene is one of the transition from the simple, if frightening, domestic situation of punishing a child to the much more intense disciplinary scene where one obliges, by the act of dominance, another to submit:

Don't look at me that way girl. Don't you dare stare me down with them strong looks. Fold your eyes down child or you'll feel my hand mighty fast. Don't move I told you. Stand there perfectly still and answer me. First I want you to lower your eyes and lower 'em good. Right down at your shoes. I want 'em pointed right on the floor. An inch in front of the toe of your shoe. One inch exactly.

At this cue, the "voice" of Sylvia startles the reader. She arrives as the innocent, incredulous, not knowing how to take this punishment seriously: "Gertrude being silly. One inch exactly. What an idiot."[41] Sylvia's willingness to play along, to disarm, her hope that if she just "cuts up a little . . . they'll break down and smile" is, for Millett, both definingly adolescent and archetypically Feminine. Submission (outside the realm of sexual play) is, after all, a defense — even if it is a failed one:

To cooperate, to assuage, to hold out the hands to be tied. To beg quietly. Not to scream because it will make him strike you. To mimic every gesture of submission even as in animals, the dog rolling on its back. Even as in women. To be "feminine."[42]

"To be Feminine . . . is to die." Even after Sylvia very quickly learns that the discipline session is serious, she demurs to what is, in her own understanding, undeserved punishment. She is a girl, and a "child"; her consent to being shamed or beaten is somehow tacit. Millett's analysis of the intimate contract of abuser and abused, of dominance and submission, derives from a set of ideas that would later give rise to such concepts as the "battered women's syndrome" and "learned helplessness." The interests of captor and captive, abuser and abused, supposedly coincide when the culture of captivity — even of extermination — is total. Millett builds on a kind of Arendtian analysis of passivity based on the experience of concentration camp survivors, a vision of sadomasochism totalized:[43]

And why shouldn't the victim be seized with the same enthusiasm, the same madness or at least the same motivations as those of the captors? . . . [T]he victims of *ideological crime* have a most difficult time keeping their minds free, even if their minds were so to begin with, were formed and set and resolute.[44]

Millett adds a kind of intellectual asperative to the phrase "ideological crime." It is a phrase that does not recur in the work, but its presence is felt everywhere. "Ideological crime," in the context of her analysis, describes a continuum of violence, institutional and individual: kidnapping, rape, torture-murder, the genocide of the Nazis. And, implicitly, the death of Sylvia Likens: an act which must have required — in that it was drawn out over months — some of the victim's tired compliance.[45] Potentially, Millett's use of the concept of "ideological crime" should militate against the otherwise essentializing direction of the work, for it is a historicizing term. "Ideological crime" implies an analytic remedy to the "othering" principles of conventional, positivist analyses of crime. Millett's ideological analysis *is* about the particular circumstances — social, institutional, and domestic — that led to the death of Sylvia Likens. Yet the wider "politics" of her tale of murder posits an archetypal violence that gives content to those modern forms of cruelty. Kidnapping, rape, murder, and genocide are all crimes achieved through the "indoctrination of terrible consequences" that constructs a victim or captive long before either the whip hand is poised to strike or the cell door is closed. The mechanism of that indoctrination is structural, and the "ideological crime" stems from an operation of hierarchy that might be called "patriarchy" or, better still, "hegemonic masculinism." But why should these crimes be distinguished so rigorously? What crime could not be called ideological? The issue of Sylvia Likens's complicity, like that of the status of Gertrude as "Kapo," is central to Millett's definition of the "ideological crime." The murderer and the victim are bonded by the very instrument of the latter's torture: not the paddle or the lit cigarette, but *femininity* itself. Both move in the same terrible gravity — the weight of sexual shame that is their heritage and their bequest.

Millett's Sylvia, meditating on the horror that has overtaken her, gestures toward the mechanism of her own implication: "*When a woman does it to you it's different.* . . . That's how Gertrude's got me so I don't know what to do."[46] Sylvia is disarmed before Gertrude not just because she too is a woman, and therefore expected somehow to be "safe," but because she is also mother to the girl. The different response of each to the burden of sexual shame is dictated by their position relative to the powerful institutions of patriarchy mentioned above. Millett's figuring of Gertrude Baniewski as murderer is a metaphorical device aimed at exposing the essential violence of the institution of family. Moreover, the bond between Gertrude and Sylvia that underlies and subverts their polarity as murderer and victim in the tale of murder exemplifies the self-defeating agency of women under patriarchy. Parent and child, mother and daughter, pastor and parish, social worker and beneficiary — each of these pairings is hierarchical, an inequivalency of power pivoting on a mistaken trust in an identity of interest.

Millett is fascinated with the death of Sylvia Likens, with the lesson of her vulnerability:

You have been with me . . . an incubus, a nightmare, my own nightmare, the nightmare of adolescence, of growing up a female child, of becoming a woman in a world set against us, a world we have lost and where we are everywhere reminded of our defeat.[47]

"A world we have lost." This rueful phrase shows the extent to which Millett's critique is about essence and archetype as well as a historically situated "oppression" of women. It is the bond of "femininity" that fascinates Millett — her own similarity to the murdered subject. Millett feels, perhaps, that she herself has narrowly missed becoming a terrible and unforgettable story. Yet that similarity is itself historically situated; it is not a more generally realized "femininity" to which Millett here alludes. The slippage between the author of the tale of murder and the vanished subject is an integral mechanism of authority in the narrative. Millett writes *to* Sylvia ("What you endured . . . emblematic") and *as* her.[48] What authority is it that the author assumes in order to speak to and as the victim and, contradictorily, about her absence? It is simultaneously essential and historically contingent: the fate of "being feminine" and the coincidence of place, time, and culture. "Because I was Sylvia Likens. She was me. She was sixteen. I had been."[49]

It is this positioning of the author and its inscription of authority in the tale of murder that makes *The Basement* distinctive. Yet Millett has not written as thoroughgoing a counternarrative of murder as has James

Baldwin in *The Evidence of Things Not Seen*. The political and ideological terms of Millett's fiction — that identity of interest binding the author to the text, just as surely as it does the murderer to the victim — cannot quite mask the depth of the author's fascination with the *disappearance* of her subject and with the relics not of a life lived, but of a drawn-out death: "Finally, it is not even faces one studies, but artifacts. The pictures of *things*. Of place and milieu and object."[50] Throughout the text Millett is struck by wonder at the material traces of the story of Sylvia's death. In that wonder is held the whole mystery of murder, of the "truth" always escaping — long gone, and irremediably so, like warmth from a corpse.

Murder and the Photograph as Artifact

In one short passage Millett spans the full spectrum of that wonder as she moves from a description of the photographs of the house in which the murder took place to her reminiscences about how the house *actually* looked:

I have seen both the house itself and its photograph; they are different. The house today has been repainted and has lost the terrible power it had in the photograph, austere in its peeling paint, its thirsty wood, that almost mythic sorrow it gave off — a power that pictures can convey into things, a force much grander at times than their own actual presence.[51]

The curiosity that makes the author visit 3850 New York Street ten years after the murder occurred is in itself hardly surprising: researchers become fascinated by even the most mundane subjects. What is startling about this passage is its unconscious enactment of the basic mechanism of authority in Millett's fiction: "a power that pictures can convey into things, a force much grander at times than their own actual presence." "Presence" in the tale of murder — with its vanished victim and its often inscrutable murderer — is always reconstructed; it relies upon the reading of traces, of "evidence" that is fragmentary, ambiguous, or contradictory. Everything about the truth of the event — its immediacy — is lost. The victim cannot testify to her own murder, and the recollection of events by witness and murderer is often suspect. The event of murder, as narrative, is supposition. It is something that must always be imagined, and that imagining is necessarily a narrative exercise. In such a narrative space, designed to recapture a moment that is lost as it occurs, even the ensuing parade of "evidence" comes to seem like an array of ciphers: signs toward a displaced truth. The photographs of the murderer on the courthouse steps; the photograph of the victim lifted from the high school yearbook; the coroner's close-up of her demolished face; exterior views of the house from the books of evidence — faces become *things*, and *things* take on a spectral identity. The peeling outer walls of 3850 New York Street and the chewed-off lips of Sylvia Likens are ultimately the same. *Relics.*

Ann Imbrie, trying to pick up the trail of her childhood friend, already then more than ten years dead, also looked to the photograph as evidence and narrative:

I've come to much of my story, what I can't know or didn't observe myself, through photographs, which I have learned to read, imaginatively, like a text. A photograph is the next best thing to being there, and the next best thing to a photograph is a good description of one.[52]

Imbrie's faith in the photograph is such that she will accept its power to tell, even if that power is only referred. What is the difference, then, between saying "I saw . . ." and describing the face once seen, and saying "There is this photograph . . ."? It would seem that the photograph has greater *presence*. Photography is the perfect medium to convey loss and mortality. The "permanence" of the medium and the idiosyncratic nature of the photographic gaze both counterpoint the fragility of the moment claimed by the photograph. Millett looks into the photographs from the books of evidence and finds in the household detritus pictured there the reality and materiality of a time long passed. And yet that "presence" is, ironically, the presence of portent. As Roland Barthes has noted, photographs testify to what was, but it is their very timelessness that makes them ominous:

[B]y attesting that the object has been real, the photograph surreptitiously induces belief that it is alive, because of that delusion which makes us attribute to Reality an absolutely superior, somehow eternal value; but by shifting this reality to the past ("this-has-been"), the photograph suggests that it is already dead.[53]

The photograph, as illusion, is perhaps *the* perfect corollary for the function of the murder narrative, and is also, therefore, its perfect accompaniment.[54] The photograph provides for the longevity of the mystery of murder, rather than its dissolution. Millett's fascination with the moment preserved in the books of evidence reflects the urgency of the story to the author — not its timelessness as such, but its immanence.

Describing the photograph of the basement in which Sylvia was kept prisoner for so long, Millett writes:

[E]ven the ordinarily inoffensive presence of a few probably empty paint cans and an overturned plastic clothes basket, even these take on the taint of what has occurred here, an aura permanent now and to remain forever after the event or any of its participants, imbued now indelibly over the indifferent paper of police and news documents.[55]

The photographic evidence of the murder, then, has a special quality. It is not "indifferent." For Millett the "stark black and white photographs of each room" were her "touchstone and . . . dramatic tableau."[56] The photographic relics invite interpretation and gain meaning through narrative. They formed the ineluctable "reality" that enabled, even demanded, the construction of the fiction. The photographs are clearly the key to Millett's "total immersion" in the murder. It is the photographs, rather than the transcript, that determine her engagement with the subject, her taking on of their voices.

Ironically, Millett's belief in the power of the photographs, in the freight of mortality they carry, betrays the distance between the author and her subject. As narrator, Millett is caught in a double bind. In order to "be" Sylvia Likens ("Because I was Sylvia Likens. She was me") the author has to be *other* to her, someone who has survived, who has come through, someone to testify. As Barthes put it, "History is hysterical: it is constituted only if we consider it, only if we look at it — and in order to look at it, we must be excluded from it."[57]

The common bond of feminine shame that obliges and enables the author to assume the position of both murderer and victim in this text is a fragile one, its fragility exposed by Millett's fascination with the past moment of murder: mortality preserved in the photographs of the corpse, the crowds, the untidy house. That fascination amounts to an acknowledgment of the mystery of murder, and to the difference between the author and her vanished subject. Even as Millett acknowledges the unknowability of the "truth" of Sylvia's murder, she forcefully reinscribes the presence of the dead woman, as if she were speaking to a photograph: "But you are Sylvia. I did not make you up. You happened."[58] For Millett, Sylvia's absence *itself* has a presence.

The assertion of identity between the Author and her vanished subject is integral to Millett's project. Yet that project can be achieved only by becoming other to that subject, by its reinvention. That apparent seamlessness — irremediable absence rewritten as presence, past time as timelessness — is part and parcel of the "mortal" text, the tale of murder. In writing *The Basement* Millett tried to sunder time and distance to re-create Sylvia Likens.[59] One mechanism for doing so was to introduce to the reader an envoy from the past, a living relic to bridge the distance between the dead and the living; between image and reality. When speaking at the University of South Florida, Millett briefly mentioned her upcoming project on the Likens's case. After the talk, a young woman came up to Millett and told her she'd attended school with Sylvia. At a following session, the girl again appeared and handed her a rose, saying, "This is from Sylvia." Millett was clearly touched, taking the offering (the girl, the rose) as a sign: "Strangest and loveliest gift, the girl herself vanishing like an apparition."[60] Later, at a gathering in a friend's studio, Millett finally spoke to the girl:

Loathe to pump, but here, after all, was someone real and alive who went to school with Sylvia, knew her or knew her a little, knew her as real and not the figure in my tale, my tabloid world of press cuttings and news photos and transcripts.[61]

The girl did, in fact, remember Sylvia only slightly, "clowning" in the art class they shared.[62] For Millett, it was not important that this girl knew Sylvia only "a little." What was important was that she had "made it through":

In those ten years since the murder this young woman had traveled very far. She was Sylvia or someone from that place and time who'd made it through. . . . Meeting her, it was as if everything had been different. As if it almost hadn't happened. At least *one* had got away. . . . As if there were one Sylvia still surviving, one who had made it out of that milieu.[63]

This girl had "made it through," had "traveled very far." Her "survival" was measured by the degree of her difference from "that milieu" of her youth: "Arsenal tech, even that neighborhood and its distance from fine arts and lesbian life-styles and radical feminism." The girl that handed Millett a rose "from Sylvia" was, perhaps, the most unusual "survivor" of those times, and her presence in Millett's company signifies the writer's definition of "survival" as something more than merely living through one's times. This girl had joined the relatively small ranks of scholarship students; had become part of youth's diaspora, escaping the hometown to the more exciting, cosmopolitan subculture of a large university. Even more significantly, this girl had taken the children, had left a marriage and "somehow in the changes sweeping along, she had become a lesbian and a feminist and a painter and was just now finishing a Master of Fine Arts."[64] In other words, this envoy from Indianapolis's working class-district of 1965 had become *like* the author: lesbian, feminist, artist, arts graduate. Other contemporaries of Sylvia that Millett might have met had not "made it through" to *that* extent. Indeed, how could she have recognized those more typical "survivors": women sunk into early marriages, or poorly paid service jobs, tired faces that scanned the supermarket shelves for better buys to feed the children? Yet it is this most unusual emissary from the "milieu" of the murders who imparts to Millett the vital "clue" to the killings:

[T]he thing that helped me, that made me understand — looking not only for traces as I was but clues (the old riddle of why did they do it and why did she let them) . . . Sylvia's peer gave me the key. Because when I asked what it was like to be a girl that age there and Sylvia's classmate when the thing came to light, she said it was to be ashamed.[65]

The "clue" and the "trace" become one another. The envoy brings a rose "from Sylvia" and the news of what it was, in the end, that killed her. The figure of the girl is a complex one: she is real, but she is atypical, she is real but she "vanishes like an apparition"; she "is" Sylvia, yet she brings tidings from Sylvia;[66] she "is" Sylvia, yet she is a younger version of the author. By combining such qualities, it is not surprising that the girl with the rose carries the "key" to Sylvia's story, which is and cannot help but be — by then — Millett's story.

Locked in the dark basement, waiting for her captors to begin the abuse again, Millett's Sylvia realizes the key to her capitulation: "When a woman does it to you it's different."[67] In Millett's narrative of murder, it is the qualitative nature of cruelty that signifies. Her working of the concept of *ideological crime*—that mechanism of masculinist hegemony that constructs murderer and victim as dependent terms (in a sense that exceeds mere semantics)—relies upon her understanding of the *difference* of women. Women simultaneously occupy the position of subject and object, and their status as historical agent is accordingly difficult. Yet the line of that difference is also one of identification, a delimiting mark that allows Millett, the author, to merge with *her* subjects—murderer and victim alike. Read through the lens of an essentialized concept of feminine difference that demolishes actually the subtle mechanisms of differentiation that have operated historically, the story of the murder of Sylvia Likens becomes a parable about shared identity. The identity of interest that Millett envisions is problematic: the largely illusory identity of "sisterhood" and, ironically, the *unacknowledged* shared identity of race. In Millett's writing of difference as similarity, via the notion of the shared burden of sexual shame, that "kinship"—however treacherous—is the analytic flaw of this counternarrative of murder.

The generic voice of true crime tends to speak for the majority (from the position of a generally undefined "normality") about chaos at the subcultural and psychological margins. Despite the identification of author and murderer so integral to the genre, the narrator becomes a kind of moral umpire, on the side of "fair play" and a society whose set rules the murderer has defied. In the previous two chapters I have discussed ways in which that particular order has been taken to task. For Baldwin and Millett, murder occasions a discussion of the context of the violent act in a culture and history organized around dominance. To differing degrees, for Baldwin and Millett, it was the scene of murder, and not its instrument, that gave meaning to the murder. The killing ground for Wayne Williams and Gertrude Baniewski was white, patriarchal, capitalist America—a world that co-opted Williams and Baniewski to kill "their own."

Both writers spoke from the margins of those killed at the margins. Baldwin, an African American, homosexual, sometime activist (though cushioned by his literary reputation, his émigré status, and his income), had himself been a subject of scrutiny by one of America's most powerful law-enforcement agencies: the FBI. His dossier ran to thousands of pages. Millett, a white, lesbian feminist, artist, and "dropout" (despite the respectability of her class and education) could also, by definition, be regarded as an outsider. Both writers admitted to being implicated in the terms of their project, and, notwithstanding Millett's obsession with her subject, they successfully countered that imposture of objectivity that speaks volumes about the voyeuristic nature of generic true crime. Millett's ethical narrative (however compromised) and Baldwin's counternarrative of murder speak *against* the normative dictates of a culturally defined ethics.

9. The Cast in Order of Disappearance

Murder is an inherently frustrating subject because it keeps moving away from us, evading us. We want to ask big questions; more than anything else, we want to get the answers to big questions. Yet all we can get at, finally, are the details.
Wendy Lesser

You should understand that I would not think of writing *your* story. It would be *my* story. Just as *The Onion Field* was my story and *In Cold Blood* was Capote's story.
Joseph Wambaugh

Americans have a stake in the telling of their tales of murder, an interest possibly best defined by the popular and expert controversy surrounding executions — death being a punishment now reserved, in practice, solely for murder.[1] Media critiques of capital punishment, by their minute attention to the ritual, drama, and pathos of the execution, may serve only to make less dispensable the fatal bureaucracy involved in the production of the murderer's corpse. The original tale of murder (the crime for which the murderer was sentenced) is told yet again — to help a dubious and possibly forgetful public understand why the state is killing in its interest — and a second, entirely *new* tale of murder arises from the execution. While one act is criminal and the other is "justice," how much difference lies between them in the telling?

In her recent wide-ranging study of the place of murder and execution in modern American culture, Wendy Lesser writes: "I am interested in our interest in murder." Positioning this interest in the context of a more general predilection for the murder narrative in American culture, Lesser reveals her own particular tale of murder.[2] I also intend to tell *my* tale of murder, which this work, thus far, has circumnavigated. Given the terms of my critique of the "interestedness" in murder of the works examined in the preceding chapters, what is the presumption of A/authority in my own work? What, in short, is my "interest" in murder?

Lesser tells the story of a young man she once taught who submitted for assessment a piece of short prose describing a gang fight that culminated in a killing. Lesser recalled her feelings of shock and confusion — her *awe* — on discovering that the writer was the subject of his own tale, a *murderer*. This anecdote, among much else in the book, is a vital point of reference for Lesser as she sets about defining the appeal of the tale of murder. After all, she herself reads and writes about murder (the first activity not necessarily occurring solely by reason of the second). Hers is a fascination that she feels a certain need to explain which, in this case, is born of that epiphanous moment when she witnessed the convergence of author and murderer: "In front of us, in our own classroom, sat a self-confessed murderer, if he could be believed (but none of us doubted him for a moment) — *a murderer who was nonetheless, or therefore, an extremely talented writer.*"[3] Lesser's description captures, retrospectively, both the degree of the shock and the listeners' naivete. What is more, Lesser seems to have remained impressed by the A/authority of that tale of murder, despite its ambiguity. Was the murderer a talented writer *despite*, or *because* of, his act? (Indeed, the stress in the above sentence would appear to be on the word "therefore," rather than on "nonetheless.")

Placing this incident as the genesis of her *motivated* interest in murder casts the author in an intriguing light. She is fascinated by the murderer as author, by — effectively — his representation of the unimaginability of murder's reality. She gives to the author of that once-told tale the ability to get right to the paradoxical heart of murder. It always turns into a story, its agents into characters:

"You got to remember," he said, "that when you're out on the street there, it doesn't feel like real life. It's like you're in a movie all the time. That's how you think about it — like you're a character in a movie."[4]

"That was the final remark," Lesser admits, "that stayed with me." Lesser's analysis of her own interest in murder (and the interest of others) is shot through with an anxiety about the tendency of murder's visceral "reality" always to "escape" into its representations, into its no less dramatic (indeed, often more dramatic) incarnation as narrative.[5]

Documentary, Drama, or Schlock?
Televising Executions in a Specular Culture

The focus of *Pictures at an Execution* is the 1991 case, *KQED* v. *Daniel B. Vasquez*, in which a San Francisco community television station sued the warden of San Quentin for the right to enter the witness area of the gas chamber and film the execution of Robert Alton Harris. Harris was the first man scheduled by the State of California to be executed for nearly twenty-five years. The ramifications of this case form the framework for Lesser's critique of the public's interest ("interest" as curiosity and "interest" as implicatedness) in murder. "A story about an execution . . . is initially a story about a murderer."[6] For Lesser's purposes, one of the most interesting things about *KQED* v. *Vasquez* was the complexity of the legal, moral, and aesthetic argument it engendered within and without the courtroom. These included, on the part of KQED, First Amendment issues (specifically, the public's "right to know" about acts committed in its name). The prison administration directed its lawyers to press argument around the Eighth Amendment (the "right to privacy") and to highlight concerns about security (that televised executions would inflame feelings in the general prison population and on death row).[7] Contained within the relatively delimited terms of that debate were wider issues about the *effect* of televising executions, issues which, once raised, brought with them an assortment of ethical and aesthetic questions regarding the nature of the execution as event or spectacle.

For Lesser, several ideas are in play behind the complex volley and return of the legal arguments heard before Judge Robert Schnacke. Would a videotape recording of an execution convey more or less of the essential horror of the event to its audience than, say, the oral, written, or sketched reports of the news media witnesses present? Is, indeed, any feeling implicit in the event (the horror is not *there* — it must somehow be conveyed)? What would motivate an audience to watch such a document, and to what effect? Argument over these issues tended to cross the boundaries of the separate adjudicatory sides, for both were forced to fight on the moral high ground of what was also an aesthetic territory.

In the recent controversy over the wisdom of televising executions, the ambiguity that Lesser critiques continues to trouble the terms of argument.[8] The defining question of the debate would seem to be whether the televised videotape of an execution would merely titillate the morbid interests of an audience with a growing taste for the sensational, or whether it would prick the conscience of a community that refuses to deal with the consequences of its continuing mandate for the death penalty. What both these possibilities call into doubt is the status of the representation of murder (in its guise as legal homicide).

Lesser's brilliance lies in the subtlety of her analysis of the precariousness of meaning as affect in the mediated tale of murder. The impact of the tale of murder tends to rely not upon its realism, but its artfulness (although that "artfulness" may take a realist guise). The implications of that fact are profound, given that the source of the tale of murder in modern American culture is, very often, actual killings. Only inside the smaller or wider circle of friends and relatives of the murderer and victim do people experience the direct and inchoate effect of a murder. The emotional impact of that shock forbids the organization of "what happened" into a generic murder tale. For someone with a direct interest in a particular tale of murder, it may ironically be more difficult to tell an effective (i.e., producing *affect*) tale of murder.

Lionel Dahmer recently published a memoir reflecting upon his son's crimes. In *A Father's Story* the elder Dahmer constructs the tale around his horrified bafflement at his son's brutality.[9] The father's text becomes a sort of confession to murder, for he seems to feel that he is in some way responsible (or at least implicated) in those crimes he knew nothing about. Unlike the generic conventions of the true crime tale identified in Chapters Three to Five above, Dahmer's narrative is generated by a complete mystification about the origin of the murders. He simply *cannot believe* what his son has done, although he knows "what happened" and will not let himself avoid the detail of Jeffrey's crimes. *He* will not be vague or coy — the responsibility having somehow devolved upon him to "face up" to the crimes. (Dahmer is less willing to face up to his son's homosexuality, which tends by and large to be elided or to be taken up as always already tainted, pathological — an inflection merely of the warped sexual being that is Jeff the murderer.)[10]

Dahmer scrutinizes what he remembers of his son's childhood for an early indication of that murderousness. This anxious reassessment of previously innocent memories, though reminiscent of the way in which portent functions in the generic tale of murder, marks the *a*uthor's bafflement (rather than the *prescient* power of the *A*uthor). Lionel Dahmer's perceived failure to predict the destiny of his son and grasp his true nature marks not the murderer, but his sire, as the focal point of censure in the text. Dahmer is forced to see his son's "madness" in himself: obsessive thoughts thankfully and luckily controlled; potential murderousness forestalled. This painful self-criticism produces an identification of author and murderer that is, perhaps, the complete opposite to the vicarious identification of author and murderer in the generic tale. Where the latter conjures the murderer from out of the disparate but portentous evidence of his or her past, the elder Dahmer cannot connect the boy he raised with the killer he became: "This . . . sense of something dark and shadowy, of a malicious force growing in my son, now colors almost every memory I have of his childhood. *In a sense, his childhood no longer exists.* Everything is now a part of what he did as a man."[11] The *fact* of the murders is absolute here. Their irrevocability is an unscalable wall that casts such a shadow on the past that the search for origins is not just futile, but impossible. The troubling and troubled "confession" of Jeffrey Dahmer's father should be viewed as a counternarrative of murder, and those critics who howled that he was "trading" on his son's crimes could not be more wrong.[12]

To everyone *outside* the circle of intimates and acquaintances of murderer and victim — no matter the extent of their sympathy, their moral outrage, or their fear — the murder, as a historical event, is understood on the basis of its various cumulative reconstructions.[13] The transmutation of event into narrative may not lose the affectivity of the act, but neither does it necessarily ensure it. When an execution is televised there is no guarantee that the *documentary* nature of the broadcast will make the death of the condemned man actually believable. Meaning as affect cannot be guaranteed by the kind, but only by the *quality* of mediation.[14] The disputes comprising *KQED* v. *Vasquez* indicate to Lesser that there is no inherent "truth" status to the videotape document of an execution, for the lack of context and the framing of the event might decrease rather than increase its affective power.[15] The "theatre of actual murder" is an unknown quality. Surprisingly, Lesser does not discuss in any depth the implications of the possible video representation of the execution as a *live event*.[16] Although the same ambiguities would remain in play as to the affective power of the document, the stakes — in terms of the power or "truth" of the text and its appropriateness — would be raised.[17] "Murder stories hinge on the tension between endlessness and finality," Lesser tells us. And she is quite right. The simultaneous sense of dread and regret, of portent, that is at the heart of the tale of murder is a function of the doubling-back of the tale of origins that constructs its own end. It is also a function of the *aporia* that is death in the tale: that which vanishes with the victim; the unimaginable that must, nevertheless, be imagined.[18]

The "paradoxical relation to time" of the "murder story inherent in *KQED* v. *Vasquez*" is accentuated by the video medium. A locked-down camera, recording in "real time" the execution — from the entry of the condemned into the chamber to the moment of his/her being declared dead — would appear to offer a particularly dramatic or "true" rendition of the metered ritual of scheduled murder. And yet, "real time" is fragile. It is hard to imagine a television network broadcasting an unedited version of the execution. Quickly the "real time" that marks the documentary integrity of the piece fragments and decays into the episodic highlights so dear to tabloid television. Only a *live* broadcast might retain the dread of "real time" in the execution chamber. But it might also, simultaneously, change the nature of the document from "news" into rank spectacle.[19] "Real time," as a cinematic technique, purports to close the distance between fiction and the "real," imitating the absolutism of *lived* time: every moment freighted and disappearing. Yet, like all film, its iterability marks a surreal, rather than a real, quality. A live broadcast — because the moment is documented — stands both as testament to the irrevocability of the killing (the moment of death) and to the iterability of the historical event which that killing becomes. The dread and regret implicit in the tale of murder (or, as Lesser puts it, "the tension between endlessness and finality") finds its perfect accompaniment in film, whether the still photograph or the videotape. These all are mortal texts.[20]

The uncertain affective power of any documentary medium stands as testament not to the complete relativity of meaning, but to its vicissitudes in culture. A television movie about an asteroid colliding with the earth, recently screened by a major American network, caused in some of its viewers a panic remarkably similar to that caused half a century before by Orson Welles's "War of the Worlds" broadcast.[21] Although (as a simple phone call to the station could clear up the confusion) people did not load up their Ford trucks and head for the hills, what is remarkable about this story is its testimony to the power of the audience to bestow upon even an unlikely story the authority of a threatening "truth." If fantastic fiction can be mistaken for fact, then certainly documentary media can be taken as other than "real." And one cannot with certainty say that the panic caused by Welles's radio program was merely an effect of the times: the greater ambiguity of a voice on radio; the inability of people to check the reality of that voice; the supposed lack of sophistication of an isolated, rural audience. Although these things cannot be discounted, the fact that a similar panic can occur in a vastly different world suggests that the technical sophistication of media and medium has not affected the basic mechanism of belief (the way in which narratives are constructed and received) in that culture.

Closure in the Tale of Murder as Execution

The "interestedness" of a culture in the murderousness that it ethically deplores is a phenomenon that fuels, perhaps contradictorily, both (*a*) the continued existence of active capital-punishment statutes (plus a super due process which augments the effects of that legislation by an increasingly detailed moral analysis of just punishment)[22] and (*b*) the *market* for murder evidenced by the media circus and public protests attendant on executions. Executions continue because they are still rhetorically, symbolically potent—not merely as "just punishment," deterrence, or retribution, but as analogical closure to the forever open-ended tale of murder. Each murderer killed settles the score for the hundreds of others who are not, who continue (their own lives outstripping the deaths of their victims) forgetful, reformed, lying, denying: "I'm not that person anymore." Only execution provides (however erroneously) the sense that something is settled. The murderer, like the victim, is irrevocably attached to the moment of the crime (death returns him or her there). This "closure" is very unlike the closure touted by supporters of the death penalty and by certain of the grieving relatives of the killed as a "psychological" or "moral" benefit of execution.[23]

Lesser deplores the mealymouthed humanitarianism of media that react to the grim spectacle of state-sponsored murder with a sentimental refashioning of the condemned: "the executed murderer doesn't have to be an *innocent* victim to be a victim."[24] In other words, one does not need to clamor over the greater or lesser merits of the personality of the condemned. Whether they have reformed or not, the *act* of homicide (legal or otherwise) should be the subject of moral scrutiny, all other issues aside:

[T]he victim's inherent sweetness or innocence has little bearing on the severity of the crime; but I am now making the even more extreme assertion that even the murderer's character is largely irrelevant, except insofar as it bears directly on his reasons and motives for committing the murder. Our usual standards for judging human worth are useless in the face of the enormity of murder; normally admirable qualities like sobriety or honesty or generosity or intelligence or artistic talent do not weigh in the balance against this single catastrophic act. *This does not mean that the murderer's only character is his character as a murderer.*[25]

As part of her analysis of the redundancy of capital punishment, Lesser argues for this more instrumental approach to murder in legal terms that are also, inescapably, cultural. The logic of such an equation can be interrupted only by the inclusion of the random — and largely irrelevant — factor of the criminal. Of course, Lesser's intent in suggesting that the "character" of the killer has little bearing on the issue of either the crime or the punishment (except where it directly relates to motive and execution) is to promote a different kind of uniformity to replace that of the absolutist deterrence of sure and swift punishment. Historically, the liberal approach to punishment has failed to eradicate the death penalty but has cumulatively constructed a discourse of power that sifts those "deviants" who are too bad to live from those who are not.[26] For Lesser, the sentimental drift of that kind of carceral power must be halted. Like Susan Jacoby, who critiqued the insufficiency of public vengeance to codify a fitting response to the diverse, distinct, and unquantifiable kinds of violent acts that constitute murder,[27] Lesser suggests that the person of the murderer is functionally irrelevant in the face of the gravity, the irrevocability, of the crime. In concentrating on the execution — the possible implications of its specular qualities, the ethical implications of the continued practice of the ritual — Lesser clearly demonstrates her revulsion for the death penalty. Yet her premise that execution is in itself a tale of murder reinscribes uncritically a supposedly self-evident relationship of crime to punishment, of murder to execution. The two stories are attached, but their functions are different. Both are tales within which American culture and the American public are implicated (are "interested"), uniquely so, however, in the tale of execution.

Whether the execution is a distinctive subgenre to the tale of murder or an exemplary murder narrative, we are, regardless, left with the irreducible presence of the murderer in the text. In that sense, the "murderer's character" *can only be* "his character as a murderer." Lesser tries to maintain a distinction between a process of "ethical or legal accounting" which may take into consideration only those "contradictory 'motives' . . . that led directly or indirectly to the murder" and a wider sorting process whereby "readers, writers, news collectors, citizens, fellow human beings" construct a narrative of murder.[28] Yet that distinction is less clear than it sounds. The "ethical or legal accounting" that defines the crime and leads to the disposition of the murderer may issue, at first glance, from the narrow and well-defined edicts of due process, but it is a formal process constructed under the same conditions, and impelled by the same cultural forces, as those tales of murder which are "of interest" to those of us outside the confines of the law.

Within the solid structure of Lesser's analysis appear troubling wraiths. The subject of her analysis is the representation of murder: specifically, the interest and the interestedness of culture in murder. Her analysis is simultaneously literary, legal, and sociological. Lesser asks the "big questions," the answers to which seem evasive (that resistance, I would argue, is itself constitutive of the tale of murder). The empirical basis of Lesser's work — her interrogation of those details that form the cement of the murder narrative — revolves around the unanswerable core of the matter: the mystery at the heart of murder. While there is nothing outwardly mysterious about the process of an execution (the procedure is codified down to the minute), the bureaucratic veneer masks a murderousness that has no single agent but culture itself. Lesser is torn between her own interest in the appeal of the tale of murder and her desire to demystify that tale in order to make less viable the future of legal homicide. Despite the empirical context to her study, and vital disclaimers notwithstanding, Lesser's discussion of real and fictional murder — which travels between ethics and aesthetics without an acknowledgment of their essential contiguity — is written as a metaphysics of murder.[29] She, too, must ask the "big questions" and, without answers, gesture wide into that great and baffling territory which is mortality.

Like others who write about murder, Lesser cannot avoid the imperatives of a narrative genre that structures absence as presence, that is circular, that thrives on portent.[30] As a subject, murder obliges grandiloquent obfuscation from those who write about it. Lesser constantly reflects upon her own position as a commentator on what, in the debate represented by *KQED* v. *Vasquez*, is actually a story about one man's death at the hands of the state. Her final chapter, therefore, concludes the story of the legal battle, as well as describing her reaction and that of the media to the last moments of Robert Alton Harris's life, extinguished by the State of California on 21 April 1992. Her fascination with the tale of murder comes at the price of her implication in it, a fact of which she seems largely aware. The metaphysics of murder that she has constructed itself nominates the terms by which that deal is struck:

Perhaps in part because I was writing this book, Harris's death had a profound effect on me. It filled me with anxiety and sadness, so that for days I was able to think of nothing else and for months was unable to write about it. Such tribulations are minor, of course, compared to what happened to Robert Alton Harris. *But then, that is part of the terrible irony of the death penalty: we take personally something that is not actually happening to us, so that even the suffering — the one thing left to the condemned man, the one thing we have not deprived him of — becomes our own rather than, or as much as, his.*[31]

In her last sentence, Lesser claims the very thing she has so guiltily disclaimed in the sentence before. Spectacle and empathy combine to rob the condemned of his suffering, his confusion, his abject fear. But this is presumption and, sadly, sophistry — however well motivated. Lesser can only guess at the content of Harris's suffering. As her analysis repeatedly demonstrates, even the witnesses to the execution — who are as well-placed as anyone to report on the condemned man's "suffering" — give quite different accounts of the same event.[32] *Demeanor* is all that the reporters can, finally, describe. The experience of dying belongs only to the one who dies (although "experience" is a decidedly problematic concept here). This is a story of death that the watchers tell.

Lesser's implication in the terms of her own analysis is a foregone conclusion. Simply, there is no getting around it. As a responsible author, she retains her self-reflexive stance wherever possible. But the act of authorship, the obligation of authority, forbids innocence in those who tell the tale of murder. Only a counternarrative, like James Baldwin's *Evidence of Things Not Seen*, is "innocent" — if innocence can be taken as a refusal of the generic imperatives of the tale of murder. Baldwin's metaphysics, his grandiloquence, arise from a quite different place than that obliged by the tale of murder. His "sermon" is not a meditation on the hereafter, but on the here and now; not an apologetic paean to death but a commentary on life in the terms it must be lived. It is not circular, but speaks *from* a history *to* the present. While Lesser's discourse is grounded in particular ethical concerns, it cannot be said to be a counternarrative of murder. Her critique of the conventions and implications of murder's representation begets the telling, nonetheless, of another tale of murder.

Interrogation, Confession, and Authority in the Tale of Murder

All of which brings me nearer to the point where I must make overt my position as author in *this* particular tale of murder. I can no more avoid being implicated in the terms of my own analysis than Lesser can, which makes it doubly difficult to avoid the irritating tone of confession that infuses so much self-criticism. Yet, the confession must be made, so great is the temptation that strikes even those who have much to lose, like the murderer who throws up her hands and says, finally, to her captors: "*Yes, I did it, just like you said.*" One tells the story in the way it *must* be told, an imperative only partly explained by a desire to approximate the tale as closely to the facts as possible. Martha Beck and Ray Fernandez, for instance, signed statements that told the story of their murders in some depth, much of which was suggested to them by the detectives leading their interrogation. The disputed material — the difference, say, between not only Martha's and Ray's version of events, but also between Martha's first and second statement — could not all be *true*, but was all *necessary* for the construction of the prosecution case against them (see Appendix). That case consisted of a set of strategies more diverse than any sequence of actual events that the prosecution adhered to during the trial. Alleged motives were raised and discarded in argument; whole versions of the meaning of the murder might be made redundant by a change in strategy.

Likewise the defense chopped and changed its tactics, and with those changes the nature of the underlying tale of murder altered too. When former Federal Judge Marvin Frankel wrote that "trials occur because there are questions of fact . . . [and] the paramount objective in the principal is the truth," he showed the weird and unwordly optimism, the pedantry, of legal formalism.[33] Long before the "truth," or those "facts" which are its supposed foundation, there must be a structure of belief within which the "true" and its actual sediments can be weighed. The story comes first.

When Martha and Ray tendered their statements,[34] they did so in the hope that their cooperation would secure them an indictment in Michigan, rather than one under the lethal murder statutes of New York.[35] The contradictory detail of their retelling of the events leading up to Janet Fay's death could not have mattered so much to them when they faced what would be — given the amount of physical evidence available to connect them to the Downing killings — a *fait accompli* conviction and life sentence. Saying *too* much seems to have been a response to that inexhaustible curiosity of their interrogators, but it may also have been coincidental to the process of confession itself.

Confession, historically defined in the Christian sense of an act of conscience, would appear to be about the reassertion of a subject's authority over himself. And yet, following Foucault's various meditations on the development of the confession as religious ritual (and, as a distinctive development, as legal process), the confession should be seen not as the assertion of the subject, but as a site of intervention.[36] Whether to the priest, the psychoanalyst, or the prosecutor, the story told by the subject as *what is felt* or *what happened* is given over to the use of the one who listens — to the discourse that structures the listener and the teller, and that defines the contract of power which is confession itself. Martha Beck and Ray Fernandez found themselves at the mercy of the renegade meaning of the stories they themselves initially told, because their confessions were caught up in the migratory paths of meaning that constitute both legal process and the "news." The helplessness of the accused in the face of their "own" tale of murder is not just the result of their suppliant position before the law, it is also consequent to the general direction of meaning in culture. The story of murder that Beck and Fernandez told to Detectives Clarence Randle and James Toohey,[37] and to the county prosecutor, must have caused enough outrage to prompt their accusers to begin a process of extradition that was hardly standard procedure. The disposition of the case, and the growth of the competing and authoritative tales of murder to which it gave rise, were not simple effects of the orderly march of due process. The tale of murder as received by police, prosecutor, judge, defense, jury, news media, and public dictated the extremity of the circumstances that eventually killed the tale's protagonists. Simply, the story of the Hearts Killers was *too much*, and its meaning and effect changed radically from that originally intended by Beck and Fernandez when they "sold" their stories to the Kent County authorities in the hope of lenient sentencing.

Those of us — like Wendy Lesser, or Joe McGinniss, or Ann Rule (or, indeed, myself) — who write about actual murders are troubled by the murderer, but cannot afford to dispense with the way in which he or she is figured. And the confusion of the person of the killer with the figure of the murderer is pretty much unavoidable, part and parcel of the discourse of murder itself, and not merely an effect, as Janet Malcolm would have it, of the "moral ambiguity of journalism."[38] While murders might be called banal (predictably unpredictable, they often occur under the most prosaic of circumstances), murder is nevertheless a subject that tends to invite decidedly unprosaic responses. The teller of the tale of murder touches upon grand and unanswerable questions; and that teller, as subject, may not be confined to a desk or computer well removed from the more immediate scene of the crime. Sometimes the subject of that tale is a lawyer, trial judge, consulting psychiatrist, or the murderer him or herself.[39]

Norman Mailer's *The Executioner's Song* demonstrates how the subject in the tale of murder has a tendency to escalate and multiply. Mailer's tale of murder has no single author, despite the quite extraordinary A/authority of Gary Gilmore in his own story of murder (as execution). After all, Gilmore successfully directed a legal effort to expedite, rather than delay, the execution of his sentence.[40] Primed for the event, the media death watch had more time, more territory in which to work. Everyone seemed to want "in" on Gilmore's death, and, as an extra piece of pie at the feast, "in" on the deaths of his victims, Jensen and Bushnell.[41] The media extravaganza attendant to Gilmore's execution was a circus, the excess of which Mailer is brilliant at exposing. There are so many potential angles to the story that media entrepreneurs determine their plot line on the basis of which "characters" in the real-life drama will sell the rights to their story. And there is a peculiar tension between the idea of detailed general coverage and the concept of the "exclusive" — which is about who gets into print first, rather than who attempts responsibly to sketch the "whole" story (i.e., the "facts" that say depressingly little). If there is an essence to the story of Gilmore's murder/s that Mailer tells, then that essence must be *dilation*. The story does not get reduced to the "facts," it outgrows them rapidly.

Let us return for a moment to that proposition of W. H. Auden's that murder is "unique in that it abolishes the party it injures" and "is the one crime in which society has a direct interest."[42] Society takes a "direct interest" because it must "demand atonement" or "grant forgiveness" on behalf of the vanished victim. That "direct interest" arises, necessarily, as supposition and presumption. The death of the victim, the fact that murder often occurs without witnesses, and the ambiguous status of the murderer's recollection of motive and event are factors that make the account of murder extraordinarily opaque. And yet there must be an account. Murder fascinates, and its ambiguity — the mystery at the heart of murder — is not merely an effect of the factual unreliability of individual accounts of murder. Like all tales of death, the narrative of murder is freighted with a kind of awed bafflement at something visceral, yet inscrutable. As Wendy Lesser has so aptly written, "Our death, which is intended for us alone, is the one experience in our life we can't directly experience."[43] Leaving aside for one moment what problems there may be with the concept of "direct experience" here, we can see that the beguiling paradox described by Lesser is enhanced in the tale of murder. Her formulation of the phrase recalls an earlier proposition that "a story about murder . . . is also, obliquely, a story about the existence or absence of God."[44] There is no marker for human mortality but the divine. Lesser herself proves that. Despite her obviously secular analysis, the insertion of the word "intended" gives an oddly divine ring to the first quote above. We all must die. But is there a God to decree that death? Time's immolation is as coincidental as it is inevitable: a slow wearing-down of the flesh. Death is no agent, merely a biological (and a metaphysical) certainty. Yet the tale of murder contains both death as event and death as agency. Death has a *presence* — however confused, humble, or maniacal — in the figure of the murderer. It is that metaphysical investment in the murderer that explains his or her dominant position in the narrative of murder: his or her body, his or her psyche is the trail down which death comes.

In Cormac McCarthy's recent novel, *All the Pretty Horses*, the two protagonists witness a peremptory execution. While they are en route from one jail to another, the boys' captors take one of the company to a stand of trees and there, with singular dispatch, shoot him. In the passage describing the survivors' meeting with the officer who had been in charge of the killing, the reader is positioned, with the prisoners, at an insurmountable distance from their captor. On top of the difference of culture, and of relative power, there is an idiosyncratic but vital distinction: the irrevocable act of murder that has severed the killer from the world, even that of the murder's witnesses. McCarthy writes:

The captain inhabited another space and it was a space of his own election and outside the common world of men. A space privileged to men of the irreclaimable act which while it contained all lesser worlds within it contained no access to them. For the terms of election were of a piece with its office and once chosen that world could not be quit.[45]

This is an almost perfect inscription of the mystery of murder. He who inhabits the "space privileged to men of the irreclaimable act" is linked by the history, effectively, of *another person* (the murderer before the murder) to the world they have left. It is this problematic transition of one who has *not* killed to one who *has* that defines irrevocability in the discourse of murder. Not only is the victim abolished, but so, too, is the one who has not killed. At this paradoxical border the whole imperative of murder's origin arises. How does one explain the murderer (and therefore tell the story of the murder) when his or her history is that of another person: *the one who has not killed*? That demarcation is visible in Lionel Dahmer's horrified statement that his son's "childhood no longer exists." Although Dahmer goes on to say of his son that "everything is now a part of what he did as a man," the murderer's colonization of the past before the murders cannot be complete. The elder Dahmer attempts to invoke the integrity (meaning the *difference*) of the Jeff he knew as his son before the revelation of the horrors in apartment 213. That obligation to remember his son is opposed by as weighty an obligation to confront the murderer. *A Father's Story* is about precisely this struggle, and its inevitable failure. The site of that struggle is the collision of "Jeff" and the murderer, "Jeffrey

Dahmer" — a collision the force of which is measured by Lionel Dahmer's deflection of guilt onto himself. The link of son and murderer is, therefore, a device. Dahmer cannot unite the two "truths," and he sets *himself* at the place of their meeting to make traversable (and intelligible) that border.

The search for murder's origin would seem to be the unifying impulse of all murder narratives, whether legal, psychoanalytic, "literary," or generic. That search is equally an obligation upon the counternarrative of murder, although the difference of both means and ends defines its status as counternarrative. Bridging the paradoxical border of the one-who-has-not-yet-killed and the murderer requires a definite re-Authoring of the crime. In Chapter Three I demonstrated how the "high literature of true crime" of Fredric Wertham and Curtis Bok proposed a social origin for the individual violent acts they studied. That social context could be provided, however, only via a thorough investigation of the murderer's psyche — an investigation which entailed a reinvention of the murderous subject. That reinvention — achieved by the intervention of the analyst or lawyer and his drawing out the meaning of the murder from the accused — appeared to foreground the murderer as authoritative subject, while actually foregrounding the authority of the analyst.

The issue of A/authority in the tale of murder is therefore more complicated than the concept of "identification" can suggest. The identification of author and murderer (or that of vicarious reader with the figure of the murderer) is something of a trick. The reader identifies with the *figure* of the murderer, remaining always at a sufficient remove (theoretically) to maintain an ethical position on the crime while aesthetically appreciating it. The identity of author and murderous subject is more complicated. Janet Malcolm would argue that that "identity" is strategic, allowing the pecuniary-minded author access to the perspective of the murderer for the profit of his or her text.[46] The integrity of the subject and that of the journalistic contract are sacrificed for the (false) integrity of the text established under the terms of such a claim to identity. While Malcolm's point of view as a watchdog of journalistic ethics is laudable, it is also rather one-dimensional. In the instance of the actual murderer finding a mediator for his or her story — whether an author, a psychoanalyst, or a lawyer — the person who mediates the tale of murder establishes identity with the subject at the fault line of the other's subjectivity as *murderer.*

The Author in the tale of murder arises at the place of greatest uncertainty: at the point where the murderer exists unexplained, his or her new identity as murderer unconnected to the past before the killing. Regardless of the *project* of the particular tale of murder (to classify the pathology of the killer, to provide his or her defense, to write the "definitive" account of the crime and trial), the business of the author is to bridge that paradoxical border. Under such conditions, there can be no definitive tale of a given murder. Versions do not necessarily even succeed one another but coexist in complement or opposition. Every tale of murder arises in and on uncertainty, and no definitive tale can exist.

In two of the most renowned nonfiction novels about murder, *The Executioner's Song* by Norman Mailer and *In Cold Blood* by Truman Capote, the author's literal presence is shadowy. In *The Executioner's Song*, Larry Schiller — the entrepreneur gathering the rights to Gilmore's story — performs the function of the actual *author* of the story, Mailer. Capote's presence in his text is veiled, generic; he becomes "The Journalist" on those occasions when he must make overt his presence as narrator. However coded the presence of the author, and however scrupulous the documentary evidence that forms the basis of both works, the A/authority of Mailer and Capote seems solid. But the case of *In Cold Blood* is peculiar. There is an authorial presence that Capote, "The Journalist," erases. Unlike Mailer, who completed many of the interviews for *The Executioner's Song* himself, Capote was less than comfortable in his role as researcher in Holcombe, Kansas. Much of that research was done by Harper Lee, and it was she who did the "people work" from out of which comes much of the finely worked portraiture that makes *In Cold Blood* so affecting.[47] In Mailer's work, the wraiths are not veiled: they speak out in the exact meter and nuance of the voices bequeathed in tapes and letters to the author. However, those "actual" voices exist only by virtue of the narrative appetite of both the author and his surrogate in the text. Neither Mailer nor Capote makes naive claims to tell the truth of "what happened," unlike the true crime writers (or the publisher's blurbs) that promise definitive, "true," and "uncut" accounts. It is not the documentary nature of the texts *but the status of fiction* that grants these two novels their explanatory power.

For Mailer and Capote the axis of affectivity in the text is the transition of murderer into victim enacted by the execution. While both authors successfully preserve the identity of the *murderer* in the face of that metamorphosis,[48] the price of that supposed integrity is the elision of his character "other than as a murderer." The double bind obliged by the backwards narrative in the tale of murder is inescapable. The preservation of the figure of the murderer at the point at which he himself becomes a victim is achieved by the dominance, overall, of the story of the murderer's genesis. The "tainted" innocence that is the murderer before he has killed forms a narrative counterweight to the guilty innocent about to be executed by the state.

The "becoming" of the murderer forms a large part of both novels, although *In Cold Blood* more closely follows the generic tradition by initiating the search for murder's origin in the latter part of the book (through the lens of forensic psychiatry). Mailer's search for the origins of Gilmore's murderousness even extends beyond the text, a curiosity that can be read, inferentially, from the published selection of letters Mailer received from Jack Henry Abbott in prison. Abbott's replies are long and thoughtful, but we cannot tell from the book what questions and prompts from Mailer Mr. Abbott is responding to. And yet the substance of the conversation remains: *How did you get here? How has imprisonment changed you?* The story of Abbott's mental and physical demolition at the hands of the correctional authorities is much like Gilmore's. Both had to bear long periods of isolation and the more deadly assault of antipsychotic drugs like Prolixin. Both were "recidivists" who, since adolescence, had spent only a few months out of prison. Abbott is one of the wraiths in *The Executioner's Song*. Despite Mailer's contention "the two men could not be more different,"[49] Abbott stands in the place of the Gilmore who died before Mailer could ever meet him.[50]

The context within which Mailer and Capote set about placing the figure of the murderer is topological. The "character of the murderer" represented by Gilmore, Hickock, or Smith, exists in apposite relation both to their own prior innocence and to the murderousness of others, whether the "organized" or "disorganized" psychoses of the "serial killer" or a more ordinary fury and frustration that leads daily to murder. Mailer's topology continually refers back to the institutions that produce the machismo of the "good con" — one who can be both spiritually and physically demolished, yet *survive:*

Here in prison the most respected and honored men *among us* are those who have killed other men, particularly other prisoners. It is not merely *fear,* but *respect.*

Everyone in prison has an ideal of violence, murder. Beneath all relationships between prisoners . . . is the ever-present fact of murder. It ultimately *defines* our relationship among ourselves.[51]

Correctional institutions culture violence in administrators and wards alike, and the news media—implicated both in the operations of due process and in regenerating narratives of murder—provide the wider stage upon which that violence plays. Gilmore's murderousness can become intelligible, can be understood in its full horror, *only* in the context of the topology of indifference and violence to which it belongs.

In Capote's work, the topology to which Hickock and Smith belong is a simpler one than Mailer's; indeed, it forms a kind of a distinct *set:* those men who make up the small community of the condemned on death row. Capote remained fascinated by that typology of murder long after his completion of *In Cold Blood.* He interviewed and corresponded with convicted and condemned murderers throughout his career,[52] and although the focus of his interest seemed to be the *convicted* murderer, Capote did produce a second "nonfiction" account of a set of murders twenty years after *In Cold Blood.*[53] Like *In Cold Blood,* the genius of "Handcarved Coffins" lies in its evocation of place and character; unlike it, there is no getting near to the murderer who, in escaping detection but not suspicion, cannot seem to fill the figural space of the murderer. The crimes remain a mystery, beautifully achieved, but not anchored in meaning by origin. What sense there is in Capote's topology of murder comes from his rendering of its constituent parts, his faith in the relation of each oddity, each coincidence, each particularity, to its other.

Capote was fascinated by the signifying quality of idiosyncratic detail. In the grip of that enthusiasm he was quite capable of overlooking the casual function of the signs he sought to interpret in the context of the tale of murder. When interviewing Robert Beausoleil in his cell in San Quentin, Capote veered from the subject of conversation, distracted by the bare chest Beausoleil had just revealed. He mused aloud: "It's odd about tattoos. I've talked to several hundred men convicted of homicide—multiple homicide, in most cases. The only common denominator I could find among them was tattoos. A good eighty percent of them were heavily tattooed. Richard Speck. York and Latham. Smith and Hickock."[54] To find a "common denominator" among murderers in their tattoos is hopeful, if not downright naive. Capote would likely have found tattoos ubiquitous in the general prison population, the amount of tattooing determined by the length of sentence. Tattoos form a part of prison culture, as well as signaling other class, work, or subcultural identities. Deeply immersed in his catalogue of killers, Capote has forgotten the institutional limits of the topology he describes.

The topological approach, even as subtly worked as it is in Mailer's hands, tends to award to the figure of the murderer both particularity and the potential to explicate the generalities of murderous violence. In the generic tale of murder — even in these self-reflexive nonfictions — the figure of the murderer is synecdochic. As the focal point of the story, the murderer stands always in reference to the meaning assigned to his act: by statute, by the courts, by the community, by the media. Yet the meaning assigned to the act itself arises from and about the murderer, who is the one apparently firm place on the shifting ground of the tale of murder. The figure of the murderer refers back continually to other murderers. His or her particularity is a ruse. Much more important is his or her supposed power to tell us something *generally* about murder. People listen closely to the tale of murder — so much of which is banal detail — and hear a mystery. A tale full of ciphers.

Telling Tales of Murder

Once upon a time, when I was a younger woman, I met — coincidentally, as one does — someone whom I instantly liked and, not much later, crazily loved. She was, like my father, an ex-Catholic and, also like my father, was born the last of several generations local to the area. While coincidence does not ordinarily lead to much, in this case it did. My lover's father, it turned out, had been in the same class as my father at Old St. Joseph's. After my father was expelled from there, and had escaped the approbation of police and priests, their paths crossed again when they took up positions in the same division of a government department. The two young men became casual drinking buddies, and my father admired the beauty of the woman Dan was dating, and would later marry. Constance had inherited her mother's beauty, but not much else from parents as remote from her as is Pluto from the Sun.

Con didn't have much to say to her parents, nor they to her. In that household the focal point of any conversation was the cat. While Con and I were together, she didn't visit home much, content instead to endure the weekly phone calls in which her mother would tell stories about the cat, or complain about not being able to understand the window locks. Con would raise her eyes heavenward, her tongue thick with the desire to tell her mother to shut up.

Unlike Con and her parents, members of our family talked regularly to one another, although strangers observed that we did so simultaneously, with much arm-waving. Dad and I *could* talk quietly, catching up, as he drove me down to the train station at the end of my visit. It was on one of these short car rides that he told me about the confidence imparted to him once by Dan, when drunk. Dan, a taciturn man, was driven to talk only partly by drink. He and my father had both just extracted themselves from a car wreck, and Dan may have been feeling sentimental. At any rate, he told my father that he'd once killed a man — had drowned an Arab trader in a barrel of oil because of an "overpriced" trinket. There were three of them, soldiers in New Zealand's Second Expeditionary Force, abroad for the first time in their short lives.

After my father told me this story, I stepped out into the drizzling autumnal day to await my train.

I wondered why Dan had confessed such a thing to my father. If he knew him at all, he'd have known that Ray would despise him for it. Perhaps Dan had not told this story as blithely as my father seemed to suggest he had. Or should Dan's confession not be considered as a confession to murder, but merely a "war story," re-creating an act of indifference or, more pointedly, of racist "superiority" (the "colonists" abroad) — an "adventure" sanctioned by circumstance? Certainly, the *victim* in the story (and maybe even the story itself) seems dispensable, almost throwaway. (For, after all, is there not something careless, flippant about the mode of the killing: to drown someone in a *barrel of oil*?) I do not now think that Dan would have spoken with such drunken largesse if the man he had drowned had not been an Arab.

And then I wondered why my father had told *me* the story. Maybe he offered me the story to help explain why Con's relationship with her parents was so unlike our own. But that assumed she knew what her father had done, which I doubted. To me it was unnecessary detail, unassimilable, a fact I could not organize into the overall story of my loving Con.

Over the following days, I tried hard to ignore the story of the murdered Arab. I had decided, after all, that it bore no relevance to our relationship, that knowing the fact could be no benefit to Con. But the nature of the story — as it had always been — was such that I was finally compelled to tell it, to pass on the anomaly in the hope of making some sense of it. It was a cruel thing to do, because the burden of sense could only fall on Con, could register only in confusion and silence. The story carried within it the unfulfillable promise of a revelation. Con's coolness toward her father was formed out of habit, out of familiarity, out of indifference. Con found it impossible to react to this new piece of information about her father. The story went round her, past her, under her — like cloven water that seals, seamless, behind the ship that has broken it. The difference it made to her I could not fathom, but the difference it made to me was obvious: I was guilty of telling a story for the sake of the story alone.

She who tells the tale of murder is telling, inevitably, the story of her own "finer feelings." That vanity — the affective power of a conscientiously told tale of murder — means that the definition of a well-told tale is not its "truth," nor even its strength as a moral fable, but how well one signals one's own pity (and, thereby, the pity of others). I told Con the story of her father's murderousness more to say something about myself than about him. For I knew myself in the telling of the tale much better than I knew its subject. In *telling on* Dan I was defining my difference from him, while also positioning myself in alliance with Con, to whom I was confiding. While the impulse to lay bare and to exercise those "finer feelings" may not hold true for some of the more tabloid forms of true crime, it is certainly true of the more finely worked pieces of true crime writing. The sensibility of the author is the measure by which both the literal insensibility of the corpse and the metaphorical insensibility of the murderer are thrown into relief. The foregrounding of the figure of the murderer can occur only through his or her being reauthored — by the sensitivity of the analyst's diagnosis, the writer's art, the lawyers understanding of justice and human weakness.

The *sensibility* of the author in the tale of murder was the first thing to fascinate me about narratives of murder. My own sense of pity, mirroring that of the author, appalled me. The sensibility of the author — comprising in equal measure pity, regret, and horror — was clearly signaled to me by two quite different tales of murder as execution. The implicatedness of the observers struck me in George Orwell's essay "The Hanging"[55] and in the closing scenes of Richard Brooks's film version of *In Cold Blood*. Orwell and Capote both acted as witnesses at the execution. Their revulsion at the scene of death was the sum, therefore, of their empathy, their outrage, *and* their guilt.

At twelve years old, reading "The Hanging," I remember the impact of Orwell's description of the prisoner's walk to the gallows. It had rained the night before, and the pitted ground of the prison yard was covered with water. As he was led across the yard, the condemned man stepped aside from a puddle to avoid getting his feet wet. This fastidiousness seemed bizarre and unintelligible. What was so frightening about this scene was its portrayal of the very tenacity of life; its dumb, habitual, unconscious willfulness.[56]

Not long after reading Orwell, I watched *In Cold Blood* on the Saturday night TV feature. Richard Brooks had faithfully rendered the atmosphere of Capote's nonfiction novel: a feeling of dread and, simultaneously, of regret. When Hickock and Smith are taken by car to the building where the gallows are erected, we see the black sedan enter the prefab, rainwater running in thick rivulets from the gleaming hood of the car. Overhead, rain drums on the corrugated-iron roof. I remember wondering what it would be like to meet one's scheduled death in the rain, which spoke so loudly of life. In both readings, my shock seemed a good measure of the intention of the author (or, in Brooks's case, of the director's faithfulness to Capote's sense of affect) to convey his own horror and bafflement. Like them, I was fascinated by my own morbid attention to detail in the death scene, the depth or shallowness of my empathy for the condemned, the affective power of the execution. That fascination is produced by the sudden awareness of one's own senses: *I* have outlived the subject of the tale. One is witness to a death that seems to bequeath to the survivor a greater portion of life, however confounding that inheritance may be.

In *A Father's Story* Lionel Dahmer writes of the thousands of letters directed to his son in prison, letters which he collected and read on Jeffrey's behalf. Fan mail directed to the famous and infamous alike seems to indicate a need in the sender to relate his or her own everyday setbacks and miseries (which have no limit on depth merely because they are ordinary) to the extraordinary grandeur or horror of others' lives. The letters directed to a murderer, though, carry an even greater freight of hopelessness: the burden of a confused desire for recognition from the person to whom the confession is made. In that recognition is sought redemption. Many of the letters directed to Jeffrey Dahmer seemed, in his father's words, "to embrace . . . the whole vast sadness of the world":

"I know what it's like to be lonely," one woman wrote. "My husband was my whole world, and when he died, I wanted to go with him." Letter after letter formed a long chain of immemorial complaint: "My fiance is an alcoholic." "I've just broken up with my boyfriend." "I get dizzy spells." "I am on Dilantin for my epilepsy." "I have this problem with my husband. . . ." "No one likes my music." "No one understands me." "No one cares." "Sometimes all I feel is hate."

Some of these letters clearly deepened into grave emotional distress: "When I go to sleep, I die," wrote one woman. "I feel so miserable, I just don't care," said another. To these were added dozens of similar complaints: "I can't sleep anymore"; "I am always shaking"; "I feel so lost"; "I feel so numb"; "I seem so negative all the time"; "I am so limited."[57]

The murderer is an emissary of mortality itself. All of the half-promises and prevarications of mortality live in the murderer. For the hopeful, the murderer is both an oracle of a God to whom they are subject but do not understand and the staunchest enemy of that God. Here the minor and major miseries of the readers' lives are offered up in the context of greater cruelties, greater mysteries. The tale of murder — which makes so much of detail — seeks to make the prosaic mysterious. Portent inevitably reminds the reader both of chance and fate. Their lives are not in their own hands; they have not failed. Contradictory and coexistent, chance and fate in the tale of murder measure mortality, in all its possibility, always foreclosed.

Responding to an earlier version of this work, a reader gently pointed out that, for all the laudable insights of the overall critique, I had failed to work out my own position on the tale of murder; that is to say, I had not sketched a means by which some of the worst generic impulses could be avoided. Perhaps, in reply to that, I can only cite the means (and end) by which this argument resolves itself: with a confession, a guilt-inflected version of Baldwin's, Millett's, or Dahmer's "witnessing." Their tales of murder might be termed a "better," wiser, or more compassionate response to murder than that of the earlier writers examined here. Although neither compassion nor imagination are modern inventions, the recent history of race, class, and gender activism (not to mention its rich accompaniment in theory) has cut out a space within which the "marginal" can contest their position at the limits, defined by the interests, material and epistemological, of others. Such a contest, quite apart from its immediate aims, tends to throw "authority" into doubt — asking what the power to speak actually means. Indeed, if "death is both superlatively real and superlatively tropic," as Elisabeth Bronfen would have it, then death does have an agent, has specific interests, works against some and for others.[58] What is distinctive about the works of Baldwin, Millett, and Dahmer is the way in which the authors are present in the text, as if they themselves were ghosts, sent to testify for the silenced dead. Capote, present at the execution of Hickock and Smith, for whom he unquestionably felt compassion and, certainly in the latter's case, sympathy, somehow betrays that presence by recalling himself in the text only as a generic witness. *He* is not there; a *reporter* is there. Orwell, on the other hand, *testifies* to the hanging he witnesses: his is a conscientious, self-conscious, and implicated presence. The later writers, Baldwin, Millett, and Imbrie, also testify. Theirs is a *witnessing*. And that, indeed, is what I must nominate as a "fitting" way of writing about murder.

But, for all that such witnessing is fitting, it is also *rare*. It is the murderer that remains at the center of the tale of murder, a tale told by the living to bring death, the spectral visitor, into their presence. It is a tale in which death's usually blind agency has a face, a name, and a life all its own in the figure of the murderer. Dennis Nilsen, murderer, once quipped that a miniseries about his crimes ought to credit its cast "in order of disappearance."[59] Sadly, in the tale of murder it is the figure of the murderer that is the last to disappear.

Appendix:

Varying Accounts of the Murder of Janet Fay

Statement of Martha Beck

Janet Fay had accompanied Ray, her fiancé, and his "sister," Martha, to their house at 15 Adeline Place. Ray was sleeping on the couch in the living room and Martha and Janet took the bed. Janet was talkative all night, asking questions of Martha. Around three or four in the morning she asked for a telephone book, saying she wanted to look up her dead husband's sister who lived in New York. Discouraged from that, she got agitated about the checks she'd signed over to Fernandez the evening before. "Fed up," Martha went into the living room and told Ray, "For God's sake, give this woman back her checks and take her to the train and send her back to Albany." Worried, Mrs. Fay said she didn't want to go, but didn't know what she did want. She was agitated and rambling. Ray said to Martha "in an undertone," "We have to get her quiet." Martha told Janet to go back to bed and Janet retorted in offense, "Are you being paid to make that remark?" The two then argued, Janet accusing Martha of "telling Ray what to do" and Martha accusing her of being "jealous of his sister." Janet said Ray was "soon to be her husband" and when he was they wouldn't want Martha living with them. Ray, tired of this fussing, "jumped up" and told Martha to "get her quiet" and left the room for the bathroom. Janet began to rummage in her suitcase on the floor and, taking the hammer that was lying on the armchair (it had been used to tack up some pictures) Martha hit Janet Fay on the head and "she fell kind of sideways . . . still moaning." Ray then reentered the room and "took her by the throat and tried to choke her," but this was ineffective as she was still moaning and bleeding. So Martha handed Ray her scarf from the chair, and he used the hammer to twist it tight about her neck.[1]

Revised Statement of Martha Beck

In her revised statement,[2] Martha allegedly told the visiting New York authorities that although she was "signing her own death warrant" she must "tell the exact truth." The significant changes in the earlier story were her admission that Ray brought the hammer in not to tack up pictures but because they "may have trouble tonight." When the argument in the early hours of the morning occurred, Martha hid the hammer in the sleeve of her housecoat. She held it out to Ray, but he said, "No, you have got to do it." She said she didn't want to and Ray replied, "If you love me, you will do it." "And that is when I hit her." This second account both placed Fernandez in the room at the time of the murder and gave evidence of premeditation. For those reasons, it formed the heart of the prosecution's account, for it refuted both the insanity defense and the claim that Ray was merely an accessory after the fact.[3]

Statement of Ray Fernandez

Fernandez told the Michigan authorities that Mrs. Fay had come into the living room in the early hours of the morning of 4 January, "wanting to be near" him. He told her to go back to bed and she did, only to return minutes later worried about her money. Hearing her "whimpering," Fernandez got angry and left the living room. In the bedroom Martha told him Fay had been worrying about her money. Returning to the living room, Fernandez assured Fay that her checks were safe in his coat pocket. She was not comforted. Ray again left the room, after saying to Martha, "See if you can keep that woman quiet, no matter how it is." When he returned, "she had kept her quiet by hitting her on the head with a hammer." Seeing the moaning and bleeding Fay, Ray picked up the remnants of the bottle of whiskey in the cabinet and downed it. Fernandez then "helped" Martha, as she said they had to "finish it." He put Martha's white scarf around her neck and tightened it with the hammer.[4]

Testimony of Ray Fernandez

On the stand Fernandez recanted his earlier statement. Janet Fay had kept him up the night previous to that on which the murder occurred. She had "wanted some loving" and he had reluctantly obliged. Fernandez "hugged her, kissed her, caressed her and most everything" while, not a few feet away on the bed, Martha lay silent, possibly asleep and possibly not. After this session, Mrs. Fay would pass him by on the couch every so often and "just touch me." On the morning of the murder, Mrs. Fay was also needing affection but Fernandez was "in no mood for it." Her "worrying about her money" was merely an excuse for her to leave Martha in the bedroom and be near him. Annoyed with her incessant advances, Fernandez went into the bathroom, returning in time to see Mrs. Fay crouched over her suitcase, which was full of blood. Standing over her, Martha seemed to be in something of a daze: "just looking down at Mrs. Fay and no movement." When Fernandez exclaimed "Martha, what has happened?" she only looked down in shock, echoing him: "My God . . . what has happened?" Ray began to stutter about a hospital or a doctor or something, but Martha, feeling for a pulse, said it was "too late." Fernandez strenuously denied using a hammer to tighten the scarf that strangled Fay. He said he'd seen no hammer, although he admitted he owned one. The strangling incident in both his and Martha's testimony became merely an attempt to staunch the flow of cranial blood that was ruining the carpet.[5]

Testimony of Martha Beck

On the stand, Martha enlarged upon Ray's version of the murder. Mrs. Fay had been very needy, soliciting the sexual attention of Fernandez on both of the nights before the murder as well as the night it occurred. Martha, pretending to be asleep, overheard Mrs. Fay's attempts to seduce Ray, and his justifications for the lack of response. Mrs. Fay had apparently "reached in the neck of her slip and pulled out a wrinkled, shriveled-up old breast [saying] 'Don't oo want some sugar, honeychile,'" Ray told her then that "he would give her plenty of loving after the marriage, but not before."[6] The next night, Mrs. Fay made a similar sexual foray, with better results. As Martha dozed, she heard the couple go and sit on the chair by the window, where "there was some talk and mumbling" until she slept. On the morning of the murder, Mrs. Fay was once again restless. After one of her visits to the living room, where Ray was trying to sleep, she told Martha that she was worried about all the money in the house. But her conversation soon diverted to the matter of Ray and her anxiety about whether he'd "ever had an intercourse" or "would she have to show him." Following this conversation, Mrs. Fay went back into the living room, and from there to the bathroom. While she was gone, Ray came through to the bedroom and asked what Martha had been saying to the older woman. After a while, he came in again, flustered. "My God, Martha," he said, "that woman wants to be screwed!" He asked Martha to go and talk to Janet and try to get her back to bed. In the living room, Martha surprised Janet, lying naked on the couch and "expecting Ray to come in," as she put it. Martha told her, "For a woman of your age, you're the hottest bitch I have ever seen." Janet then "rushed toward me and drew back her fist and slapped me. At the same time she slapped me she said: 'Are you being paid to make that remark?'" Beyond that, Martha could remember nothing, until she was shaken by Fernandez and found herself staring at the body slumped over a suitcase that was rapidly filling with blood. Martha did not mention the hammer — it seemed to vanish in the dry well of her memory.

Martha's attorney brought out on direct that it was not only Janet Fay whose advances were rebuffed on the morning of the murder. Martha also went to bed "hurt and angry."[7] The remainder of her account followed Fernandez's closely. Martha also insisted that Janet was dead before Ray began to strangle her with the scarf (or apply the "torniquet").[8]

The State

The version of the murder that the prosecution adhered to was that of the defendants' statements elicited in Michigan "before they had a chance to plan together a defense."[9] This was the version apparently solicited from Martha Beck by the state's psychiatrist, Perry Lichtenstein.[10] After Fernandez had conned Mrs. Fay into signing over her bank checks to them, the household settled down. Fernandez, anticipating trouble, had brought the hammer up from the set of tools in the car. Mrs. Fay kept Martha awake with her worries about the money, and when Fay tried to solicit from Ray some assurances that everything was all right he became annoyed with her, instructing Martha — who would do anything for him — to "keep her quiet, no matter how." Thus it was that Martha struck the elderly woman several times on the head with the ball-peen hammer. When Fernandez returned to the room, Janet Fay was still alive, "bleeding and moaning," and Fernandez cut short those moans by strangling her.[11] Realizing she was finally dead, the couple took "that old woman and they tie her up . . . put her knees up against her chest and her feet up against her buttocks and they wrap her up as you probably wrap a cat that has been killed, and [they] throw her in the closet," but not before Martha had stolen her jewelry. Then, because the body wouldn't fit in the trunk they had, Beck and Fernandez went to buy a bigger trunk. While out, they popped in to the bank in Jamaica, Queens, to open a deposit account with Mrs. Fay's money.[12]

The Defense

The defense stuck to the testimony of the principals, purged of the more confronting and offensive details. It is the one version where the actual event of murder appears only briefly. It is the merest of subplots, rather than the culmination of the drama. Rosenberg told the jury: "When she got into this argument with Mrs. Fay, when she saw Mrs. Fay nude on that couch, she went into a whirlpool, a blind fury. She didn't know what happened. . . . [T]he only thing she remembered after that, there was Mrs. Fay bent over bleeding and dead."[13] For the defense the account of murder is, in fact, an *accounting* of the murderers. The defense strategy was to demonstrate the lack of responsibility of both defendants for the murder — one being literally, and the other figuratively, absent. The murderers are not present at the murder, but they are everywhere else. Such a displacement is ironic. The defense account of murder explodes the frame of narrative that, in all the previous accounts, reduces murder to a moment. The later tale of murder spun by true crime writers would — if any attempt at accuracy was made — detail the events listed by the prosecution, but the actual story would be found in the meaning imputed by the defense to those events.

Martha Beck's 1951 Signed Statement

Shortly before the execution, Martha gave the psychiatrist who'd testified for the defense a quite different account of the Fay murder. She wrote that Ray intervened when Mrs. Fay slapped her, to prevent a "free-for-all." Martha "left the room crying" and returned when she heard a "frightened" call from Ray:

Ray was standing over Mrs. Fay with both hands around her neck. Blood was flowing all over the place from her head and she was moaning faintly. I ran over to him and said, "My God, Ray, stop that!" He said, "This moaning is driving me crazy!" With those words he dropped her head back on the floor and jerked a neck scarf off a chair and put it around her neck. He put the hammer in the knot and tightened it. . . . [H]e told me to hold the hammer. I said "Why? She's dead. Why did you kill her?" Then and only then do I believe that he knew what he had done because he sat down on the couch and said, "My God! My God! What have I done?"[14]

Dr. Hoffmann indicated that Martha had taken the blame on herself because she was afraid of Fernandez — a fear that impelled her to act as an accessory to murder.

Notes

Introduction

1. See Wendy Lesser, *Pictures at an Execution: An Inquiry into the Subject of Murder* (Cambridge: Harvard University Press, 1993), 93–120.

2. See U.S. Department of Commerce, *Statistical Abstract of the United States, 1995*, 115th ed. (Washington, D.C.: GPO, 1996), tables 125–128, 133.

3. David Brion Davis, *Homicide in American Fiction, 1798–1860: A Study in Social Values* (Ithaca: Cornell University Press, 1957).

4. Bill Ellis, "Death by Folklore: Ostension, Contemporary Legend and Murder," *Western Folklore* 48 (July 1989); Joel Black, *The Aesthetics of Murder: A Study in Romantic Literature and Contemporary Culture* (Baltimore: Johns Hopkins University Press, 1991).

5. Fredric Wertham, *The Show of Violence* (Garden City, N.Y.: Doubleday, 1949).

6. Willard Motley, *Knock on Any Door* (New York: Appleton-Century, 1947).

7. William March, *The Bad Seed* (London: Hamish Hamilton, 1954).

8. Curtis Bok, *Star Wormwood* (New York: Knopf, 1959).

9. Ibid., 205.

10. Ibid., 161.

11. The *New York Journal American* used this characterization frequently, particularly in the lead-up to the execution.

12. Martha Beck, quoted in Wenzell Brown, *Introduction to Murder: The Unpublished Facts Behind the Notorious Lonely Hearts Killers Martha Beck and Ray Fernandez* (New York: Greenberg, 1952), 149. I have been unable to verify this quote. Its tone, however, does match that of some of Martha Beck's reproving letters to the press published in part just after her death. It seems likely that she did say it, and she certainly had *cause*, as we shall see in Chapters 4 and 5.

13. There is, of course, the problem of that important subgenre in true crime: the unsolved murder. Where the tale lacks a murderer, the corpse must stand in. The victim and the scene of the murder become ciphers for the absent author. "How?" is asked as if it were "Why?"

14. Directed by Leonard Castle and Oliver Wood and starring Tony Lo Bianco and Shirley Stoller.

15. James Baldwin, *The Evidence of Things Not Seen* (New York: Henry Holt, 1985); Kate Millett, *The Basement: Meditations on a Human Sacrifice* (New York: Simon and Schuster, Touchstone, 1991 [orig. 1979]).

16. Baldwin is less gender-blind than Millett is inattentive to race. Baldwin's analysis of gender, however, is very much leveled at the category of the masculine.

1. Here There Be Killers

1. "Body Found," *Daily Sentinel*, 26 August 1866.

2. Michel Foucault et al., eds., *I, Pierre Riviere, Having Slaughtered My Mother, My Sister and My Brother* . . . (Lincoln: University of Nebraska Press, 1975), 206.

3. Jane Caputi has scrupulously (if rather didactically) traced the power of the narrative frame of "true crime" to mythologize both the act of murder and the murderer — obscuring the discrete characteristics of act and actor and effectively obliterating the victim. See her discussion on the creation of the Ripper mythology and the wholesale repetition of the characteristics of that myth in crime reporting (particularly of rape-murder) up to the present day. Jane Caputi, *The Age of Sex Crime* (London: Women's Press, 1987).

4. Josephine McDonagh, "Do or Die: Problems of Agency and Gender in the Aesthetics of Murder," *Genders*, no. 5 (Summer 1989): 123.

5. See Chapter Seven below for an analysis of the impact of the formalist mode of legal reasoning in contemporary American jurisprudence.

6. Foucault speaks of a need to get away from the idea of power as law, so that an analytics of power can map the operations of specific relations of power that occur at the local level, the level of bodies, of moments, of the banal, the everyday, the interior — those places, in short, which traditional analyses of power do not attend to; that which one might call the "profane." Traditional power's relation to the profane was only that of a realm to be contained and controlled; for Foucault the profane is the ground, the circuit, of power.

The disciplines have grown out of an understanding of power as a thing to be had, wielded, ameliorated, rationalized. Foucault's critique of the development of the human sciences cannot be abstracted from his work on the disciplining of bodies and populations, "anatomo-" and "bio-politics," and the "knowledge–power" relation within which the body and species are the object of scrutiny but are also subjects in process. Foucault's complex analyses of the development of the human sciences, "expert" knowledges, the carceral complex, and the production of pathology are to be found in the works he produced from the mid-1970s till his death. See particularly (but obviously not exclusively) Michel Foucault, *The Archeology of Knowledge* (New York: Harper Colophon, 1976); *Discipline and Punish: The Birth of the Prison* (London: Peregrine, 1979); *The Order of Things: An Archeology of the Human Sciences* (New York: Pantheon, 1971); and *The History of Sexuality*, vol. 1: *An Introduction* (London: Penguin, 1990).

7. For a structural and materialist account of the postwar success of the crime story, see Ernest Mandel, *Delightful Murder: A Social History of the Crime Story* (London: Pluto, 1984).

8. For an indication of the interplay between the chronicle of crime, crime literature, and the growth of the newspaper media, see Beth Kalikoff, *Murder and Moral Decay in Victorian Literature* (Ann Arbor: UMI, 1990). See also David Ray Papke, *Framing the Criminal: Crime, Cultural Work and the Loss of Critical Perspective 1830–1900* (Hamden, Conn.: Archon, 1987).

9. Michel Foucault, *The History of Sexuality*, vol. 1: *An Introduction* (New York: Penguin, 1990), 138.

10. For a discussion of the Western relationship of modernity, individualism, and death, see Philip A. Mellor and Chris Shilling, "Modernity, Self-Identity and the Sequestration of Death," *Sociology* 27, no. 3 (1993).

11. Davis, *Homicide in American Fiction*; Black, *Aesthetics of Murder*.

12. "[O]nce an event is covered, or 'mediated,' by the press or by television, it essentially enters into the same quasi-fictional, hyperreal domain of all artistic representation and misrepresentation" (Black, *Aesthetics of Murder*, 10). Although his approach is supposedly extramoral, Black retains an uncharacteristic moralism about textuality in his distinction between representation and misrepresentation.

13. Davis, *Homicide in American Fiction*, viii.

14. "During the course of our inquiry, we shall examine diverse theories and distant relationships, but the unifying core will be the knowledge that man possesses, by virtue of his intelligence, an extraordinary capacity to kill" (ibid., ix).

15. James Gordon Bennett, quoted ibid., 162.

16. Drawing heavily on Bennett's reporting, Howard wrote a full-length account of the case: *The Lives of Helen Jewett and Richard P. Robinson, by the Editor of the New York "National Police Gazette"* (New York: George Wilkes, Printer, 1848).

17. Joseph Holt Ingraham, *Frank Rivers; or, The Dangers of the Town* (1843).

18. "Helen Jewett's sexuality is attractive but taboo, therefore she must die; but in death she is even more appealing and even more forbidden" (Davis, *Homicide in American Fiction*, 164).

19. Sander Gilman's discussion of the beautiful female corpse in reference to forensic pathology is instructive here. See Gilman, " 'I'm Down on Whores': Race and Gender in Victorian London," in David Goldberg, ed., *Anatomy of Racism* (Minneapolis: University of Minnesota Press, 1990).

20. Elisabeth Bronfen, *Over Her Dead Body: Death, Femininity and the Aesthetic* (New York: Routledge, 1992), 205.

21. Introduction to Sarah Webster Goodwin and Elisabeth Bronfen, eds., *Death and Representation* (Baltimore: Johns Hopkins University Press, 1993), 14.

22. Ibid., 13.

23. Davis argues that it was a metaphorical relationship between the deranged values of the individual and the deranged values of society that fascinated American writers prior to the Civil War. In his reading of selected texts, Davis shows that the individual criminal act of violence could simultaneously be an expression of familial contest, patriarchal dominance, or even political rebellion. See Davis on the spectre of European anarchism and fears of unrestrained democracy (*Homicide in American Fiction*, 240–243). In terms of his complicated critique of changing understandings of criminal responsibility, Davis contends that the derangement of the murderous protagonist was the result of a flaw in reason, will, or morality that weakened him, enabling the full force of an outside ill to drive him to action. The model of the "ruling passion" governed much fiction of the period, just as the theory of monomania was gaining ground in American psychiatry. Davis's discussion of the progression of American psychiatric thought and its intersection with forensic psychiatry is supported by less "literary" analyses. See Janet Colaizzi, *Homicidal Insanity, 1800–1985* (Tuscaloosa: University of Alabama Press, 1989) for a view from the profession itself.

24. It is interesting to note that there have recently been popular feminist attempts to "rewrite" the nineteenth-century tale of seduction. See, for instance, Susan Fromberg Schaeffer, *The Madness of a Seduced Woman* (London: Pan, 1989).

25. Davis, *Homicide in American Fiction*, 171.

26. Ibid., 201.

27. Davis's characterization of "the Colonel's lady and Judy O'Grady" finds its refined equivalent in Fiedler's "Fair Maiden and Dark Lady."

28. Michel Foucault et al., eds., *I, Pierre Riviere, Having Slaughtered My Mother, My Sister, and My Brother . . . A Case of Parricide in the 19th Century* (Lincoln: University of Nebraska Press, 1975), xiii, 199.

29. "The event was freedom; it cut like a blade, perturbed, thwarted, or took every sort of institution in the rear. An exemplary event, murder, here aimed, in a frozen world, at the timelessness of oppression and the order of power" (Jean Peter and Jeanne Favret, ibid., 186).

30. Auden, quoted in Black, *Aesthetics of Murder*, 7.

31. See McDonagh, "Do or Die," 122.

32. Black, *Aesthetics of Murder*, 12, 13, 16.

33. Quoted in Jean Baudrillard, *Simulations* (New York: Semiotexte, 1983), 1.

34. I have placed ironic emphasis on the term "serial killer" to demonstrate that

it is not the *found* category of a new killer that criminologists would have it to be, but is itself a historically and culturally particular construction.

35. David Berkowitz, the "Son of Sam," is a case in point. The publication of his first letter to the police upped sales of the *Daily News* to over a million. The *New Yorker* accused the practitioners of such journalistic sensationalism of engaging in "self-fulfilling publicity": encouraging the killer by "transforming him into a celebrity." See Caputi, *Age of Sex Crime*, 39–41. Another writer notes the effect, after Berkowitz's capture, of the killer's rise in status: "Berkowitz, the mail clerk, suddenly finds that every word becomes important; Berkowitz, the murderer, discovers that a poem found in his pocket after capture becomes important." See Wayne Wilson, *Good Murders and Bad Murders: A Consumer's Guide in the Age of Information* (Lanham, Md.: University Press of America, 1991), 203.

36. Black, *Aesthetics of Murder*, 17.

37. Ibid., 21.

38. Susan Griffin provides one of the more metaphysical analyses of the relation of the pornographer to the violent world he inhabits: "[W]hen a madman is told that he does not see the world correctly, and when he is given evidence against his prejudices, he will refuse to see the truth, and he will even distort this evidence to support his own delusion. But, most significantly, he will even change reality so it supports his mad idea of the world. . . . *The deluded mind must try to remake the world after an illusion* [emphasis in original]." Susan Griffin, "Pornography and Silence," in *Made from This Earth* (London: Women's Press, 1982), 136. Griffin here retains a clear distinction between the mad (the unreal) and the true (the real). The critical idea of what constitutes "mad" goes unexamined, and with it an unproblematic "reality."

39. There has been a plethora of findings — supporting variously a causal link, no causal link, and the impossibility of establishing such a link! Thus the 1970 National Commission on Obscenity and Pornography, which found no causal link, had its decision reversed by a 1986 Attorney General's Commission which found the exact opposite.

40. See Caputi, *Age of Sex Crime*, 36, 167.

41. Ian Hacking, *Rewriting the Soul: Multiple Personality and the Sciences of Memory* (Princeton: Princeton University Press, 1995), 239.

42. Chapman was obsessed by J. D. Salinger's *Catcher in the Rye* and styled himself as Holden Caulfield, a "latter-day" catcher. It is well known that Hinckley modeled himself on Travis Bickle in the movie *Taxi Driver* — so dedicated to this image, in fact, that he intended to "liberate" Jodie Foster from Yale, where she was then studying (Foster had played the teen prostitute Bickle "saves" in the film).

43. Black, *Aesthetics of Murder*, 25.

44. Ibid.

45. The term "urban legend" can be a little misleading if it is taken to restrict the circulation of these modern apocrypha to metropolitan areas.

46. Ellis, "Death by Folklore," 202.

47. Ibid., 208.

48. Ellis details the possible occurrence of murder by ostension in the killing near Logan, Ohio, of Annette Cooper and Todd Schultz, whose corpses were found dismembered and inscribed with signs. Although Cooper's stepfather was convicted of the murder (the verdict was overturned on appeal), both popular belief and forensic evidence point to the murders as being an incidence of cult sacrifice. Ibid., 209–218.

49. Ibid., 219.

50. "[N]ot only can facts be turned into narratives but narratives can also be turned into facts" (Linda Degh and Andrew Vaszonyi, quoted ibid., 202).

2. Parens Patriae

1. One critic has identified the appeal of the "idea of degeneration" for American writers in the period up to World War II: "For American writers, heartbreakingly earnest about warning their countrymen that America not only was failing to live up to its ideals but was becoming a plutocracy in which money was the one true God, the idea of degeneration as a means to dramatize their concern was so attractive for so long because of its dynamism. Unlike such static abstractions as the Fall and innate depravity, degeneration was a secular, historical process. . . . [I]t allowed for the possibility that the degenerative process could be reversed in time." George Spangler, "The Idea of Degeneration in American Fiction 1880–1940," *English Studies*, no. 5 (1989): 435.

2. Motley, *Knock on Any Door*.

3. March, *The Bad Seed*.

4. The present book is in many ways indebted to the work of Michel Foucault, although I have tried to maintain the theoretical precepts of the work as implicit in order to avoid the scholarly genealogies that often form such an unwieldy part of scholarly texts (and that seem to be, more often than not, relics of the dissertation stage). Undeniably, however, my critiques have been shaped by Foucault and, particularly, by his introductory volume in *The History of Sexuality*.

5. Foucault, *The History of Sexuality*, vol. 1: *An Introduction*, 130.

6. Ibid., 147.

7. These unities are, briefly,

1. *A hystericization of women's bodies:* . . . whereby it [the feminine body] was integrated into the sphere of medical practices, by reason of a pathology intrin-

sic to it; whereby finally, it was placed in organic communication with the social body (whose regulated fecundity it was supposed to ensure), the family space . . . and the life of children. . . .

2. *A pedagogicization of children's sex.* . . .[A]ll children indulge or are prone to indulge in sexual activity, and that, being unwarranted, at the same time "natural" and "contrary to nature," this sexual activity posed physical and moral, individual and collective dangers. . . .

3. *A socialization of procreative behaviour.* . . .

4. *A psychiatrization of perverse pleasures.*

This whole section (ibid., 104–105) is crucial to my project here.

8. Ibid., 104.

9. While this is obvious in many ways, both in the tone and the thematic preoccupations of the work, it is best evidenced by the use of popular songs throughout the text, all of which hit the charts prior to 1940. Motley wrote the bulk of the work from 1940 to 1943 (but revised it extensively thereafter). Its genesis, however, dates from the much earlier short fictional works eventually integrated into the novel. See Robert Fleming, *Willard Motley* (Boston: Twayne, 1978).

10. In critical and popular terms, this was the best received of all Motley's novels. After two years of sale, 350,000 copies were in print, 47,000 of which had sold in the first two weeks. One (white) reviewer thought that it invited comparison with Richard Wright's *Native Son*, and that it was the better work. See ibid., 59–63, for an overview of the critical response.

11. See *The Diaries of Willard Motley*, ed. Jerome Klinkowitz (Ames: Iowa State University, 1979), particularly the introduction and the years 1938–1941.

12. The plot of *Knock on Any Door* mirrors elements of both those other seminal works. But this mirror gives back different reflections. Motley tackles the sexual double standard, as does Dreiser in the sequence involving Clyde's sister's sequestration during her pregnancy (she was unmarried). Clyde is quite helpless before his sister's shame. But when Nick's sister comes to him for help about getting an abortion, Nick is disposed and able to help her get it. Ang retains her respectability; Nick never attains his. This reflection of the earlier naturalistic work shows critical engagement, not plagiarism. An analysis of apparent parallels between *Knock on Any Door* and *Native Son* would likely show a similar critical engagement.

13. Motley, *Knock on Any Door*, 478.

14. See Chapter Seven below for an analysis of Baldwin's coding of degraded manhood in relation to the concept of "sorriness" in the African American community.

15. See Ian Hacking (*Rewriting the Soul*, 210–220) on the historical development of the concept of "trauma." Although Hacking is concerned with the de-

velopment of the categories of "child abuse" and "multiple personality disorder," and their relationship to the investment of Western modernity in the idea of memory, his work is an illuminating exercise of some of Foucault's critical work around the "pedagogicization of children's sex."

16. Note that Foucault does not differentiate in his discussion of the "pedagogicization of children's sex" between the "child" and the "adolescent," yet the discursive differentiation is important here because of the salience that juvenile (meaning adolescent) sexuality was assuming in discussions about juvenile delinquency in the United States when Motley wrote his novel.

17. Motley, *Knock on Any Door*, 123.

18. Ibid., 119, 123, 128, 155.

19. Ibid., 128.

20. Ibid., 129.

21. Ibid., 147.

22. Ibid., 151.

23. Ibid., 181–182, 184.

24. Ibid., 292.

25. Ibid., 296–297.

26. Indeed, the novel — though not well remembered now — can boast to be the originating text for this phrase.

27. Ibid., 481–482.

28. The film foregrounds the murder in a way that suggests the diminution of the materialism of the novel in favor of "suspense." Its reworking produced a hybrid of detective and courtroom drama (the primary search being for motivation).

29. Motley's novel seeks to dispel the "legitimacy" of certain forms of state-sanctioned violence, most particularly that of the police, the judiciary, and corrections.

30. *Parens patriae* is a paradoxical phrase connoting the generative fatherland as well as the feminine (conveyed by the Latin gender of both words of the phrase). It is an apt phrase for Motley's critique of authority and the masculine.

31. If Nick had been able to make love to Emma, she would not have killed herself; had she not died, he would not have killed Riley; had he not killed Riley, his mother would be happy.

32. Stanley Hyman (untitled review), *New Republic*, 8 February 1943, p. 188.

33. March told his friend, Clint Bolton, that the novel was to be a portrait of "planned evilness." See Bolton, quoted in Roy Simmonds, "Cathy Ames and Rhoda Penmark: Two Child Monsters," *The Mississippi Quarterly* 39 (Spring 1986): 99.

34. Bolton, quoted ibid., 98.

35. It is worth remembering at this point that Willard Motley extensively

researched the various institutional settings for his novel, from the reformatory through to the trial process. He is said to have used real characters he encountered in that research. See Fleming, *Willard Motley*, 36–40.

36. "Already she [Christine] missed her husband, and although she had become reconciled to these necessary absences, she had never become used to them; and standing quietly in her living room she thought that all her life she had waited for someone — first her father, and now her husband" (March, *The Bad Seed*, 44–45).

37. Ibid., 188.

38. Looking at a photograph of her husband, Christine sees the brown eyes that "looked out at the world with a sort of innocent eagerness" (ibid., 126). A description remarkably similar to that of August Denker.

39. While Christine's suspicions were aroused by the peculiar circumstances surrounding the death — to which Rhoda was sole witness — of an elderly neighbor in Baltimore, her husband cannot even begin to entertain doubts.

40. Ibid., 99.

41. Christine writes in another letter that cannot be sent to Kenneth: "I feel now more strongly than ever that the problem of Rhoda is not the joint one I considered it: the problem is mine, and I must solve it alone. I alone am responsible. It was I who carried the bad seed that made her what she is, not you" (ibid., 206).

42. Ibid., 210–211.

43. Ibid., 33.

44. Rhoda is portrayed as an atavistic throwback, and the description of her "peculiar character" in regard to her acquisitiveness is naturalizing even at the point when it is considered merely a curiosity, not a threat: "She was like a charming little animal that can never be trained to fit into the conventional pattern of existence" (ibid., 46).

45. Ibid., 64.

46. This dangerous naivete is demonstrated by Monica Breedlove's attitude toward Leroy, and Monica's brother and friends all counsel her to dismiss Leroy. She ignores both Leroy's surliness and their advice "not because she condoned his actions, but because she considered him disturbed and hardly responsible for some of his acts" (ibid., 26). March is making a frontal assault here on the tendency of certain powerful schools of forensic psychiatry to abolish personal responsibility for criminal or "antisocial" acts. Monica Breedlove, a passionate devotee of Freudian psychoanalysis, is frequently used as a device to attack the dangerous vanities of a science of mind.

47. Leroy nurtures his grievances against the society that has deprived him, grievances apparently backed up by a sociological model that holds an oppressive society to account for the individual's actual and potential wrongs: "his mind rehearsed eternally the inequities forced upon him — inequities which he must

endure in silence, since he was one of the underprivileged ones of the world: the unfortunate son of an unfortunate sharecropper, the pathetic victim of an oppressive system, *as everyone who knew anything at all admitted, and had admitted for a long time* [emphasis mine]" (ibid., 20). Leroy is enamored of the hierarchy of privilege that excuses him anything — so much so that he has invented wholesale his own lowly position in that hierarchy (ibid., 64).

48. Ibid., 39.

49. "A few of the gravestones, with their authentic dates, and affirmations of a quainter morality than our own, had been left as they were, as though they, too, were shrubs of a sort; as though they could put the earnest reader into that mood of sadness, that sense of the transience of life, which is the reason of the philosopher's reading" (ibid., 215).

50. In the film version of *The Bad Seed* Reginald Tasker is called not "that true crime writer" but that "criminologist" — a handy confusion which inadvertently reduces criminology from a scholarly discipline to a journalistic fairy tale for bombasts (which it arguably is). This slippage makes quite clear the interdependence of scholarly and popular discourses of criminality.

51. Ibid., 50.

52. Ibid., 147.

53. Nurse Earle Dennison's murder indictment was contemporary with March's writing: she was executed in Alabama in September 1953. Also mentioned are Beulah Hunnicutt, Norma Jean Brooks, Richard Walsh, Milton Drury, Houston Roberts, and the poisoners Tillie Klimek and Daisy de Melker (ibid., 153–154). Amy Archer-Gilligan, Belle Gunness, Bertha Hill, Catherine Wilson, Anna Hahn, Jane Toppan, and Susi Olah are all listed as precursors to the fictitious Bessie Denker (pp. 164–165). Eva Coo, Madeleine Smith, Lizzie Borden, and Lydia Southard also get "favorable" mentions in comparison to Bessie Denker (pp. 179–180). Of all the real murderers drawn on, the most crucial are Belle Gunness and Ruth Brown Snyder — from whom the composite figure which is Bessie Denker is made.

54. A definition very unlike the more recent "motiveless" crime that is a catchall descriptor for the apparent rise in the "thrill-killing" of strangers.

55. Ibid., 51–57.

56. Wertham did write on murder as a popular forensic psychologist, but he would probably have been horrified to have himself tagged as being in the true crime genre. I would argue, however, that Wertham wrote in what I term the "high literature" of true crime. See Chapter Three below.

57. Ibid., 55.

58. See Hayden White on the ironic mode of narrative in his *Tropics of Discourse: Essays in Cultural Criticism* (Baltimore: Johns Hopkins University Press, 1978).

59. March, *The Bad Seed*, 129, 169, 180.

60. There are other examples of this. Tasker's case notes on Bessie Denker are full of speculation from "Bessie Denker's admirers" concerning her involvement in the mysterious deaths among her family when she was a child (ibid., 187).

61. "[F]or years he'd read, collected, annotated, and digested cases of the type . . . and it seemed to him that environment had little to do with its persistent appearance, although, conceivably, environment might modify its outward aspects. The simplest way to understand the type was to regard them as the normal human beings of fifty thousand years ago, before man began his task of civilizing himself, or built his code of axioms into the moral codes that govern us" (ibid., 178–179).

62. Ibid., 244–245.

63. Ibid., 215, 244.

64. Belle Gunness (1860–?) was never apprehended after her flight from the La Porte, Indiana farm where authorities located the grisly remains, buried around the property, of her various wealthy suitors (mail-order husbands who traveled there in response to her offer of property and romance). Her story features at length in various murder dictionaries. See J. R. Nash, *Murder America: Homicide in the United States from 1850 to the Present* (London: Harrap, 1961); Ann Jones, *Women Who Kill* (New York: Holt, Rinehart, and Winston, 1980), 129–39; and Kerry Segrave, *Women Serial and Mass Murderers: A Worldwide Reference, 1580– 1990* (Jefferson, N.C.: McFarland, 1992) for several different extensive treatments. Belle may also have been a particularly tempting choice for March because of the media circus that surrounded the exhumation of the bodies of Belle's successive suitors. Trainloads of sightseers arrived to watch the proceedings, practically dismantling the farm for souvenirs.

65. March, *The Bad Seed*, 243.

66. The phrase is Adrienne Rich's, from her poem "For Ethel Rosenberg."

67. The best discussion of Snyder's case is in Jones, *Women Who Kill.*

68. March, *The Bad Seed*, 150.

69. See Clint Bolton, quoted in Simmonds, "Cathy Ames and Rhoda Penmark," 98.

70. March, *The Bad Seed*, 137.

71. Ibid., 138.

72. Ibid.

73. Ibid., 208. Earlier in the novel Christine observes Rhoda's enthusiasm for her Sunday school lessons, no doubt an enthusiasm encouraged by the presentation of prizes for lessons well learned. But the passage for that day's text foreshadows Christine's recognition of Rhoda's affinity for the "bloodier precepts of the Old Testament: . . . it centred around the damnation and most cruel destruc-

tion of those who had been unable, or unwilling, to conform blindly to some Hebraic party line of that day. . . . Christine read the text slowly, shook her head and thought, 'Is there nothing but violence everywhere?' " (pp. 70–71).

74. Ibid., 39.

75. In the novel, Christine's research is mainly done by *reading*, a highly undramatic activity.

76. Again, the progress of Christine's awful discoveries and the increasing complexity of her dilemma are described in the novel by means of her internal monologues — difficult to transcribe onto the screen (although the voice-over had been a staple of the *film noir* detective genre).

77. Cold War discourse on the family has received a good deal of attention in recent scholarship on gender and the family in Cold War culture. See, for instance, Elaine Tyler May, *Homeward Bound: American Families in the Cold War Era* (New York: Basic Books, 1988); Arlene Skolnick, *Embattled Paradise: The American Family in the Age of Uncertainty* (New York: Basic Books, 1991). I am indebted also to Dr. Geoffrey Smith, of Queens University, Kingston, Ontario, for access to his forthcoming study of gender and sexuality in the Cold War era.

78. Rather than a quantitative view like March's. For a thoroughgoing interdisciplinary discussion of the history of quantitative and qualitative theories of pathology, see Georges Canguilheim, *The Normal and the Pathological* (New York: Zone, 1991).

79. In a letter to a friend, Motley described MGM's reaction to the screenplay of his novel (which they'd just promised to purchase when *Knock on Any Door* was chosen as "Best Novel of the Year" in their studio contest). The deal fell through when the Breen office reported that the novel "encouraged juvenile delinquency, was immoral, indecent, etc." (Klinkowitz, ed., *The Diaries of Willard Motley*, xix).

3. Min(d)ing the Murderer

1. Wertham, *Show of Violence*; Bok, *Star Wormwood*.

2. For two quite different interpretive directions taken from the mythical archetypes of murder, see René Girard, "The Sacrificial Crisis," in *Critical Theory since 1965* (Tallahassee: Florida State University Press, 1986) and Nicole Ward Jouve, *"The Streetcleaner": The Yorkshire Ripper Case on Trial* (London: Marion Boyars, 1986).

3. "It is the historical function of psychiatry in relation to law at the present time to introduce into criminal cases facts and interpretations of facts which psychiatry and psychoanalysis have taught us. This will not only help in the proper disposition of cases but will aid in the prevention of crime and will lead

more and more to the principle of safeguarding the community" (Wertham, *Show of Violence*, 24–25).

4. In this I follow Michel Foucault's construction of the development of the discourse of the "human sciences," explicated in *The Order of Things* and *The Archeology of Knowledge*.

5. Wertham, *Show of Violence*, 128.

6. See Fredric Jameson's discussion of generic systems, implementing Edmund Husserl's theory of "sedimentation," in *The Political Unconscious: Narrative as a Socially Symbolic Act* (London: Methuen, 1981), 139–141n32.

7. Wertham considered himself lucky to have had an opportunity to study at length this young man, who became his patient years before he would commit the triple murder for which he became infamous. Irwin features largely in *The Show of Violence*.

8. Wertham, *Show of Violence*, 111.

9. See, for instance, the way in which Wertham's suggestion to Irwin that he had a "love-hate relationship" with his mother structured the highlighting of certain "revelatory" recollections by Irwin of his mother. Ibid., 125–126.

10. See Russell Grigg, "Subject, Object, and the Transference," in E. Ragland-Sullivan and M. Bracher, eds., *Lacan and the Subject of Language* (New York: Routledge, 1991), 108–109.

11. Michel Foucault, "About the Concept of the 'Dangerous' Individual in 19th Century Legal Psychiatry," in D. Weisstub, ed., *Law and Psychiatry* (New York: Pergamon, 1978).

12. This compromise is explored at length by Thomas Berger's novel, *Killing Time* (New York: Delta, 1967), structured loosely around the story of Irwin as mediated by Wertham, Quentin Reynolds, and the media at large. For an analysis of *Killing Time* as a critique of the discourses that circumscribed Irwin, see Jon Wallace, "A Murderous Clarity: A Reading of Thomas Berger's *Killing Time*," *Philological Quarterly* 68, no. 1 (1989). Although I would like to deal with Berger's novel, space does not allow me to do so here.

13. These included charitable institutions and psychiatric clinics. The timing of Irwin's incarceration — during the lean years of the Great Depression, when Irwin could find no work and little afford lodgings — begs the question of the reason for Irwin's "flight into custody."

14. Wertham, *Show of Violence*, 101–102. For a complete rendering of Irwin's first interview with the police and his statement, see Quentin Reynolds, *Courtroom: The Story of Samuel S. Leibowitz* (New York: Farrar, Straus, 1950), 123–128.

15. Wertham provided a definition of "catathymic crisis" in an earlier case study in *The Show of Violence*. Explaining the murder of her children by a woman he calls "Madeline," Wertham writes: "Madeline suffered from a reactive depres-

sion with delusions. The aberration of reasoning under the impact of emotional complexes (technically called *catathymic*) accounted for the crisis — that is, the outbreak of violence. Psychiatrically we speak of such a condition as catathymic crisis" (*Show of Violence*, 76).

16. Quoted ibid., 139.

17. Reynolds, *Courtroom*, 114. Emphasis mine.

18. For an interesting explication (in an entirely different context) of the problem of "retroactive anticipation," see Jane Gallop, "Where to Begin?" in *Reading Lacan* (Ithaca: Cornell University Press, 1995).

19. Reynolds, *Courtroom*, 114.

20. Wertham, *Show of Violence*, 170.

21. Ibid., 140.

22. Wertham, *Show of Violence*, 170.

23. For Lacan and Freud, a pact based upon the "free consent and liberty of the patient." See Grigg, "Subject, Object, and the Transference," 104–109.

24. Wertham, *Show of Violence*, 125.

25. The "glory" of Irwin's "attainment" was to be arrived at by the development of the psychic skill he called "visualization." Visualization was a means to redeem the insufficiencies of memory, to recall from the past, in their nuanced entirety, works of art and literature, historical figures and, eventually, the past itself "as living." It was Irwin's professed belief that he could develop such a skill that led him to tell the police in his initial statement that the lives of his victims were not "lost": "theirs are borrowed lives, and if I live I will repay them." Statement by Robert Irwin, 27 June 1937, quoted in Reynolds, *Courtroom*, 127.

26. Wertham, *Show of Violence*, 178.

27. According to Wertham, Irwin had a "consuming drive to excel for the favor of his mother" and "he was very close to her, but she unwittingly stimulated his ambivalent feelings about her" (by calling him, for instance, "a regular girl"). Ibid., 172. The doctor went on to explain Irwin's "abnormal attachment to his mother," as follows: "The mother-image, distorted in his mind and loved and hated at the same time, prevented him from making a normal love adjustment to other women without leading to a dominant homosexual pattern. He acted as if he wished to keep indefinitely an overwhelmingly pure love for his mother. . . . [H]e repeatedly showed friendliness for older women who were like mothers to him. He would leave these mother substitutes as abruptly as he had left his mother" (p. 177).

28. Riviere's bid for fame is complicated by the production of the memoir. The act of writing and the murder constitute, in effect, a single act: "the fact of killing and the fact of writing, the deeds done and the things narrated, coincided since

they were elements of a like nature." Michel Foucault, "Tales of Murder," in Foucault et al., eds., *I, Pierre Riviere*, 200.

29. Quoted in Foucault et al., eds., *I, Pierre Riviere*, 108, 105.

30. Wertham, *Show of Violence*, 170 (emphasis mine), 122, 123.

31. Ibid., 123.

32. Ibid.

33. Ibid., 178.

34. Ibid., 177.

35. Statement by Robert Irwin, quoted in Reynolds, *Courtroom*, 126.

36. Wertham, *Show of Violence*, 136.

37. Ibid., 105.

38. See L. Stephens, "Still Ripping One Hundred Years On: Regarding the 'Ripper Centenary,' " *Antithesis*, 3, no. 2 (1990), for a discussion of this process of the murderer's sexualization of the female victim/corpse and the following discursive desexualization of the crime by its commentators through the reduction of what constitutes the sexual. The discourse that denies the sexual metaphor in the Ripper's murders does so only by its repression of such knowledge of the sexual.

39. Statement by Robert Irwin, quoted in Reynolds, *Courtroom*, 126.

40. Ibid., 126–127.

41. Ibid., 127.

42. See Jacqueline Rose's introduction to the set of readings by Lacan on the problem of feminine sexuality and the creation of the female subject—the double bind of feminine subjectivity—in Jacqueline Rose and Juliet Mitchell, eds., *Feminine Sexuality: Jacques Lacan and the ecole freudienne* (New York: Norton, 1985), 27–59.

43. On the tropic relation of Woman and Death in Western culture generally, see Bronfen, *Over Her Dead Body*.

44. She becomes both Irwin's literal mother and representative of the archetypal devouring Mother.

45. Some years earlier and before the self-emasculation attempt that would land him in the hospital and first bring him into contact with the doctor, Irwin wrote to a girlfriend that he wanted to "cut off his penis in order to 'bottle up his sexual energy' for higher purposes" (Wertham, *Show of Violence*, 122).

46. Irwin, quoted in Reynolds, *Courtroom*, 137.

47. As distinct from the *phallus*. It might seem that the omission of this critically important signifying term is even more surprising—an omission that indicates both Wertham's relative lack of fidelity to the rigors of Freudian analysis and the distance of the Anglo-American school from its Lacanian-influenced Continental counterpart.

48. Wertham, *Show of Violence*, 154.

49. Inevitably, this relocation of the borders of the self results in a radical redefinition of the divine. Irwin's investment of himself into others naturally does away with the differentiation that leaves the divine "out there," elsewhere. This philosophical tendency of Irwin's bamboozled his later analysts, leading them to suggest that he thought himself to be God. As the following exchange between Dr. Hinsie and Irwin makes clear, this was not quite the case:

Q: . . . You and divinity and God and the universal mind are all one[?]

A: So are you, of course.

Q: Then I can only conclude or reframe your statement to read as coming from you, "I am God."

A: Yes. Absolutely! Since you limit your whole statement to me, exactly.

[. . .]

Q: Do you wish to cancel anything that you said here?

A: No, I do not. If you leave it to me, I prefer to say that I am divinity, but you are too.

Quoted in Reynolds, *Courtroom*, 136.

50. A model that figures the flawed link between Irwin and his mother: his need to find, then annihilate, her surrogate.

51. Such an explanation is not uncommon among people charged with homicide. The protestation that everything "passed in a blur" could indicate either a strategic response (in preparation for the defense of insanity or diminished responsibility) or a genuine description of shock.

52. Wertham, *Show of Violence*, 153.

53. Ibid., 170.

54. Just before sentencing, when asked by the court whether there was anything he wished to say, Irwin pointedly told the press gallery: "I have nothing but contempt for you. You have lied about me continually. You have told untruths. You are dirty dogs." Quoted in Reynolds, *Courtroom*, 148.

55. Wertham, *Show of Violence*, 161.

56. Irwin, however, did redirect this sum toward paying the legal costs of his defense. Reynolds, *Courtroom*, 122.

57. The $500 Irwin charged his lawyer in exchange for his agreement to plead guilty to a lesser charge of second-degree murder was to go toward the perfection of his "visualization" skills. Significantly, it was the *change in the direction of his story* augured by the plea bargain that annoyed Irwin: "Leibowitz had quite a time persuading Irwin to plead guilty of second-degree murder. Irwin felt cheated. He wanted to appear on the stand and expound his theory of divinity to the public. It took all of Leibowitz' persuasive powers to convince him to plead guilty of

second-degree murder. Irwin made one condition. He would allow Leibowitz to have his way if Leibowitz would give him five hundred dollars" (ibid., 146).

58. Irwin's ambition to reconstruct lost places, people, time, was the source of his insistence that he had only "borrowed" the lives of the Gedeons and Byrnes.

59. "In a human being's life, murder is one of the most crucial, experiment-like events that can possibly take place. It reveals the innermost springs of the individual's life and is a profound self-revelation of character" (Wertham, *Show of Violence*, 245–246).

60. Ibid., 253.

61. Ibid., 164.

62. This distinction can also be identified in Wertham's treatment of the ideological nature of the concept of murder. He asks, for instance, why it is that industrial accidents — caused by the callousness and greed of employers (he denounces the theory of worker carelessness) — do not earn the title of "murder." In his discussion of the concept of the criminal in Nazi Germany, he also raises interesting questions about the normalization of murder by its elevation to a system (ibid., 241–266). See, too, Wertham's article "It's Murder" in the *Saturday Review of Literature*, 5 February 1949, pp. 7–9, 33–34 for a distillation of this analysis.

63. Unlike Irwin, "Mary" had not become nationally infamous, and she therefore did not warrant the use of her real name. One effect of the lack of the "real" Mary is the tendency for her to become a sign of something else — whether the incarnation of a mythic child murderer or a benchmark of the state of working-class motherhood.

64. See Hilary Allen, "Rendering Them Harmless: The Professional Portrayal of Women Charged with Serious Violent Crimes," in P. Carlen and A. Worrall, eds., *Gender, Crime and Justice* (London: Open University, 1987).

65. Wertham, *Show of Violence*, 235. It would seem that Irwin's symbolic matricide, part of his multiple murder, in no way approaches the "extreme horror" of the outcome of Mary's frustrations. In such a reading, then, mothers make more logical *victims* than they make *agents* of destruction.

66. Who was deported after the trial, although innocent of any criminal wrong.

67. Ibid., 218.

68. Medea's role as statusless foreigner is defined in direct reference to the civil role of wife/mother which she is denied.

69. "Mary," quoted ibid., 224.

70. See A. Shapiro, "Disordered Bodies? Disorderly Acts: Medical Disclosure and the Female Criminal in Nineteenth Century Paris," *Genders*, no. 4 (Spring 1989): 68–86.

71. Wertham, *Show of Violence*, 247.

72. As is very much the case with Kate Millett's *The Basement*, examined in Chapter Seven below.

73. Bok, *Star Wormwood*, 3.

74. "From somewhere deep within him an old memory flashed: 'Part of me would stick out!' " Ibid., 39.

75. Ibid., 49.

76. "The state" is a problematic concept, but a fundamental one in the liberal lexicon and the term that best fits the tone of Bok's critique. He does recognize the power of certain jurisdictions to judge and punish with greater compassion than others, but it is the system that tolerates such differences which is the focus of his critique. As a Pennsylvania Supreme Court judge (the court of last resort in Pennsylvania) Bok was perhaps thinking of the responsibility of federal law to mitigate the unnecessary force of some local capital statutes.

77. Ibid., 4.

78. Forty-six states practiced one or more forms of capital punishment up to the period of the moratorium in the early 1970s initiated by the U.S. Supreme Court's ruling in *Furman* v. *Georgia* (overturned by the *Gregg* v. *Georgia* decision). Currently, thirty-eight states impose capital punishment, as well as the federal government, which has the statutory power to execute but has not done so since 1953. See William Bowers, *Legal Homicide: Death as Punishment in America, 1864–1982* (Boston: Northeastern University Press, 1984) app. A. For a comprehensive analysis of the judicial history of death statutes, see Jeffrey Pokorak, " 'Death Stands Condemned': Justice Brennan and the Death Penalty," *California Western Law Review* 27 (1990/91).

79. For an insightful discussion of the rationalizations advanced in capital punishment's support (by an author who does not, herself, support the death penalty), see Susan Jacoby, *Wild Justice: The Evolution of Revenge* (New York: Harper and Row, 1983).

80. See Lawrence Klein, "The Deterrent Effect of Capital Punishment: An Assessment of the Estimates," in Alfred Blumstein et al., eds., *Deterrence and Incapacitation: Estimating the Effect of Criminal Sanctions on Crime Rates* (Washington, D.C.: National Academy of Sciences, 1978).

81. This revival is demonstrated by the swiftness with which successive state legislatures reformulated their death penalty statutes when their constitutionality was questioned by the *Furman* decision. These reformulations resulted in a huge increase in administrative expenditures to ensure the proper functioning of "super due process." See *Reviving the Death Penalty* (Hudson, Wisc.: G. E. McGuen, 1985); Alan Blakley, "The Cost of Killing Criminals," *Northern Kentucky Law Review* 18 (Fall 1990); F. Zimring and G. Hawkins, *Capital Punishment and the*

American Agenda (New York: Cambridge University Press, 1986); and T. Sellin, *The Penalty of Death* (Beverly Hills: Sage, 1980).

82. For an analysis of this trend, see Michael Massing's review article about recent scholarship on drug cultures and crime in America. "Crime and Drugs: The New Myths," *New York Review of Books*, February 1996, pp. 16–20.

83. See Richard Brown, *No Duty to Retreat: Violence and Values in American History and Society* (New York: Oxford University Press, 1991) for an analysis of the dire ramifications of the American conception of "justifiable homicide" for domestic and international relations, both past and present.

84. The case of Bernhard Goetz is exemplary here. When Goetz shot four black youths (permanently crippling one) on a subway train in New York, his act of preemptive "self-defense" raised great controversy. Writers have since noted that Goetz's explanation of his actions hardly supported even the legal definition of self-defense noted above. Despite the dubious nature of his claim of self-defense, the response of media and public was overwhelmingly supportive of his actions (with the notable exception of the black community). See George Fletcher, *A Crime of Self-Defense: Bernhard Goetz and the Law on Trial* (New York: Collier Macmillan, 1988); Lillian Rubin, *Quiet Rage: Bernie Goetz in a Time of Madness* (London: Faber, 1987).

85. See Chapter Eight below.

86. Using the example of Adolf Eichmann, executed by the Israeli government by virtue of extraordinary legislation, Susan Jacoby argues that the idea of the "most deserving case" for execution is both logically and ethically bankrupt. How can killing one man possibly form a balanced and just punishment for his killing of two, let alone a thousand, victims? The issue here is not numbers, but the qualitative value and meaning of individual life for which neither an equivalent nor a surrogate can be found. See Jacoby, *Wild Justice*.

87. The imbalance between murder and execution is tacitly acknowledged by the much-debated changes in the criteria under which a crime can be designated "capital." A number of these criteria are both quantitative and qualitative in their very subjective weighing of the severity of the crime. Thus many states rule that capital homicide is one that (among other things) involves torture or multiple victims. For an extensive analysis of the guidelines on "aggravating and mitigating circumstances" in post-*Furman* capital legislation, see Pokorak, "Death Stands Condemned," 271–274.

88. The problem of what to do with the "serial killer"—the bogeyman of late twentieth-century America—is a case in point. For the punishment to reflect the crime and be just, more would be required than merely killing the killer.

89. Bok, *Star Wormwood*, 11.

90. "Her mind sheered off to an easier emotion, hatred of Joe and soon of all

mankind for its cruelty and its traps. . . . [S]he could not die without devising a fitting act of revenge upon some of them" (ibid., 15). Although Bok uses the generic term "mankind" here, the context makes clear Angela's need to revenge herself on the male of the species.

91. Ibid., 36.

92. While there are identifiable positions in the text for good and bad father, the concept of bad mother appears but once and then rather elliptically. Roger is raised by an aunt, his mother having run off in his infancy: "Roger . . . could not have borne his aunt if she had been a roaring, noisy woman intent on shattering him with her glowing affection. Most boys are shamed, bored, and sustained by violent maternal emotion, so that to the end of their lives they utter the sound Mother in a tremulous voice as if it were a holy and self-executing word." Note here too the discrimination between sound—void of content—and meaning. Ibid., 19.

93. Ibid., 45.

94. "Grown-ups rarely bothered about kids, but when they did they had the strength to beat down any opposition. All they had to do was try, because other grown-ups were always preoccupied and would pay only half-attention" (ibid., 46). And, as Roger hears the verdict of guilty, he reflects that "the grown-ups had won after all" (pp. 123–124).

95. Ibid., 161.

96. Ibid., 6.

97. I use here the Derridean concept of "supplementarity"—a paradoxical excess that is part of (supplementary to) the story, but also is needed to *complete* it. For a demonstration of the quality of the concept, see Jonathan Culler's discussion of Woman treated as supplement by psychoanalytic discourse. Culler, *On Deconstruction: Theory and Criticism after Structuralism* (New York: Cornell University Press, 1982), 102–106, 160–171, 195–199.

98. Bok, *Star Wormwood*, 69.

99. Ibid., 161.

100. Ibid., 50, 58.

101. Ibid., 69.

102. Ibid., 137–138.

103. Ibid., 138.

104. Ibid., 129, 173, 177.

105. Ibid., 165.

106. Which, in Lacanian terms, can be read as entry into the Symbolic, the Law of the Father.

107. Ibid., 174.

108. Ibid., 180.

109. Ibid., 182.

110. Ibid., 187, 205.

111. "So long as we permit the death penalty at all, let us kill off the right people, the homicidal maniacs and the insane killers. We need not do it vengefully or in bad blood, but rather with relief, once they have been determined to be fit candidates for the gas chamber or the electric chair. Then let us quietly, dispassionately, painlessly, even apologetically, return them to Mother Earth." Ibid., 194.

112. Ibid.

113. Ibid., 50.

4. True Crime Romance I: A Genre Defiled

1. Retired Assistant District Attorney Henry Devine, notes from conversation with author, 2 December 1993. I am much indebted to Mr. Devine for his cooperation, to Barry Grennan, chief of the Major Offenses Bureau, District Attorney's Office, Nassau County, and to the staff of that office for extending me every courtesy.

2. Fay was killed at the house in Valley Stream, but the body was eventually interred at a house rented just for that purpose.

3. Beck and Fernandez were given various monickers by the media — the most favored contemporary one being the "Lonely Hearts Killers," abbreviated for headline brevity by Hearst's *New York Journal American* to "Hearts Killers."

4. The name is occasionally given in sources as "Dowling," but here I follow the transcript's usage.

5. Mr. Devine particularly recalled the circumstances of the extradition because of the parallel with a recent case in which a man, wanted for murder in New York, was arrested in Oklahoma. Governor Mario Cuomo of New York had apparently requested extradition to *save* him from a capital charge in that state. Henry Devine, conversation with author, 2 December 1993.

6. A charge leveled by the defense throughout the trial and not satisfactorily countered by the prosecution. See the transcript of *People* v. *Fernandez* 301 NY 302 (1950): vol. 2, cols. 2164–2165; vol. 3, cols. 4597–4599; vol. 5, cols. 7301–7302, 7327, 7333–7335, 7383.

7. By the 1960s their deeds had paled in comparison with those by such mass killers as Charles Starkweather, Richard Speck, and Charles Manson.

8. *People* v. *Fernandez*, vol. 1, col. 42.

9. "I was questioned by different officers . . . every state in the U.S. I am sure. Q. Questioned by some officers from the Middle-West? A. Well, every crime that

was committed in the U.S., I was asked if I had been the one." Testimony of Ray Fernandez, *People* v. *Fernandez*, vol. 2, col. 3373.

10. The prosecution only mentioned Myrtle Young (whose "suspicious" death was linked to Beck and Fernandez) and the Downings elliptically and rarely.

11. This was the prosecution story, developed from Martha's second, revised statement to police and from the story allegedly told by Beck to the examining psychiatrist for the people, Perry Lichtenstein. See Statement of Martha Beck, 3 March 1949, quoted in *People* v. *Fernandez*, vol. 6, cols. 10621–10678, and Testimony of Dr. Lichtenstein, vol. 6, cols. 9348–9359.

12. Essentially this was the defense position. See Summary for the Defense, *People* v. *Fernandez*, vol. 6, cols. 10355–10359, and Testimony of Dr. Richard Hoffmann, vol. 5, cols. 9119–9125 passim.

13. A confusion noted by Judge Ferdinand Pecora in his charge to the jury: "That kind of abnormality, assuming that it exists or is possessed by one charged with crime, does not in and of itself constitute the kind of insanity which under our law will excuse a person from the consequences of an act" (*People* v. *Fernandez*, vol. 6, col. 10884). The term "abnormality" had entered the arena of forensic psychiatry with the famous expert defense of Leopold and Loeb marshaled by Clarence Darrow. Darrow, however, was not trying to prove insanity and was accepting the legal responsibility of his clients. The deployment of his clients' "abnormality" was purely a strategy to mitigate sentence.

14. Testimony of Ray Fernandez, *People* v. *Fernandez*, vol. 3, cols. 5388–5403, 5460–5475.

15. "Well, certainly, the things that he has told us about would make one callous to death, absolutely callous. Death would mean nothing to him." Summation for the People, *People* v. *Fernandez*, vol. 6, col. 10410.

16. Summation for the Defendants, *People* v. *Fernandez*, vol. 6, cols. 10307, 10337–10338.

17. See Colin Wilson and Patricia Pitman, *Encyclopaedia of Murder* (London: Pan, 1984), 236.

18. There were also different versions given of the Downing killings, but these were never tested at trial.

19. The tale of murder consists both of all other murders, known and unknown, for which the principals were responsible and the life stories that, as they are told, lead to the execution of their subjects.

20. Brown, *Introduction to Murder*, 200.

21. Who, the story goes, was shot in the head by Fernandez.

22. I have been unable to consult an authoritative source on the Downing murders (i.e., the police files). See Introduction.

23. Recross Examination of Ray Fernandez, *People* v. *Fernandez*, vol. 3, col. 3721.

24. As evidenced by the entry for Beck in a recent "true crime" reference manual: *"Victims: 4–20(?). Method: poison, beating, shooting, drowning."* See Segrave, *Women Serial and Mass Murderers*, 26.

25. Ralph Willett, *The Naked City: Urban Crime Fiction in the U.S.A.* (New York: Manchester University Press, 1996), 6–7. Willett's work is especially useful for deunifying historically and culturally (notably in terms of race and gender) the crime genre.

26. Testimony of Ann Mason, *People* v. *Fernandez*, vol. 1, col. 812.

27. Joe McGinniss noted the results of a spot poll of North Carolinians in which 81 percent of those contacted (*prior* to the 1979 trial) professed knowledge of the so-called Fort Bragg killings. McGinniss wryly observed that it was "rare for 81% of those polled to identify the president of the United States." Joe McGinniss, *Fatal Vision* (New York: Putnam, 1983), 494. Even though this high figure is not entirely reliable, it is fair to surmise that a notorious murder is not only big news but is common conversational currency.

28. That "abnormality" was of prime importance in defining the crime and its severity. One writer would note a couple of years later that the jury, "confused by the psychiatric testimony," had rendered their guilty verdict on the basis of the "general undesirability of the defendants." Brown, *Introduction to Murder*, 179.

29. *New York Journal American*, 25 July 1949.

30. Dorothy Kilgallen, "Mrs. Beck Facing the Chair Worries about Her Weight," ibid., 28 June 1949.

31. The more pertinent fact about Graham was that she was left-handed, whereas the blow was struck by a right-handed assailant. See Bernice Freeman Davis and Al Hirschberg, *The Desperate and the Damned* (New York: Crowell, 1961).

32. *New York Journal American*, 27 June 1949.

33. Ibid., 25 June 1949.

34. It is difficult, writing in the 1990s, to find a language to describe these events with historical accuracy. Such terms as "date rape," "child abuse," and "sexual harassment" simply did not exist in any meaningful sense during the late 1940s, although the activities they describe today (which were then probably experienced differently) certainly did. However, to try to remedy some of the problems facing the historian who must contend with a punitive and expansionist modern discourse on abuse, I'll let Martha Beck describe how she felt. After the second time her brother forced sex on her, Martha said: "I tried to cleanse myself, but from that day forward I haven't felt like I've been physically clean" (Testi-

mony of Martha Beck, *People* v. *Fernandez*, vol. 4, col. 6456). When Martha eventually told on her brother, her mother blamed her for bringing shame on the family: "she told me that I was a bad girl and I may not be respected; that I had caused the family to lose our self-respect and that of the community; she wouldn't be able to face any of her friends anymore, and she held it against me" (vol. 4, col. 6461).

35. A strategy often pursued in the penalty phase of recent capital trials.

36. *New York Journal American*, 25 July 1949.

37. Represented, in part, by the glandular condition they tried to get the expert witnesses to testify to.

38. Summation for the People, *People* v. *Fernandez*, vol. 6, cols. 10463–10464.

39. *New York Journal American*, 26 July 1949.

40. Testimony of Ray Fernandez, *People* v. *Fernandez*, vol. 4, cols. 5567–5577.

41. Testimony of Martha Beck, *People* v. *Fernandez*, vol. 4, col. 6484.

42. "Her abnormal bodily structure made normal sexual gratification impossible, while at the same time her pituitary-ovarian deficiency created unduly strong urges" (Brown, *Introduction to Murder*, 34).

43. *New York Journal American*, 26 July 1949.

44. Ibid., 1 June 1949.

45. Ibid., 13 June 1949.

46. See A. Cranny-Francis, *Feminist Fiction: Feminist Uses of Generic Fiction* (New York: St. Martin's Press, 1990); Margaret Jensen, *Love's Sweet Return: The Harlequin Story* (Toronto: Women's Press, 1984).

47. Dennis Porter, "Backward Construction and the Art of Suspense," in Glenn Most and William Stowe, eds., *The Poetics of Murder: Detective Fiction and Literary Theory* (San Diego: Harcourt Brace, 1983), 328.

48. And, in one important instance, as nanny.

49. This summary account is drawn from a series of articles on the Lonely Hearts Killers appearing in the *New York Journal American* (June–August 1949 and February–March 1951).

50. Testimony of Martha Beck, *People* v. *Fernandez*, vol. 4, cols. 6499–6501.

51. *New York Journal American*, 25 July 1949.

52. Testimony of Martha Beck, *People* v. *Fernandez*, vol. 4, col. 6503. It is possible that Beck is using "affair" in the colloquial sense, meaning "that business" or some such. However, her use of "the affair" rather than "that affair" suggests otherwise.

53. *New York Journal American*, 25 July 1949.

54. The defense brought out a lengthy work record from both defendants. Their mobility, and the short duration of some of Fernandez's jobs, was consistent

both with labor demographics in the late 1940s and with the pattern of work in the building industry. See Statement of Ray Fernandez, People's Exhibit 57, *People v. Fernandez*, vol. 3.

55. The prosecution contended that Martha lost her position as superintendant of the home for crippled children owing to a "morals" charge: the board of directors had heard of her liaison with Fernandez. Martha testified that she had returned to Florida from New York (where she'd been visiting Ray) to find that she had lost her job; she did not know why. Testimony of Martha Beck, *People v. Fernandez*, vol. 4, cols. 6840–6848.

56. Testimony of Martha Beck, *People v. Fernandez*, vol. 4, cols. 6515–6516.

57. *New York Journal American*, 30 June 1949.

58. In one version, Delphine Downing is killed because she surprises Fernandez without his hairpiece. See Bruce Sanders, "The Incredible Lovers," in *Murder behind the Bright Lights* (London: Herbert Jenkins, 1958), 11–12.

59. Fernandez testified that he "never wore a toupee except once for about 15 minutes" (*People v. Fernandez*, vol. 4, col. 5488). He bought the toupee in Chicago, late in 1948 (vol. 3, col. 4121; vol. 4, col. 5642).

60. Testimony of Martha Beck, *People v. Fernandez*, vol. 4, col. 6788.

61. *New York Journal American*, 26 July 1949.

62. Martha's own account of her desire for Fernandez is an eminently practical one, bound up in her desire for a trustworthy and kind mate: "it gave me a feeling I had never experienced before — to think that there was a person there that seemed to like my two children . . . that . . . liked me, and it was certain that my children liked him." Testimony of Martha Beck, *People v. Fernandez*, vol. 4, col. 6788.

63. Cross-examination of Dr. James McCartney, *People v. Fernandez*, vol. 6, col. 9826–9827.

64. Summation on Behalf of the People, *People v. Fernandez*, vol. 6, col. 10432.

65. *New York Journal American*, 26 July 1949.

66. A surprise witness for the prosecution testified that Martha had faked at least one of these suicide attempts in order to get sympathy from Ray. See Testimony of Dorothy Lynn, *People v. Fernandez*, vol. 5, cols. 9260–9280.

67. Fernandez had a wife and children in Spain to whom he would regularly send money. His marriages in the United States were, therefore, bigamous.

68. Testimony of Ray Fernandez, *People v. Fernandez*, vol. 4, cols. 5753, 5759.

69. "Q. Are these relationships embarrassing to you? A. Very much so." Testimony of Ray Fernandez, *People v. Fernandez*, vol. 4, col. 5569.

70. Testimony of Martha Beck, *People v. Fernandez*, vol. 5, cols. 7716–7717.

71. *New York Journal American*, 18 August 1949.

72. "A crowd of 150 persons, most of them women" (ibid., 17 August 1949);

"precautions were taken to prevent a recurrence of yesterday's near riot when 150 women fought for admission to the trial. . . . [S]till there was a terrific pressure as the spectators, mostly middle-aged housewives, pressed and pushed before the doors were opened" (ibid., 26 July 1949); "hair was pulled and clothing ripped as the women fought to gain entrance" (ibid., 25 July 1949).

73. Note, in *Star Wormwood*, Curtis Bok's vitriolic jibes at the local towns-women's call for Roger's blood. Damon Runyan, covering that earlier sensation on Long Island, the April 1927 trial of Ruth Snyder and Judd Gray, had this to say about the audience:

Among the other spectators comfortably chaired, or standing on tired feet, were ladies running from a couple of inches to three yards wide. They were from all parts of Long Island, and the other boroughs of the large and thriving City of New York, the inmates of which are supposed to be so very blasé but who certainly dearly love their murder cases.

A big crowd waited in the hallways and outside the courthouse. Tearful females implored the obdurate cops guarding the stairs and the court room doors to ease them through somehow.

Damon Runyan, "Mrs Snyder and Mr Gray," in Jonathan Goodman, ed., *The Pleasures of Murder* (London: Sphere, 1983), 180. Runyan went on to condemn those "solid-looking citizens" with a "morning to waste" as a "fine commentary on what someone has mentioned as our vaunted intelligence." He also later refused an invitation to the execution that was so capitalized upon by the media (for it was there that a *Daily News* reporter with an ankle camera photographed Ruth Snyder's electrocution, an image described in depth in Chapter Two above).

74. The *New York Journal American* made this their favorite description for Martha in the week leading up to her execution. See the issues of 2 and 5 March 1951.

75. Quoted in Brown, *Introduction to Murder*, 149.

76. Quoted in Paul Buck, *The Honeymoon Killers* (London: Xanadu, 1990), 139.

77. *New York Journal American*, 8 March 1951.

78. Sigmund Engel, quoted ibid., 5 July 1949.

79. Ibid., 2 July 1949.

80. Henry Devine, conversation with the author, 2 December 1993.

81. *New York Journal American*, 12 October 1950, 5 and 8 March 1951.

82. Testimony of Martha Beck, *People* v. *Fernandez*, vol. 4, cols. 6446–6462.

83. Summation on Behalf of the People, *People* v. *Fernandez*, vol. 6, cols. 10425–10427.

84. *New York Journal American*, 8 March 1951. An earlier report described Martha as the "strong 'man' of the hideous team of killers, the aggressor in their sorties of murder, egging the weaker Fernandez on" (ibid., 2 March 1951).

85. Also executed on 8 March 1951 were John King and Richard Power, electrocuted for the felony murder of a man in Queens.

86. Ibid., 8 March 1951.

87. Leon Racht, "Martha, Last of Four . . ." ibid., 9 March 1951.

88. Ibid.

89. The infinitely more temperate and respectable *New York Herald Tribune* did print Beck's charge that the press had represented her as "unfeeling, stupid and moronic," but even they declined to print the section decrying the abuse of her appearance, despite the fact that the *Tribune* had refrained from the name-calling that was the specialty of the Hearst press. See the *New York Herald Tribune*, 9 March 1951.

90. *New York Journal American*, 28 June 1949.

91. Leon Racht, "High Court Rejects 'Hearts' Killers Plea to Cheat the Chair," *New York Journal American*, 4 March 1951.

92. *Time*, 14 March 1949, p. 14.

93. Racht, "High Court Rejects . . . Plea."

94. Ibid.

95. *New York Journal American*, "Hearts Killer's Cries Bare His Fear of a Lonely Death," 6 March 1951.

96. *New York Journal American*, 5 March 1951.

97. On 12 June 1949 the *New York Journal American* devoted a couple of columns to a man indicted in New Hampshire for "suffocating a girl last summer by cramming her silk panties down her throat." Another sensation was the nonfatal shooting of the Cubs ballplayer Eddie Waitken by one Ruth Steinhagen, a devoted fan whom he didn't know. She reported that she'd shot him "for the thrill of it" (ibid., 14 June 1949).

98. Brown, *Introduction to Murder*, 4.

99. According to Brown, "90% of all members are women" (ibid., 208).

100. Ibid., 82–83.

101. Ibid., 216.

102. Ibid., 166.

103. Martha had, after all, been selected from a list of Mother Dinene's Lonely Hearts by Ray Fernandez. Beck later remarked on the irony of that "joke" played on her by her friend Elizabeth Swanson (sending her name in to Mother Dinene), for "if it hadn't been for that joke . . . I wouldn't be in the courtroom now." Testimony of Martha Beck, *People* v. *Fernandez*, vol. 4, col. 6758.

1. For an astute analysis of the cultural work of such a strategy (and of the case in general), see Paula S. Fass, "Making and Remaking an Event: The Leopold and Loeb Case in American Culture," *Journal of American History* 80 (December 1993).

2. Reginald Medlicott, "Paranoia of the Exalted Type in a Setting of *Folie à Deux:* A Study of Two Adolescent Homicides," in W. Black and A. Taylor, eds., *Deviant Behaviour: New Zealand Studies* (London: Heinemann, 1979), 119. Dr. Medlicott made his career on the application of the type to the case of Pauline Parker and Juliet Hulme, who murdered the former's mother in June 1954.

3. Brown, *Introduction to Murder.*

4. Ibid., 7.

5. "He became firmly convinced that he possessed supernatural powers, and he took a keen interest in voodoo, Obeah, and other forms of black magic" (ibid., 2–3). This information was apparently given by one of Fernandez's sisters, but it remains purely anecdotal. Numerous writers (probably following Brown) told how the Valley Stream house was decorated with voodoo symbols and Catholic paraphernalia arranged into the context of pagan worship (ibid., 118). The detailed photographs of the crime scene fail to support that claim, showing an ordinary interior with a few holy pictures and a greater number of family portraits adorning the walls of lounge and bedroom. See *People* v. *Fernandez*, vol. 7, exhibits 48–53.

6. Brown did note that Fernandez may have been guilty of murder before meeting Martha. At least he was suspected of it by the Spanish authorities. He was apparently "under indictment in La Linea" (a claim made at the trial that was not supported by evidence). See Brown, *Introduction to Murder*, 88.

7. Ibid., 3.

8. Porter, "Backward Construction and the Art of Suspense," 328. Emphasis mine.

9. Fredric Wertham can be so identified in his texts, perhaps most clearly in his analysis of the "serial" child killer, Albert Fish. See Wertham, *Show of Violence*, 65–99.

10. Brown, *Introduction to Murder*, 31.

11. Ibid., 221–222.

12. Ibid., 30–31.

13. Ibid., 99.

14. The testimony of both Fernandez and Beck made it clear that their sexual life at the outset was not particularly satisfactory; both also denied that they had sex the first time they met. The tale of Martha's promiscuity and the meaning

ascribed to her "frigidity" is completely at odds with anything the couple offered in testimony; the power of that reading is in its very remoteness from the facts.

15. Ibid., 36.

16. Her first job was as librarian of the "Women's Club" in Milton, Florida. See Testimony of Martha Beck, *People* v. *Fernandez*, vol. 4, col. 6498.

17. Brown, *Introduction to Murder*, 37.

18. Ibid., 36.

19. An ill-defined condition the existence of which was debated at the trial. The cause of Martha's obesity is not resolved in the transcript.

20. Ibid., 34, 53.

21. Testimony of Martha Beck, *People* v. *Fernandez*, vol. 4, cols. 6714–6720.

22. Brown, *Introduction to Murder*, 227.

23. Ibid., 166.

24. Ibid., 108.

25. Which was a good few years before it was purchased in reality. Ibid., 82.

26. Pages 129–144 were ripped out of the sole copy of Brown's book held by the New York Public Library. This irritating and fateful piece of vandalism resulted in a reading of the text that must admit to being more than usually interpretive.

27. Ibid., 121.

28. "Fernandez seized Martha's arm. 'What's happened? What did you do?' he shouted. Martha replied, 'I don't know. I had no idea what I was doing'" (ibid., 120).

29. Ibid., 121.

30. Ian Brady of the Moors murderers, as well as Richard Loeb, the "unredeemed" killer friend of Nathan Leopold, are obvious examples. The pattern exists for lesser-known couples: Pauline Parker is commonly depicted as dominating her lover Juliet Hulme in the 1954 murder, in Christchurch, New Zealand, of the former's mother. Such readings must always arise on the back of certain assumptions about — in these examples — class and gender.

31. H. Montgomery Hyde, *United in Crime* (London: Heinemann, 1955), 139–143; David Rowan, "The Lonely Hearts" and "The Death House," in *Famous American Crimes* (London: Frederick Muller, 1957); Sanders, "The Incredible Lovers."

32. Sanders's account is distinguished in that it claims this honor for the pair throughout the history of modern crime in the West as a whole.

33. This was a common facet of his work when dealing with executed felons. Montgomery Hyde was staunchly opposed to capital punishment. His reservations in the Hearts Killers case recall those of the later case of Barbara Graham: "Martha subsequently asserted that it was not her hand which struck the fatal blow that killed Janet Fay, and some grounds for this belief are provided by the

fact that she was left-handed, while Mrs. Fay was killed with a right-handed blow" (Montgomery Hyde, *United in Crime*, 142–143).

34. Ibid., 142.

35. *The Honeymoon Killers*, 35 mm, 108 min., directed by Leonard Castle and Oliver Wood, 1970.

36. The first line of the text: "Raymond Fernandez was feeling pleased with life. He had seduced more than twenty women" (Rowan, *Famous American Crimes*, 82). Rowan's rather stuffy Englishness is demonstrated here by his assumption that the seduction of twenty women is anything to write home about.

37. Martha had not, for instance, been "married three times"; nor did she have three children. Rowan also consistently misspelled "Downing" as "Dowling" (yet even *Time* had managed to screw up the widow's first name: printing "Deliphene" instead of "Delphine"). See ibid., 83–84.

38. Ibid., 89.

39. Roland Barthes, stumbling upon a "Basque style" house in Paris, wrote that he felt as if "this chalet has just been created on the spot, for me, like a magical object springing up in my present life without any trace of the history that has caused it" (quoted in Dean MacCannell, *The Tourist* [New York: Schocken Books, 1989], 159).

40. Rowan, *Famous American Crimes*, 91.

41. Fernandez heard rumors that Martha was flirting with one of her wardens and, in his fury, requested his lawyers to ask that his execution be moved up to dispatch him from his misery. Naturally, this extraordinary request was not seriously considered, but the ruction was sufficient to cause the prison warden to transfer certain of the death house staff and to order the doors between wings closed. The warden's investigations revealed there was no substance to the story anyway. Buck, *The Honeymoon Killers*, 138; Rowan, *Famous American Crimes*, 99–100.

42. For a detailed discussion of the Rosenbergs' infringement of that discourse, see my article "The Genealogy of Treason: Ethel Rosenberg and the Masculinist Discourse of Cold War," *Australasian Journal of American Studies* 12, no. 1 (1993).

43. A genre in which the protagonists are largely solitary, masters of duplicity and strategy, acting without the impediments of conscience or heart.

44. The spy as lover did appear in the guise of the confessions of Elizabeth Bentley, the so-called Blonde Spy Queen, who, with her lover Jacob Golos, supposedly passed information to the Soviets. Her tale came from her status as communist apostate. In using her love for Golos as the explanation for her commitment to communism, Bentley, a "woman who loved too much" (and who had learned her lesson) became easier to grasp (and harder to impeach) than someone who had once been infatuated by an ideology.

45. Rowan, *Famous American Crimes*, 105.

46. The execution drew an audience "in excess of the legal number of witnesses" (Brown, *Introduction to Murder*, 187).

47. Rowan, *Famous American Crimes*, 104.

48. Sanders, "The Incredible Lovers," 13.

49. Reprinted recently in Richard Glyn Jones, ed., *Couples Who Kill: Terrifying True Stories of the World's Deadliest Duos* (London: True Crime, 1993).

50. Wenzell Brown's *Introduction to Murder* and Paul Buck's *The Honeymoon Killers* are the most extensive.

51. Sanders, Introduction, *Murder behind the Bright Lights*, 6.

52. Partly in response to the furor caused by the execution of Bentley, the Royal Commission on Capital Punishment recommended, six to five, that no one below age twenty-one should be liable to the death penalty. See "Capital Punishment in the Case of Women and Adolescents," *Justice of the Peace and Local Government Review*, 17 October 1953. The Homicide Act of 1957 did not, however, implement that recommendation. Although the act did more clearly state the conditions of capital homicide, both Bentley and Ellis would still have been condemned under the terms of the new legislation.

53. Wertham, *Show of Violence*, 242.

54. If the killings of Delphine and Rainelle are taken as a single act. The child was actually killed two days after her mother.

55. In every other version (following the depositions) Martha gives Delphine a large (though necessarily fatal) dose of barbiturates, after which Ray shoots the widow in the head.

56. Sanders, "The Incredible Lovers," 13.

57. Ibid., 14.

58. The police arrive at the door of the Downings' home, now empty but for Ray and Martha, enquiring about a "Mrs. Fay from New York" (ibid., 15). In point of fact, the police had not connected the Fay murder to Beck and Fernandez until after their statements were tendered to the Kent County authorities.

59. One of her typical lines: "Better put your thinking cap on, Ray. We've settled for six thousand bucks and a body. It's the body we've got to dump in a hurry, sweetheart" (ibid., 34).

60. Ibid., 22.

61. Not to be confused with its European equivalent in the *série noir*.

62. Ibid., 24.

63. An entirely appropriate title for Sanders's purposes when deployed in the context of dominance and submission.

64. Ibid., 30.

65. Ibid.

66. "She developed the soul-destroying qualities of a smiling ogress" (ibid., 33).

67. Sanders's true crime account is also completely contrary to the portrait of Martha that emerges from the trial transcript.

68. The film also owed much, stylistically, to Roman Polanski's film *Repulsion* (1965).

69. Wertham, "It's Murder," 33.

70. Stanley Cohen laid the foundations for an analysis of the "homicidal" tendencies of a society stratified by race and class. See Cohen, *Against Criminology* (London: Transaction Books, 1988).

71. See the President's Commission on Law Enforcement and the Administration of Justice, *The Challenge of Crime in a Free Society* (Washington, D.C.: GPO, 1967), as well as the *Wickersham Report* of 1968 (National Commission on Law Observance and Enforcement, Crime and the Foreign Born [Wickersham Commission Report, no. 10], Montclair, N.J.: Patterson Smith Reprints, 1968 [1931]).

72. Even the most supposedly conservative media were not immune. The superhero comic — for all its patriotism and morals-mongering — underwent profound changes in the 1970s. The most startling evidence for this phenomenon is the transformation of "Captain America" into "The Nomad" when, demoralized by the president's betrayal of his precepts of high office (a thinly veiled restaging of the Watergate crisis), Cap dons black garb instead of his famous red, white, and blue.

6. True Crime Romance III: *The Honeymoon Killers*

1. Buck mentions the 45,000 pages of court records, but I am doubtful that he read the transcript very closely or in its entirety. In the retelling of the murders, he does use material that has not appeared before, but his acceptance of some of the worst apocrypha and rumor is worrying.

2. Buck, *The Honeymoon Killers*, 151. Emphasis mine.

3. "An alluring dramatization of the shocking real-life 'Lonely Hearts' murders that took place in the Sixties [*sic*]," wrote Richard Skorman. Both the film's resetting of the crimes in the 1960s and this critic's belief that that *was* when the murders occurred demonstrates how much *The Honeymoon Killers* is a text of its times. Skorman typed the film as a "crime docudrama." See Richard Skorman, *Off-Hollywood Movies: A Film-Lover's Guide* (New York: Harmony, 1989), 176.

4. This exhortation was drawn from his "last official words" and reprinted across the country in the major evening papers.

5. The filmmakers were poor chemists. Ammonia is actually used to neutralize chlorine.

6. Buck, *The Honeymoon Killers*, 145, 131.

7. Hugo Adam Bedau, *The Death Penalty in America* (New York: Anchor, 1964), 238–241.

8. See the Summation for the People, *People v. Fernandez*, vol. 6, col. 10475.

9. Testimony of Martha Beck, *People v. Fernandez*, vol. 4, cols. 5828 and 5841.

10. Although both Martha and Ray testified to Janet Fay's desire for sex with him, the prosecution refused to accept the picture of a respectable, aged, Catholic widow at the mercy of her long-starved libido: "And then she wants you to believe that she is telling the truth and saying that that poor Irish woman went over to that defendant Fernandez and in honeyed talk of the South, if you please, said to him: 'Don't oo want some sugar, honeychile?' An Irish woman, living there, apparently most of her life, pulling out a shriveled old breast and using that sort of Southern dialogue" (Summation for the People, *People v. Fernandez*, vol. 6, cols. 10476–10477). Notwithstanding this pointed questioning of Martha's account, the credibility of the couple's story of Fay's affection remains untestable.

11. Buck, *The Honeymoon Killers*, 126.

12. Statement of Ray Fernandez, *People v. Fernandez*, vol. 3, col. 4070.

13. Supplementary Statement of Martha Beck, *People v. Fernandez*, vol. 3, col. 4154.

14. On seeing the peculiar object attached to Janet's head, Ray is shocked back to his native tongue, crying "¡Jollín!" Martha is more effusive because she has a moment more in which to react and because she, as a woman, is more versed in strategic exchanges, such as flattery.

15. Buck, *The Honeymoon Killers*, 143, 156, 157.

16. Martha testified to a relationship with a Navy man called Carmen. The liaison failed, but he apparently consented to her using his name to bestow a little respectability on the child she was soon to have (to another man). Testimony of Martha Beck, *People v. Fernandez*, vol. 4, cols. 6665–6681. The existence of Carmen has been disputed, but without stating the evidence for disbelief. It seems that many writers were willing to extrapolate from Martha's confessed lie about the marriage to the idea that Carmen himself was a lie.

17. The character of Myrtle Young, for instance, gives Ray $4,000 to marry her and make her pregnancy legitimate. Yet despite the up-front nature of the agreement, she soon tells Martha she is in love and that she thinks they'll "make a go of the marriage." Buck, *The Honeymoon Killers*, 56.

7. Killing Grounds

1. "One in eight persons arrested for murder is a woman." Elizabeth Rappaport, "Some Questions about Gender and the Death Penalty," *Golden Gate*

University Law Review 20 (Fall 1990): 504. By 1993 that percentage is only slightly higher: 9.4 percent of those arrested for homicide are women. U.S. Department of Commerce, *Statistical Abstract of the United States, 1995,* 115th ed. (Washington, D.C.: GPO, 1996), 207.

2. An even greater statistical rarity.

3. There is also a weird typicality in the figure of femininity undone: the "masculinized" female criminal who represents a much more variegated and complex pool of actual women murderers. See Lynda Hart's discussion of Aileen Wuornos in her book, *Fatal Women: Lesbian Sexuality and the Mark of Aggression* (Princeton: Princeton University Press, 1994), 135–154.

4. Information derived from the figures for 1992 in U.S. Department of Commerce, *Statistical Abstract, 1995,* 202.

5. Of the "circumstances" given for homicides investigated, 27.7 percent are listed as "unknown." It is that figure which is commonly taken to indicate the rate of "stranger killings." Ibid. However, there has been some dispute about this figure recently. The most current of the FBI's *Uniform Crime Reports* has attempted to factor in a declining rate of "cleared" homicides. According to one commentator, if one takes statistical cognizance of the up to 50 percent of "uncleared" homicides (in the urban centers where the falling clearance rates are most dramatic), then "up to 53 per cent of all homicides are being committed by strangers." See Adam Wallinsky, "The Crisis of Public Order," *Atlantic Monthly,* July 1995, p. 46.

6. With the highest rate being that of the District of Columbia at 78.5 per 100,000 population. The highest urban rate is New Orleans, at 80.3 per 100,000. U.S. Department of Commerce, *Statistical Abstract, 1995,* 200–201.

7. National Center for Health Statistics, U.S. Department of Health, Education, and Welfare, *Homicide in the United States, 1950–1964* (Washington, D.C.: GPO, 1967).

8. Brian Lane, *Murder Update* (London: Robinson, 1991), 12.

9. Wallinsky, "The Crisis of Public Order," 47.

10. U.S. Department of Commerce, *Statistical Abstract, 1995,* 14, 93.

11. Even discounting death by violence, a black male aged nineteen to forty is three times more likely than his white peer to die before reaching age forty-one. Ibid., 14, 95.

12. Lane, *Murder Update,* 12. The *Statistical Abstract* also indicates that whites in the age range fifteen to thirty-four are more likely to kill themselves or die in motor vehicle accidents than they are likely to be murdered. U.S. Department of Commerce, *Statistical Abstract, 1995,* 93.

13. James Baldwin, "The Devil Finds Work," in *The Price of the Ticket* (London: Michael Joseph, 1985), 631.

14. As demonstrated by *City of Richmond* v. *J. A. Croson Co.* (1989) and, more recently, the associated ruling in *Northeastern Florida Chapter of the Associated General Contractors of America* v. *City of Jacksonville, Florida* (1993). In the former case, the majority found against the constitutionality of "affirmative action" programs (viz., a municipal "set-aside" clause guaranteeing to minority business enterprises in the building trade a percentage of business by subcontract). Richmond, it was shown, is an urban area with a majority African American population. The basis for the Court's finding was the failure of the appellant, the City of Richmond, to establish a prima facie case, for "none of the evidence . . . pointed to any identified discrimination in the city's construction industry, and . . . past societal discrimination alone could not serve as the basis for such a rigid racial preference [as that entailed by the 'set-aside' provision]." *City of Richmond* v. *J. A. Croson Co.* 488 US 469, 102 L Ed 2d 855 (1989). See also Gordon Clark, "The Legitimacy of Judicial Decision Making in the Context of *Richmond v. Croson*," *Urban Geography* 13, no. 3 (1992), for an analysis of the implications of that decision. Although the legal issues in the associated case of *Florida General Contractors* v. *Jacksonville* are different (viz., the petitioner's standing and whether or not the case is moot) the general reasoning is similar; that is, the majority found against the constitutionality of the city's "set-aside" clause, even after that clause was substantially altered so as to meet *exactly* the "present effects of past discrimination." See the dissenting opinion of Justices Sandra Day O'Connor and Harry Andrew Blackmun, *Northeastern Florida Chapter of the Associated General Contractors of America* v. *City of Jacksonville, Florida* 508 US—, 124 L Ed 2d 586 (1993): 602–603. The Court—issues of mootness and standing aside—ruled against the principle of "preferential treatment."

15. Pokorak, "'Death Stands Condemned': Justice Brennan and the Death Penalty," 296.

16. Ibid., 296–302.

17. "Baldus found that prosecutors sought the death penalty in 70% of the cases involving black defendants and white victims; 32% of the cases involving white defendants and white victims and 19% of the cases involving white defendants and black victims." Ibid.

18. According to Justice Lewis Powell, who wrote the majority opinion, the evidence from the Baldus report which McCleskey's lawyers presented could not prove that the "decisionmakers in *his* case acted with discriminatory purpose." Powell, quoted by David Baldus et al. in Kermit Hall, ed., *The Oxford Companion to the Supreme Court* (New York: Oxford University Press, 1992), 703. Baldus et al. go on to remark that "one surprising effect of this Fourteenth Amendment holding is that equal protection claims of purposeful race discrimination in death sentence cases will now be subjected to a far heavier burden of proof than is

applied in ordinary jury discrimination and employment discrimination cases" (ibid.).

19. The law was overruled later on other grounds. However, *Pace & Cox* is still used to demonstrate the requirements of equal protection. *Pace & Cox* v. *State of Alabama* (Ala 1 S Ct 637, 106 US 583 27 L Ed 207, 1883). Emphasis mine.

20. It might be argued, too, that this indifference also applies to the poor in general and to women and children. See Chapter Eight below.

21. Baldwin, *Evidence of Things Not Seen*, 10.

22. See Martin Amis, "The Killings in Atlanta," in Sebastian Wolfe, ed., *The Book of Murder* (London: Xanadu, 1992), 190; Baldwin, *Evidence of Things Not Seen*, 10–13.

23. Baldwin, *Evidence of Things Not Seen*, 6.

24. Ibid., 5.

25. "[W]hat was one to make of a 'pattern' that included, as cause of death, gunshot wounds, strangulation, head injury, stabbed, asphyxiation, and undetermined?" Ibid., 64.

26. "In the last twenty months, twenty children have been murdered in Atlanta" (Amis, "The Killings in Atlanta," 190).

27. Baldwin, *Evidence of Things Not Seen*, 15. Emphasis mine.

28. Ibid., 72.

29. Ibid., 39.

30. See Bernard Headley on the "Race-Class-Region dialectic" in his article "Killings That Became 'Tragedy': A Different View of What Happened in Atlanta, Georgia," *Social Justice* 16, no. 4 (1989): 67–70.

31. I use the term "black" here, rather than the more contemporary "African American," in deference to Baldwin's own use of the term.

32. "I could not interview her [Ms. Camille Bell, the mother of the fourth victim, Yusef Bell] because I simply did not know what to say to the mother of a murdered child, still less what to ask" (Baldwin, *Evidence of Things Not Seen*, 54).

33. For an interesting and complex view of this form of hypertypicality, see Mark Seltzer, "Serial Killers I," *Differences* 5 (Spring 1993) and "Serial Killers II: The Pathological Public Sphere," *Critical Inquiry* (Autumn 1995).

34. That silence may not and need not be literal. Even with pages of testimony from the accused, and with all the confessions and statements, there is always so much doubt about the relationship of the "facts" to these statements that the intervention of an "interpreter" is essential.

35. Many infamous American criminals were aficionados of detective fiction and/or true crime. Leopold and Loeb lifted their ransom note from a recently published mystery story. Loeb actually followed around the crime reporters who were investigating the murder (for which he and his lover were responsible),

proposing various theories and scenarios of the crime. See Fass, "Making and Remaking an Event," 922, 950n62. Bonnie Parker was so taken with the myth of the outlaw that she took to writing her own ballads about the Barrow gang, verse which was later published in the *Dallas Evening Journal*. Martha Beck apparently read stacks of true crime and detective magazines in prison.

36. I shall discuss later in this chapter the very significant difference of Millett's *The Basement* in this regard.

37. Baldwin, *Evidence of Things Not Seen*, 125. Emphasis mine.

38. For Baldwin's impression of Williams, see ibid., 75–77, 111–112.

39. Ibid., 16, 71–72, 106.

40. Ibid., 16, 72.

41. Feminist criminologists have intensively critiqued that school of expert opinion which has made its fame from tabulating the "causes" of the psychopathology of serial killers. See Deborah Cameron and Elizabeth Frazer, *The Lust To Kill: A Feminist Investigation of Sexual Murder* (London: Polity Press, 1987); Caputi, *The Age of Sex Crime*. Dr. Joel Norris, an "expert" in the psychopathology of the serial killer, suggests that a serial killer is likely to have been either sexually abused, unloved by his mother, or to have suffered some organic brain defect. Believing such preconditions policeable, Norris treats serial murder as, in his words, a "disease" — the cure for which can be found in regulating the maternal environment from the perinatal period onward. See J. Norris, *Sexual Killers: The Growing Menace* (New York: Dolphin, 1988), 1–21.

42. For a fine example of the interdependence of both critiques, see Sherene Razack, "What Is to Be Gained by Looking White People in the Eye? Culture, Race and Gender in Cases of Sexual Violence," *Signs* 19, no. 4 (1994).

43. Baldwin, *Evidence of Things Not Seen*, 125, 95.

44. Ibid., 56, 85.

45. Baldwin's own opinion of liberalism was formed by his witnessing of the cataclysmic betrayal and intellectual perfidy of Cold War liberalism. Writing of the intellectual community that, by and large, allowed or even assisted in the destruction of Alger Hiss and the Rosenbergs, Baldwin opined that "their performance, then, yet more than the combination of ignorance and arrogance with which this community has always protected itself against the deepest implications of Black suffering, persuaded me that brilliance without passion is mere sterility." (Baldwin, "No Name in the Street," in *The Price of the Ticket*, 465).

46. Baldwin, *Evidence of Things Not Seen*, 79.

47. Baldwin, "Words of a Native Son," in *The Price of the Ticket*, 400.

48. Compare, for instance, two representative texts on American violence from the liberal and the neoconservative eras, respectively. Charles Silberman's *Criminal Violence: Criminal Justice* (New York: Random House, 1978) was very much a

product of "new criminological" liberalism, representing its most sophisticated edge. Silberman's analysis of the effects of poverty and racial oppression on crime and the administration of criminal justice was an incisive one. His work refuses definitively the "othering" process of other sociological tracts bent on containing the "underclass," and his criticism of the criminal justice system reflects the radical assumption that "criminality" and injustice are not the sole reserve of those parts of society that are the object of policing. Brown's *No Duty to Retreat*, on the other hand, is very much a neoconservative tract, regardless of the liberal overtones of its historical analysis of the implications of the right to self-defense in American history. Brown seems to accept two mutually distinct groups: the law-abiding citizens (who deplore crime and support "tougher measures") and the criminal "underclass" (pp. 139–142).

49. Baldwin, *Evidence of Things Not Seen*, 38.

50. "There is no such thing as a Negro Problem — but simply a menaced boy." Baldwin, "Words of a Native Son," 400).

51. U.S. Department of Commerce, *Statistical Abstract, 1995*, 99.

52. This figure was thought to be a low estimate, based only on the bodies actually found. See Diana Russell and Candida Ellis, "Annihilation by Murder and by the Media: The Other Atlanta Femicides," in Jill Radford and Diana Russell, eds., *Femicide: The Politics of Woman Killing* (New York: Twayne, 1992).

53. Baldwin, *Evidence of Things Not Seen*, 44, 36, 33.

54. "For the action of the White Republic, in the lives of Black men, has been, and remains, emasculation" (ibid., 21).

55. Ibid., 19.

56. See Baldwin on the killing of Emmett Till for whistling at a white woman. Ibid., 40–41.

57. Ibid., 19.

58. Willard Motley's *Knock on Any Door* was also much preoccupied with the devastations caused by that morally duplicitous culture of manhood. While Motley's ideas on masculinity did not engage the overtly racial category of "sorriness," it was, I believe, informed by it.

59. Baldwin, *Evidence of Things Not Seen*, 17, 20–21.

60. Ibid., 21.

61. There is a great deal of recent feminist scholarship that critiques the construction of black "consciousness" and "experience" as well as the racist, ethnocentric, and colonizing impulse of much of Western feminism. See, for example, bell hooks, *Ain't I a Woman: Black Women and Feminism* (Boston: South End Press, 1981); Paula Giddings, *When and Where I Enter: The Impact of Black Women on Race and Sex in America* (New York: Bantam Books, 1984); Hazel Carby, *Reconstructing Womanhood: The Emergence of the African-American Woman Novelist* (New York:

Oxford University Press, 1987); and, for more general critiques of the inclusive strategies of feminism, Denise Riley, *"Am I that Name?" Feminism and the Category of Women in History* (Minneapolis: University of Minnesota Press, 1988) and Judith Butler, *Gender Trouble: Feminism and the Subversion of Identity* (New York: Routledge, 1990).

62. Carby critiqued at length a nineteenth-century concept of woman that, by its definition, excluded black women as the female black *animal.* See Carby, *Reconstructing Womanhood.*

63. "If women dream less than men — for men know very little about a woman's dreams — it is certainly because they are so swiftly confronted with the reality of men." Baldwin is here speculating in the generic; he is also idealizing and naturalizing the figure of "unfathomable" woman. Baldwin, *Evidence of Things Not Seen,* 20.

64. For an analysis of the hegemony of the "much man," see bell hooks, "Reconstructing Black Masculinity," in *Black Looks: Race and Representation* (Boston: South End Press, 1989).

65. Baraka, quoted ibid., 98.

66. Baldwin, "Here Be Dragons," in *The Price of the Ticket,* 683, 685, 681.

67. Ibid., 680.

68. Of his early casual sexual liaisons, Baldwin remarked with sadness that "sexual rumor concerning blacks had preceded me" (ibid., 683).

69. "[W]hich, as I have understood it, simply means our endless connection with, and responsibility for, each other" (Baldwin, *Evidence of Things Not Seen,* 122).

8. Ghosts

1. See Allison Morris and Ania Wilczynski, "Rocking the Cradle: Mothers Who Kill Their Children," in Birch, ed., *Moving Targets.*

2. See Rappaport, "Some Questions about Gender and the Death Penalty," 554–565.

3. Millett, *The Basement,* 247.

4. West and Fenstermaker have developed a useful analytic model for understanding the constructive power of race, class, and gender in culture. That model gets away from influential but inaccurate mathematical metaphors for the interrelationship of these constructs, promoting instead an ethnomethodological understanding of the "situated accomplishment," between specific individuals in discrete contexts, of the behavior that simultaneously defines, classifies, and reproduces such constructs. For West and Fenstermaker, no one is exempt from the

constructive power of these three categories which, as cultural constructs, are mechanically similar. See Candace West and Sarah Fenstermaker, "Doing Difference," *Gender and Society* 9, no. 1 (February 1995).

5. Perhaps the most exemplary general feminist studies of women who kill are Jones, *Women Who Kill*; Birch, ed., *Moving Targets*; and, more recently, Kerry Greenwood, ed., *The Thing She Loves: Why Women Kill* (St. Leonards, N.S.W.: Allen and Unwin, 1996). There are many feminist studies of "spousal homicide" and the battered women's defense, as well as analyses of specific cases. In addition, there is a substantial body of work in the true crime genre, dealing with women who kill, "black widows," *femmes fatales*, etc. In the latter group is an extensive literature that treats the continuum of men's violence against women, including sexual and "domestic" murder. See, for example, Cameron and Frazer, *The Lust To Kill*; Caputi, *The Age of Sex Crime*; Mary Daly, *Gyn/Ecology: The Metaethics of Radical Feminism* (Boston: Beacon Press, 1978); Liz Kelly, *Surviving Sexual Violence* (Cambridge: Polity, 1988); and Jill Radford and Diana Russell, eds., *Femicide: The Politics of Woman Killing*. The theorists Susan Griffin, Andrea Dworkin, and Catherine McKinnon, though addressing the phenomenon of men's sexual violence more generally, have contributed significantly to the conceptualization of what Radford and Russell call "femicide." There are also, of course, "nonfeminist" works on the subject of women's violent deaths at the hands of men. This scholarship issues from within the criminological discipline and is concerned with "trends" in spousal homicide or with the psychopathology of sexual murderers.

6. Jill Radford, "Introduction," in Radford and Russell, eds., *Femicide: The Politics of Woman Killing* (Buckingham, UK: Open University Press, 1992), 4.

7. Feminine subjectivity and the question of "victim agency" are intelligently canvassed in an article by Janice Haaken concerned with the phenomena of hysteria and multiple personality disorder, respectively, and the relationship of both to authorizing narratives of trauma. See Haaken, "Sexual Abuse, Recovered Memory, and Therapeutic Practice: A Feminist Psychoanalytic Perspective," *Social Text* 40 (1994): 115–145.

8. Millett, *The Basement*, i.

9. Ibid., 2.

10. Ibid.

11. Ibid.

12. Ibid.

13. Ibid., 14.

14. Ann E. Imbrie, *Spoken in Darkness: Small-town Murder and a Friendship beyond Death* (London: Penguin, 1994), 191.

15. Millett, *The Basement*, 3, 4, 6.

16. For Jenny's complicity, see ibid., 79, 246–247, 283–286.

17. When Gertrude Baniewski agreed to take on the care of Sylvia and Jenny Likens, she was already sole caretaker for her own family of seven children, one of whom was an infant.

18. Ibid., 221, 78.

19. Baldwin, *Evidence of Things Not Seen*, 8.

20. Millett, *The Basement*, 14.

21. Baldwin, *Evidence of Things Not Seen*, 79.

22. Millett, *The Basement*, 100.

23. Ibid., 3.

24. Ibid., 131.

25. Gertrude had apparently been abused by both her husbands and by her more recent boyfriend.

26. Ibid., 259.

27. Ibid., 290–291.

28. For the problem of this negative definition, see Georges Canguilheim on the instability of the normative standard in the "healthy man." Canguilheim, *The Normal and The Pathological*.

29. She never came right out and accused any of the children, but merely said that she had been asleep or absent or busy during much of the fatal persecution of Sylvia:

Q: Are you telling the jury your children did it?

A: No, I am not telling the jury my children did it.

Q: Who else was in the house?

A: There were a number of children in the house.

Testimony of Gertrude Baniewski, quoted in Millett, *The Basement*, 133.

30. Ibid., 258.

31. Ibid., 256–263.

32. According to Diane Shoemaker in the *Indianapolis News*, 2 November 1965, quoted ibid., 64.

33. Ibid., 31.

34. Ibid., 329–331.

35. This is evident in a number of ways, but it is perhaps most starkly evidenced by the treatment meted out to African American and Hispanic women as mothers and potential mothers. See Jennifer Terry, "The Body Invaded: Medical Surveillance of Women as Reproducers," *Socialist Review* 19, no. 3 (1989).

36. Wertham, *Show of Violence*, 213.

37. As defined in a recent text: "the logic of opposite extremes and ideological norms of female behaviour combine either to deny her any agency, to make her

the innocent victim of a psychopathic megalomaniac, or to cast her as essentially wicked." Helen Birch, "If Looks Could Kill: Myra Hindley and the Iconography of Evil," in Birch, ed., *Moving Targets*, 61.

38. Millett, *The Basement*, 99.

39. Ibid., 105, 58, 43.

40. Sylvia was tortured with whatever came to hand: she was submerged in scalding water, forbidden to use the toilet, had a Coke bottle forced up her vagina. In one incident she was whipped with a piece of curtain railing.

41. Ibid., 199.

42. Ibid., 70.

43. The underground classic movie *The Night Porter* is a complex exposition of this particular body of ideas. Its plot pivots around the collapse of sadomasochism as fetish into the institutionalized sadism of Nazi fascism.

44. Ibid., 77. Emphasis mine.

45. The preceding quote continues: "What sixteen-year-old girl has not already been undermined by the guilt of modesty, the shame of sexuality? An indoctrination of terrible consequences, in these circumstances even mortal" (ibid.).

46. Ibid., 247. Emphasis mine.

47. Ibid., 11.

48. Ibid.

49. Ibid., 14.

50. Ibid., 54.

51. Ibid.

52. Imbrie, *Spoken in Darkness*, 199–200.

53. Roland Barthes, *Camera Lucida: Reflections on Photography*, trans. Richard Howard (London: Fontana, 1984), 79.

54. This is evidenced by the appearance recently of a number of works reproducing the archives of police photographers whose *oeuvre* consists largely of crime and accident scenes. These gruesome, evanescent, and sometimes beautiful images seem to appeal both as art and as sensation. For a brief review essay detailing the phenomenon, see Ralph Rugoff, "Crime Seen," *Art and Text*, no. 55 (1996): 34–35. Also see Luc Sante, *Evidence* (New York: Farrar, Strauss, and Giroux, 1992); Eugenia Parry Janis, "They Say I and I Mean Anybody," in *Harm's Way: Lust and Madness and Murder and Mayhem* (Santa Fe: Twin Palms), 1994.

55. Millett, *The Basement*, 55.

56. Ibid., 54.

57. Barthes, *Camera Lucida*, 65.

58. Millett, *The Basement*, 105.

59. There are slightly different issues involved with her re-creation of the murderer, Gertrude Baniewski. Although the murderer survived the murder, was

tried for her crime and jailed, her living through and beyond the murder changed her. The Gertrude that Millett envisions is the Gertrude of the months of torture, a different person. That demarcation between Gertrude, the murderer, and the later Gertrude is quiet clearly indicated by Millett's discussion of the photographs taken of her during the trial: "[I]n all succeeding photographs through the course of the trial her face loses, magically, its haunted quality, her body gains weight, takes shape, grows in health, flourishes. . . . There is nearly something flirtatious in her energy. She has become 'normal,' acceptable, credible, a woman now in place of the wraith at the time of her apprehension" (ibid., 16).

60. Ibid., 67.

61. Ibid.

62. Ibid., 68.

63. Ibid.

64. Ibid.

65. Ibid.

66. Even the rose the girl carries is an unlikely gift, if a gift from Sylvia. It is, instead, very much a late-sixties token: a gift from a younger to an older lesbian who is also a feminist and an artistic "patron."

67. Ibid., 247.

9. The Cast in Order of Disappearance

1. Federal statute still allows the sentence of death for acts of treason against the state. That statutory right has not been exercised since the executions of Julius and Ethel Rosenberg in June 1953.

2. Lesser, *Pictures at an Execution*, p. 1. Although Lesser's work, like Joel Black's, examines the figure of the murderer in texts derived from a variety of cultures and periods, the starting point for her analysis (in terms both of her own "interest" and the choice of her primary material) is the cultural phenomenon of murder in modern America.

3. Ibid., 12. Emphasis mine.

4. "Crip," quoted ibid.

5. "Events can become a 'story' — news, in that sense, can become art — only when the case is closed and the pattern is viewed in retrospect" (ibid., 16–17).

6. Ibid., 25.

7. Ibid., 30–31.

8. Consider the recent Phil Donahue program that previewed the execution of David Lawson in Raleigh, North Carolina. Donahue's characteristic high-energy style was fueled by an obvious frustration at not being allowed to film the execu-

tion for the show (*Donahue*, "The Execution of David Lawson," 15 June 1994). It is worth noting that Donahue was less than clear about what particular purpose he wished to serve by broadcasting the execution, despite his appeal to his First Amendment rights to do so.

9. See Lionel Dahmer, *A Father's Story: One Man's Anguish at Confronting the Evil in His Son* ([London]: Little, Brown, 1994).

10. Which begs the important question of what place sexuality has in the figuring of the murderer in the foreground of the tale of murder. As that very question is the basis of my next work, I will defer its full analysis, although the germ of that analysis can, I hope, be found here.

11. Dahmer, *A Father's Story*, 54. Emphasis mine.

12. Which Thomas Cook heatedly points out in his preface to the work. Upon opening the book, the reader is immediately struck by the dedication: a lengthy list of names that — one realizes as one counts them through — are the names of Jeffrey Dahmer's victims. A portion of the proceeds of the book's sale was given to the families of the murdered.

13. For an analysis of the process of storytelling — as a means of dealing with the remote but possible threat of murder, as chronicle, and as entertainment — see Amma A. Davis, "Narrative Reactions to Brutal Murders: A Case Study," *Western Folklore* 49 (January 1990). Davis found that the local response to three women having been rape-murdered featured "two clear narrative cycles": "The first cycle included reactionary rumors and narratives that took several forms — cautionary stories, stories of vicarious involvement (usually in the subgenre of Narrow Escapes), and stories of accusation — and were told before the murderer was apprehended. Almost all of the narratives were told by women" (p. 100). Also see Bill Ellis on the tenacity of the folk renderings of a particular tale of murder in the face of the much more banal alternative aired in the actual trial ("Death by Folklore," 209–212).

14. Lesser would understand "quality" in its fullest sense, not merely as the refinement of the technicalities of the text's production that KQED used as an argument for the inclusion of the video camera as a tool of the reporter's trade.

15. Lesser, *Pictures at an Execution*, 156–215, 250.

16. Ibid., 212, 235.

17. See Lesser on "The Sleaze Factor," ibid., 93–120.

18. "The very techniques on which the telling of a murder tale relies — foreshadowing, delay, irony, surprise, a sense of determinism, the theatrical immortalization of the main character — are techniques that play with the notion of time" (ibid., 234).

19. As there is no inherent "nature" to the document, it could be more accurate

to propose that a live broadcast would position the *audience* in a significantly different way than would a delayed broadcast.

20. Compare my own analysis with Lesser's discussion of the "strange relation" of the photograph to murder: "Photography focuses on surfaces, murder stems from and speaks to hidden depths; photography celebrates distance and removal, murder condemns the failure to interfere; photography is commemorative, murder seeks oblivion; photography freezes time, making a moment last forever, whereas murder creates irrevocable change" (ibid., 175). I disagree with the polarity of the relation described here. Lesser falls short of the point in her description of the viewer of the photograph bringing to the text that vital mortality — "the passage of time" — which is not implicit in the medium itself. The relativity simply does not work, because the photograph is always about the viewer as much as it is about the subject. Photography does not "freeze time," it testifies to time's passing. It assumes both that someone *must see* and that what is seen is already lost. See Barthes, *Camera Lucida*, 79.

21. As reported on 3 November 1994. The television movie was entitled *Without Warning*. It is tempting to suspect that the only people sucked in were those who turned on their TV sets halfway through the movie (say at the scene where the TV cameras report from the site of the impact), in which case the degree of misapprehension is perhaps more comprehensible. Viewers may have assumed they were seeing an actual news report. It is impossible, however, to speculate on just how much of the fictional "frame" to the story of catastrophe was ignored by viewers because of the tenacity of their belief, their hope even, that such things *could* happen.

22. As evidenced by the statutory construction of first-degree murder and the "aggravating" and "mitigating" factors raised in the penalty phase of capital trials.

23. See Lesser's reply to a friend of hers who wondered, angrily, "What is all this closure business?" (*Pictures at an Execution*, 258).

24. Ibid., 252.

25. Ibid., 224. Emphasis mine.

26. The phrase "discourse of power" adequately conveys the breadth of the institutional and cultural mechanisms that govern the final result of the narrowly "judicial" process which decides whether a murderer (*a*) is indicted for first-degree murder, (*b*) receives a recommendation for death by the jury, (*c*) is sentenced to death by the trial judge, or (*d*) does not have the sentence commuted on appeal. All of these stages are influenced by extrajudicial considerations, no matter what the law may claim about the hermetic nature of due process. While all punishment may be said to be arbitrary as applied under the present legal system, the application of the death penalty is relatively more arbitrary when one con-

siders the potentially irrevocable end to what is — till the final moment — a judicial guessing game.

27. Jacoby, *Wild Justice.*

28. Lesser, *Pictures at an Execution,* 225.

29. Ibid., 3, 232, 248.

30. Fredric Wertham, William March, and Kate Millett are examples from my own analysis.

31. Lesser, *Pictures at an Execution,* 249. Emphasis mine.

32. "There was a panel discussion afterward about whether he jerked or twitched, whether he lowered his head or moved it to the right, whether his left finger moved." Dr. Calvin Frederick, quoted ibid., 249–250.

33. Judge Frankel, quoted in Daniel Kornstein, "Twisted Vision: Janet Malcolm's Upside Down View of the *Fatal Vision* Case," *Cardozo Studies in Law and Literature* 1, no. 2 (1989): 152. Naturally, I also strongly disagree with Kornstein's contention that "truth begins, journalistically and legally, with the facts."

34. Not all of which were signed, although all were admitted as evidence.

35. "[O]nce you have been sentenced and serve your time . . . no other state can bring the charge against you that you have mentioned previously to me." Thus Martha Beck characterized the offer allegedly made by Prosecutor Roger McMahon to her in Michigan, should she confess to the Fay murder. See Testimony of Martha Beck, *People v. Fernandez,* vol. 5, cols. 7310–7311.

36. See Foucault, *The History of Sexuality,* vol. 1: *An Introduction;* Foucault et al., eds., *I, Pierre Riviere,* 206–210; Foucault, "The Confession of the Flesh," in *Power and Knowledge: Selected Interviews and Other Writings* (New York: Pantheon, 1980), esp. 214–217.

37. Who, when they came to investigate a neighbor's complaint of suspicious goings-on, had found the bodies of Delphine and Rainelle Downing cemented into the cellar of the widow's Grand Rapids home. The pair arrested Beck and Fernandez, who were still on the premises.

38. Janet Malcolm, *The Journalist and the Murderer* (New York: Knopf, 1990), 161.

39. Gary Gilmore and Jack Henry Abbott could be taken as examples here. Of course, both had in common their relationship with Norman Mailer, although Gilmore's relationship was one that he — in fact — knew nothing about. Much of what we know about Gilmore's "philosophical" nature is the result of Mailer's mediation. Abbott is quite another matter. On the murders of Max Jensen and Ben Bushnell by Gary Gilmore, see Jack Henry Abbott, *In the Belly of the Beast: Letters from Prison* (London: Hutchinson, 1982), 129–134; also see Jack Henry Abbott and Naomi Zack, *My Return* (New York: Prometheus, 1987).

40. In 1976 Gary Gilmore, who would be the first American to be executed

domestically since the moratorium, obstructed his own appeal process in order to bring about a speedy execution by firing squad in the state of Utah.

41. Mailer had Barry Farrell ruminate on Gilmore's love of "literary questions and highly formulated approaches," concluding that Gilmore was attracted to them because they "dignified his situation." Norman Mailer, *The Executioner's Song* (London: Arrow, 1980), 802. Yet Gilmore's esoteric response to the situation in which he found himself, and his reflection upon the murders, was at times less than dignifying. The interviews show that — even while ruminating on his "remorse" and what the murders meant to him — Gilmore would forget or mispronounce the names of the men he'd killed (p. 693). That callousness demonstrates that Gilmore was *figuring* himself as the murderer, and his concentration on that project demolished the *murdered* yet again.

42. Quoted in Black, *Aesthetics of Murder*, 7.

43. Lesser, *Pictures at an Execution*, 134.

44. Ibid., 17.

45. Cormac McCarthy, *All the Pretty Horses* (New York: Knopf, 1992), 179.

46. Malcolm, *The Journalist and the Murderer*, 45–54, 141–143.

47. Harper Lee did nearly all the research in the township of Holcombe, while Capote confined himself to the officers of the Kansas Bureau of Investigation, and, of course, Richard ("Dick") Hickock and Perry Smith. This division of labor seems to suggest a number of things about the assumed gifts (sympathy? identity of interest?) of female and male interviewers, respectively. One wild card in that neat division of roles along gender lines is the sexuality of both interviewers: Capote was homosexual and Lee a lesbian. The supposed lines of identification become a good deal more surprising if we take this information into account. (While it is arguable that their "queerness" might not be immediately or easily identifiable or apparent, it should be taken as given that one's sexuality is not — even when closeted — merely a garb that one can doff at will.)

48. Neither Gilmore nor Hickock nor Smith become, in Lesser's phrase, "*innocent* victims."

49. Norman Mailer, "Preface" to Abbott, *In the Belly of the Beast*, xi.

50. Mailer's correspondence with Jack Abbott began "sometime in the middle of working on *The Executioner's Song*" (ibid., ix).

51. Abbott, *In the Belly of the Beast*, 126.

52. Including Robert Kennedy's assassin, Sirhan Sirhan, and Robert Beausoleil of the Manson gang.

53. Truman Capote, "Handcarved Coffins: A Non-fiction Account of an American Crime," in *Music for Chameleons* ((New York: Random House, 1980).

54. Truman Capote, "And Then It All Came Down," in Sebastian Wolfe, ed., *The Book of Murder* (London: Xanadu, 1992), 19.

55. George Orwell, "The Hanging," in *The Collected Essays, Journalism and Letters of George Orwell: An Age Like This, 1920–1940* (London: Secker and Warburg, 1968).

56. "His nails would still be growing when he stood on the drop, when he was falling through the air with a tenth of a second to live. His eyes saw the yellow graves and the grey wall, and his brain still remembered, foresaw, reasoned — reasoned even about puddles." Ibid., 46.

57. Dahmer, *A Father's Story*, 240.

58. Bronfen, *Over Her Dead Body*, 434.

59. Dennis Nilsen, quoted in "Nilsen's Inferno," *Vanity Fair*, November 1991.

Appendix

1. Summary of Statement of Martha Beck, 3 March 1949, Michigan, *People* v. *Fernandez*, vol. 3, cols. 3850–3864; vol. 6, cols. 10621–10637. There is little significant variation between accounts of the disposal of the body.

2. It was an unsigned statement, and its veracity was denied by the defense once it was introduced over their objections.

3. Summary of Revised Statement of Martha Beck, 11 March 1949, *People* v. *Fernandez*, vol. 3, cols. 4146–4166.

4. Statement of Raymond Fernandez, 3 March 1949, Michigan, *People* v. *Fernandez*, vol. 3, cols. 4065–4074. Ray and Martha disagreed as to when they drank the Three Feathers whisky. Ray puts it before the strangling, Martha after they'd laid the body out in the back room. See vol. 3, col. 3864.

5. Testimony of Ray Fernandez, Direct and Cross, 14 July–20 July 1949, *People* v. *Fernandez*, vol. 4, cols. 5839–5849, 5957–5969, 6307–6320.

6. Direct Testimony of Martha Beck, 24 July–28 July 1949, *People* v. *Fernandez*, vol. 4, cols. 7121–7124.

7. *People* v. *Fernandez*, vol. 5, cols. 7734–7738.

8. *People* v. *Fernandez*, vol. 5, cols. 7271–7287.

9. Summation on Behalf of the People, *People* v. *Fernandez*, vol. 6, col. 10497.

10. Testimony of Dr. Lichtenstein, *People* v. *Fernandez*, vol. 6, cols. 9348–9359.

11. The coroner suggested that Fay had died from the fractured larynx, rather than the head wounds.

12. *People* v. *Fernandez*, vol. 6, cols. 10543–10556.

13. Summation on Behalf of the Defendants, *People* v. *Fernandez*, vol. 6, col. 10359.

14. Statement of Martha Beck to Dr. Richard Hoffmann, quoted in Brown, *Introduction to Murder*, 199–200.

Select Bibliography

Newspapers, Documents, and Other Media

New York Herald Tribune
New York Journal American

City of Richmond v. *J. A. Croson Co.* 488 US 469, 102 L Ed 2d 854 (1989).
Northeastern Florida Chapter of the Associated General Contractors of America v. *City of Jacksonville, Florida* 508 US — , 124 L Ed 2d 586 (1993).
People v. *Fernandez* 301 NY 302 (1950).

Donahue (television talk show). "The Execution of David Lawson." 15 June 1994.
The Honeymoon Killers (film). 35 mm, 108 min. Directed by Leonard Castle and Oliver Wood. 1970.

Books

Abbott, Jack Henry. *In the Belly of the Beast: Letters from Prison.* London: Hutchinson, 1982.
Abbott, Jack Henry, and Naomi Zack. *My Return.* New York: Prometheus, 1987.
Baldwin, James. *The Evidence of Things Not Seen.* New York: Henry Holt, 1985.
——— *The Price of the Ticket.* London: Michael Joseph, 1985.
Barthes, Roland. *Camera Lucida: Reflections on Photography.* Translated by Richard Howard. London: Fontana, 1984.
Baudrillard, Jean. *Simulations.* New York: Semiotexte, 1983.
Bedau, Hugo Adam. *The Death Penalty in America.* New York: Anchor, 1964.
Berger, Thomas. *Killing Time.* New York: Delta, 1967.
Birch, Helen, ed. *Moving Targets: Women, Murder, and Representation.* London: Virago, 1993.

Black, Joel. *The Aesthetics of Murder: A Study in Romantic Literature and Contemporary Culture*. Baltimore: Johns Hopkins University Press, 1991.

Bok, Curtis, *Star Wormwood*. New York: Knopf, 1959.

Bowers, William. *Legal Homicide: Death as Punishment in America, 1864–1982*. Boston: Northeastern University Press, 1984.

Bronfen, Elisabeth. *Over Her Dead Body: Death, Femininity and the Aesthetic*. New York: Routledge, 1992.

Brown, Richard. *No Duty to Retreat: Violence and Values in American History and Society*. New York: Oxford University Press, 1991.

Brown, Wenzell. *Introduction to Murder: The Unpublished Facts behind the Notorious Lonely Hearts Killers, Martha Beck and Ray Fernandez*. New York: Greenberg, 1952.

Buck, Paul. *The Honeymoon Killers*. London: Xanadu, 1990.

Butler, Judith. *Gender Trouble: Feminism and the Subversion of Identity*. New York: Routledge, 1990.

Cameron, Deborah, and Elizabeth Frazer. *The Lust To Kill: A Feminist Investigation of Sexual Murder*. London: Polity Press, 1987.

Canguilheim, Georges. *The Normal and the Pathological*. New York: Zone, 1991.

Caputi, Jane. *The Age of Sex Crime*. London: Women's Press, 1987.

Carby, Hazel. *Reconstructing Womanhood: The Emergence of the African-American Woman Novelist*. New York: Oxford University Press, 1987.

Cohen, Stanley. *Against Criminology*. London: Transaction Books, 1988.

Colaizzi, Janet. *Homicidal Insanity, 1800–1985*. Tuscaloosa: University of Alabama Press, 1989.

Cranny-Francis, A. *Feminist Fiction: Feminist Uses of Generic Fiction*. New York: St. Martin's Press, 1990.

Culler, Jonathan. *On Deconstruction: Theory and Criticism after Structuralism*. New York: Cornell University Press, 1982.

Dahmer, Lionel. *A Father's Story: One Man's Anguish at Confronting the Evil in His Son*. [London]: Little, Brown, 1994.

Daly, Mary. *Gyn/Ecology: The Metaethics of Radical Feminism*. Boston: Beacon Press, 1978.

Davis, Bernice Freeman, and Al Hirschberg. *The Desperate and the Damned*. New York: Crowell, 1961.

Davis, David Brion. *Homicide in American Fiction, 1798–1860: A Study in Social Values*. Ithaca: Cornell University Press, 1957.

Egger, Steven. *Serial Murder: An Elusive Phenomenon*. New York: Praeger, 1990.

Federal Bureau of Investigation. *Uniform Crime Reports*. Washington, D.C.: GPO, 1989.

Fiedler, Leslie. *Love and Death in the American Novel*. London: Penguin, 1982.

Fleming, Robert. *Willard Motley*. Boston: Twayne, 1978.

Fletcher, George. *A Crime of Self-Defense: Bernhard Goetz and the Law on Trial*. New York: Collier Macmillan, 1988.

Foucault, Michel. *The Archeology of Knowledge*. New York: Harper Colophon, 1976.

—— *Discipline and Punish: The Birth of the Prison*. London: Peregrine, 1979.

—— *The History of Sexuality*. Vol. 1: *An Introduction*. London: Penguin, 1990.

—— *The Order of Things: An Archeology of the Human Sciences*. New York: Pantheon, 1971.

—— *Power and Knowledge: Selected Interviews and Other Writings*. New York: Pantheon, 1980.

Foucault, Michel, et al. *I, Pierre Riviere, Having Slaughtered My Mother, My Sister and My Brother . . . A Case of Parricide in the 19th Century*. Lincoln: University of Nebraska Press, 1975.

Freeman, Bernice, and Al Hirschberg. *The Desperate and the Damned*. New York: Crowell, 1961.

Giddings, Paula. *When and Where I Enter: The Impact of Black Women on Race and Sex in America*. New York: Bantam Books, 1984.

Goodwin, Sarah Webster, and Elisabeth Bronfen, eds. *Death and Representation*. Baltimore: Johns Hopkins University Press, 1993.

Greenwood, Kerry, ed. *The Thing She Loves: Why Women Kill*. St. Leonards, N.S.W.: Allen and Unwin, 1996.

Hacking, Ian. *Rewriting the Soul: Multiple Personality and the Sciences of Memory*. Princeton: Princeton University Press, 1995.

Hall, Kermit, ed. *The Oxford Companion to the Supreme Court*. New York: Oxford University Press, 1992.

Hart, Lynda. *Fatal Women: Lesbian Sexuality and the Mark of Aggression*. Princeton: Princeton University Press, 1994.

hooks, bell. *Ain't I a Woman: Black Women and Feminism*. Boston: South End Press, 1981.

—— *Black Looks: Race and Representation*. Boston: South End Press, 1989.

Howard, H. R. *The Lives of Helen Jewett and Richard P. Robinson, by the Editor of the New York "National Police Gazette."* New York: George Wilkes, Printer, 1848.

Imbrie, Ann E. *Spoken in Darkness: Small-town Murder and a Friendship beyond Death*. London: Penguin, 1994.

Jacoby, Susan. *Wild Justice: The Evolution of Revenge*. New York: Harper and Row, 1983.

Jameson, Fredric. *The Political Unconscious: Narrative as a Socially Symbolic Act*. London: Methuen, 1981.

Jensen, Margaret. *Love's Sweet Return: The Harlequin Story*. Toronto: Women's Press, 1984.

Jones, Ann. *Women Who Kill.* New York: Holt, Rinehart, and Winston, 1980.

Jouve, Nicole Ward. *"The Streetcleaner": The Yorkshire Ripper Case on Trial.* London: Marion Boyars, 1986.

Kalikoff, Beth. *Murder and Moral Decay in Victorian Literature.* Ann Arbor: UMI, 1990.

Kelly, Liz. *Surviving Sexual Violence.* Cambridge: Polity, 1988.

Kerenyi, Carl. *Zeus and Hera: Archetypal Images of Father, Husband and Wife.* Princeton: Princeton University Press, 1975.

Lane, Brian. *Murder Update.* London: Robinson, 1991.

Leacock, Eleanor. *Myths and Male Dominance.* New York: Monthly Review Books, 1981.

Leopold, Nathan. *Life Plus 99 Years.* Garden City, N.Y.: Doubleday, 1958.

Lesser, Wendy. *Pictures at an Execution: An Inquiry into the Subject of Murder.* Cambridge: Harvard University Press, 1993.

MacCannell, Dean. *The Tourist.* New York: Schocken Books, 1989.

Mailer, Norman. *The Executioner's Song.* London: Arrow, 1980.

Malcolm, Janet. *The Journalist and the Murderer.* New York: Knopf, 1990.

Mandel, Ernest. *Delightful Murder: A Social History of the Crime Story.* London: Pluto, 1984.

March, William. *The Bad Seed.* London: Hamish Hamilton, 1954.

May, Elaine Tyler. *Homeward Bound: American Families in the Cold War Era.* New York: Basic Books, 1988.

McCarthy, Cormac. *All the Pretty Horses.* New York: Knopf, 1992.

McCullough, David Willis, ed. *City Sleuths and Tough Guys.* Boston: Houghton Mifflin, 1989.

McGinniss, Joe. *Fatal Vision.* New York: Putnam, 1983.

Millett, Kate. *The Basement: Meditations on a Human Sacrifice.* New York: Simon and Schuster, Touchstone, 1991. Originally published in 1979.

Montgomery Hyde, H. *United in Crime.* London: Heinemann, 1955.

Moore, Katherine. *She for God: Aspects of Women and Christianity.* London: Allison and Busby, 1978.

Motley, Willard. *The Diaries of Willard Motley.* Edited by Jerome Klinkowitz. Ames: Iowa State University, 1979.

—— *Knock on Any Door.* New York: Appleton-Century, 1947.

Nash, J. R. *Murder America: Homicide in the United States from 1850 to the Present.* London: Harrap, 1961.

National Center for Health Statistics. U.S. Department of Health, Education, and Welfare. *Homicide in the United States, 1950–1964.* Washington, D.C.: GPO, 1967.

Norris, J. *Sexual Killers: The Growing Menace*. New York: Dolphin, 1988.

Papke, David Ray. *Framing the Criminal: Crime, Cultural Work and the Loss of Critical Perspective 1830–1900*. Hamden, Conn.: Archon, 1987.

President's Commission on Law Enforcement and the Administration of Justice. *The Challenge of Crime in a Free Society*. Washington, D.C.: GPO, 1967.

Radford, Jill, and Diana Russell, eds. *Femicide: The Politics of Woman Killing*. (Buckingham, UK: Open University Press, 1992).

Rafter, Nicole Hahn. *Partial Justice: Women in State Prisons 1800–1935*. Boston: Northeastern University Press, 1985.

Reviving the Death Penalty. Hudson, Wisc.: G. E. McGuen, 1985.

Reynolds, Quentin. *Courtroom: The Story of Samuel S. Leibowitz*. New York: Farrar, Straus, 1950.

Riley, Denise. *"Am I That Name?" Feminism and the Category of Women in History*. Minneapolis: University of Minnesota Press, 1988.

Rowan, David. *Famous American Crimes*. London: Frederick Muller, 1957.

Rubin, Lillian. *Quiet Rage: Bernie Goetz in a Time of Madness*. London: Faber, 1987.

Sanders, Bruce. *Murder Behind the Bright Lights*. London: Herbert Jenkins, 1958.

Sante, Luc. *Evidence*. New York: Farrar, Straus, and Giroux, 1992.

Schaeffer, Susan Fromberg. *The Madness of a Seduced Woman*. London: Pan, 1989.

Segrave, Kerry. *Women Serial and Mass Murderers: A Worldwide Reference, 1580–1990*. Jefferson, N.C.: McFarland, 1992.

Sellin, T. *The Penalty of Death*. Beverly Hills: Sage, 1980.

Silberman, Charles. *Criminal Violence: Criminal Justice*. New York: Random House, 1978.

Skolnick, Arlene. *Embattled Paradise: The American Family in the Age of Uncertainty*. New York: Basic Books, 1991.

Skorman, Richard. *Off-Hollywood Movies: A Film-Lover's Guide*. New York: Harmony, 1989.

U.S. Department of Commerce. *Statistical Abstract of the United States, 1995*. 115th edition. Washington, D.C.: GPO, 1995.

Wertham, Fredric. *The Show of Violence*. Garden City, N.Y.: Doubleday, 1949.

White, Hayden. *Tropics of Discourse: Essays in Cultural Criticism*. Baltimore: Johns Hopkins University Press, 1978.

Willett, Ralph. *The Naked City: Urban Crime Fiction in the U.S.A*. New York: Manchester University Press, 1996.

Wilson, Colin, and Patricia Pitman. *Encyclopaedia of Murder*. London: Pan, 1984.

Wilson, Wayne. *Good Murders and Bad Murders: A Consumer's Guide in the Age of Information*. Lanham, Md.: University Press of America, 1991.

Wolfe, Sebastian, ed. *The Book of Murder.* London: Xanadu, 1992.
Zimring, F., and G. Hawkins. *Capital Punishment and the American Agenda.* New York: Cambridge University Press, 1986.

Articles

Allen, Hilary. "Rendering Them Harmless: The Professional Portrayal of Women Charged with Serious Violent Crimes." In P. Carlen and A. Worrall, eds., *Gender, Crime and Justice.* London: Open University, 1987.
Amis, Martin. "The Killings in Atlanta." In Sebastian Wolfe, ed., *The Book of Murder.* London: Xanadu, 1992.
Birch, Helen. "If Looks Could Kill: Myra Hindley and the Iconography of Evil." In Birch, ed., *Moving Targets: Women, Murder and Representation.* London: Virago, 1993.
Blakley, Alan. "The Cost of Killing Criminals." *Northern Kentucky Law Review* 18 (Fall 1990).
"Body Found." *Daily Sentinel* (Raleigh, N.C.), 26 August 1866.
"Capital Punishment in the Case of Women and Adolescents." *Justice of the Peace and Local Government Review,* 17 October 1953.
Capote, Truman. "And Then It All Came Down." In Sebastian Wolfe, ed., *The Book of Murder.* London: Xanadu, 1992.
—— "Handcarved Coffins: A Non-fiction Account of an American Crime." In *Music for Chameleons.* New York: Random House, 1980.
Clark, Gordon. "The Legitimacy of Judicial Decision Making in the Context of *Richmond v. Croson.*" *Urban Geography* 13, no. 3 (1992).
Davis, Amma A. "Narrative Reactions to Brutal Murders: A Case Study." *Western Folklore* 49 (January 1990).
Ellis, Bill. "Death by Folklore: Ostension, Contemporary Legend and Murder." *Western Folklore* 48 (July 1989).
Fass, Paula S. "Making and Remaking an Event: The Leopold and Loeb Case in American Culture." *Journal of American History* (December 1993).
Foucault, Michel. "About the Concept of the 'Dangerous' Individual in 19th Century Legal Psychiatry." In D. Weisstub, ed., *Law and Psychiatry.* New York: Pergamon, 1978.
—— "The Confession of the Flesh." In *Power and Knowledge: Selected Interviews and Other Writings.* New York: Pantheon, 1980.
Gallop, Jane. "Where to Begin?" In *Reading Lacan.* Ithaca: Cornell University Press, 1995.

Gilman, Sander. " 'I'm Down on Whores': Race and Gender in Victorian London." In David Goldberg, ed., *Anatomy of Racism*. Minneapolis: University of Minnesota Press, 1990.

Girard, René. "The Sacrificial Crisis." In *Critical Theory since 1965*. Tallahassee: Florida State University Press, 1986.

Griffin, Susan. "Pornography and Silence." In *Made from This Earth*. London: Women's Press, 1982.

Grigg, Russell. "Subject, Object, and the Transference." In E. Ragland-Sullivan and M. Bracher, eds., *Lacan and the Subject of Language*. New York: Routledge, 1991.

Haaken, Janice. "Sexual Abuse, Recovered Memory and Therapeutic Practice: A Feminist Psychoanalytic Perspective." *Social Text* 40 (1994): 115–145.

Headley, Bernard. "Killings That Became 'Tragedy': A Different View of What Happened in Atlanta, Georgia." *Social Justice* 16, no. 4 (1989).

hooks, bell. "Reconstructing Black Masculinity." In *Black Looks: Race and Representation*. Boston: South End Press, 1989.

Janis, Eugenia Parry. "They Say I and I Mean Anybody." In *Harm's Way: Lust and Madness and Murder and Mayhem*. Santa Fe: Twin Palms, 1994.

Klein, Lawrence. "The Deterrent Effect of Capital Punishment: An Assessment of the Estimates." In Alfred Blumstein et al., eds., *Deterrence and Incapacitation: Estimating the Effect of Criminal Sanctions on Crime Rates*. Washington, D.C.: National Academy of Sciences, 1978.

Knox, Sara. "The Genealogy of Treason: Ethel Rosenberg and the Masculinist Discourse of Cold War." *Australasian Journal of American Stories* 12, no. 1 (1993).

Kornstein, Daniel. "Twisted Vision: Janet Malcolm's Upside Down View of the *Fatal Vision* Case." *Cardozo Studies in Law and Literature* 1, no. 2 (1989).

Massing, Michael. "Crime and Drugs: The New Myths." *New York Review of Books*, 1 February 1996.

McDonagh, Josephine. "Do or Die: Problems of Agency and Gender in the Aesthetics of Murder." *Genders*, no. 5 (Summer 1989).

Medlicott, Reginald. "Paranoia of the Exalted Type in a Setting of *Folie à Deux*: A Study of Two Adolescent Homicides." In W. Black and A. Taylor, eds., *Deviant Behaviour: New Zealand Studies*. London: Heinemann, 1979.

Mellor, Philip A., and Chris Shilling. "Modernity, Self-Identity and the Sequestration of Death." *Sociology* 27, no. 3 (1993).

Morris, Allison, and Ania Wilczynski. "Rocking the Cradle: Mothers Who Kill Their Children." In Helen Birch, ed., *Moving Targets: Women, Murder, and Representation*. London: Virago, 1993.

"Nilsen's Inferno." *Vanity Fair,* November 1991.

Orwell, George. "The Hanging." In *The Collected Essays, Journalism and Letters of George Orwell: An Age Like This, 1920–1940.* London: Secker and Warburg, 1968.

Pokorak, Jeffrey. " 'Death Stands Condemned': Justice Brennan and the Death Penalty." *California Western Law Review* 27 (1990/91).

Porter, Dennis. "Backward Construction and the Art of Suspense." In Glenn Most and William Stowe, eds., *The Poetics of Murder: Detective Fiction and Literary Theory.* San Diego: Harcourt Brace, 1983.

Rappaport, Elizabeth. "Some Questions about Gender and the Death Penalty." *Golden Gate University Law Review* 20 (Fall 1990).

Razack, Sherene. "What Is to Be Gained by Looking White People in the Eye? Culture, Race and Gender in Cases of Sexual Violence." *Signs* 19, no. 4 (1994).

Rose, Jacqueline and Juliet Mitchell. "Introduction." In *Feminine Sexuality: Jacques Lacan and the ecole freudienne.* New York: Norton, 1985.

Rowan, David. "The Death House" and "The Lonely Hearts." In *Famous American Crimes.* London: Frederick Muller, 1957.

Rugoff, Ralph. "Crime Seen." *Art and Text,* no. 55 (1996).

Runyan, Damon. "Mrs Snyder and Mr Gray." In Jonathan Goodman, ed., *The Pleasures of Murder.* London: Sphere, 1983.

Russell, Diana, and Candida Ellis. "Annihilation by Murder and by the Media: The Other Atlanta Femicides." In Jill Radford and Diana Russell, eds., *Femicide: The Politics of Woman Killing.* New York: Twayne, 1992.

Sanders, Bruce. "The Incredible Lovers." In Richard Glyn Jones, ed., *Couples Who Kill: Terrifying True Stories of the World's Deadliest Duos.* London: True Crime, 1993.

Seltzer, Mark. "Serial Killers I." *Differences* 5 (Spring 1993).

—— "Serial Killers II: The Pathological Public Sphere." *Critical Inquiry* 22, no. 1 (Autumn 1995).

Shapiro, A. "Disordered Bodies? Disorderly Acts: Medical Disclosure and the Female Criminal in Nineteenth Century Paris." *Genders,* no. 4 (Spring 1989).

Simmonds, Roy. "Cathy Ames and Rhoda Penmark: Two Child Monsters." *The Mississippi Quarterly* 39 (Spring 1986).

Spangler, George. "The Idea of Degeneration in American Fiction 1880–1940." *English Studies,* no. 5 (1989).

Stephens, L. "Still Ripping One Hundred Years On: Regarding the 'Ripper Centenary.' " *Antithesis* 3, no. 2 (1990).

Terry, Jennifer. "The Body Invaded: Medical Surveillance of Women as Reproducers." *Socialist Review* 19, no. 3 (1989).

Walkowitz, Judith. "Male Vice and Female Virtue." In *Desire: The Politics of Sexuality*. London: Virago, 1984.

Wallace, Jon. "A Murderous Clarity: A Reading of Thomas Berger's *Killing Time*." *Philological Quarterly* 68, no. 1 (1989).

Wallinsky, Adam. "The Crisis of Public Order." *Atlantic Monthly*, July 1995.

Wertham, Fredric. "It's Murder." *Saturday Review of Literature*, 5 February 1949.

West, Candace, and Sarah Fenstermaker. "Doing Difference." *Gender and Society* 9, no. 1 (February 1995).

Index

Crime (*cont.*)
126–127, 145–149; race and, 146–149; television and, 17–18, 145–146
Criminology: feminist, 124–155, 164, 257n41; radical, 155–156

Dahmer, Jeffrey, 192–193, 203–204, 211–212
Dahmer, Lionel, 192–193, 203–204, 211–213
Darrow, Clarence, 108
Davis, David Brion, 5, 19–23, 224n23
Death: and femininity, 21–23. *See also* Mortality
Death penalty: 7, 69–72, 133, 189, 191–192, 195–196, 238n78; in United Kingdom, 122, 251n52; as racially discriminatory, 148–149, 162. *See also* Execution
Degeneration, 17, 29–30, 38, 39–43, 45, 47, 226n1
De Quincey, Thomas, 25
Detective fiction, 43, 45, 86–87, 91, 110, 122–123; hardboiled, 124–126. *See also* Crime
Devine, Henry, 79–80
Diminished responsibility, 66–67
Discrimination and affirmative action, 148–149, 255n14
Downing, Delphine, 81–82, 84, 92, 105
Downing, Rainelle, 81–82, 84, 105
Dreiser, Theodore, 31–32

Ellis, Bill, 5, 27–28
Ellis, Ruth, 122
Eschatology, 47–48
Espionage in literature, 121. *See also* Genre
Essentialism, 30–31, 42–43, 47–50. *See also* Biological determinism
Eugenics, 17
Evidence of Things Not Seen, The, 10–11, 149–162, 164, 181–182, 199
Evil, 30–31, 39–40, 42–43, 47–51
Execution, 18–19, 47, 77, 189, 197,

210–211; symbolic power of, 195–196; televising, debate regarding, 191–199. *See also* Death penalty
Executioner's Song, The, 201–202, 205–208
Existentialism, 47–49

Fatherhood, 40–41, 50; paternal symbolism and, 73–77
Fay, Janet, 79, 82, 92, 115–117, 134, 137, 215–220
Femininity: death and, 21–23; race and, 159–160; and sexual shame, 169–171, 174–176; Woman as "chosen" victim, 62, 169–188. *See also* Gender; Women murderers
Feminist criminology. *See* Criminology
Fernandez, Raymond, 7–8, 79–140, 199–200; execution of, 102; Fay murder, 215–220; masculinity of, 94, 96, 99–100, 114–115; notoriety of, 80–81, 105; portrayals of, 108–141; and prison, 98–102, 119–120; voodoo, interest in, 110, 248n5
Film noir, 87, 125–126
Folie à deux, 9, 85, 104, 107–110, 132, 140; definition, 109
Folklore, 8. *See also* Urban folklore
Forensic psychology, 5–7, 16, 53–55, 68–69, 78, 167
Formalism. *See* Legal formalism
Foucault, Michel, 18–19, 23–24, 30, 222n6
Franks, Bobby, 108
Free will, 39, 75

Gedeon, Ethel, 62
Gedeon, Veronica, 56, 60–62
Gender, 10–11, 31, 38, 50, 66–68, 129, 163–188, 213; death and, 21–23; race and, 157–162, 169, 171–172
Genre, 8–9, 43–44, 85, 91, 100, 122–123, 133. *See also* Crime; Detective fiction; Espionage in literature; Romance
Gilmore, Gary, 201–202, 206, 266n39, 267n41
Goetz, Bernhard, 239n84

Sara L. Knox is Lecturer in
Gender and Cultural Studies at the
University of Western Sydney.

Library of Congress Cataloging-in-Publication Data

Knox, Sara L.
Murder : a tale of modern American life / Sara Louise
Knox.
p. cm.
Includes bibliographical references and index.
ISBN 0-8223-2053-3 (cloth : alk. paper). —
ISBN 0-8223-2066-5 (pbk. : alk. paper)
1. Murder literature. 2. Murder in literature.
3. Murder in mass media. I. Title.
HV6515.K64 1998
364.15′23′0973 — dc21   97-23086